Memories of
Summer

BOOKS BY ROGER KAHN

*The Era* (1993)

*Games We Used to Play* (1992)

*Joe and Marilyn* (1986)

*Good Enough to Dream* (1985)

*A Season in the Sun* (1977)

*How the Weather Was* (1973)

*The Boys of Summer* (1972)

*The Battle for Morningside Heights* (1970)

*The Passionate People* (1968)

*Inside Big League Baseball* (Juvenile, 1962)

NOVELS

*The Seventh Game* (1982)

*But Not to Keep* (1978)

COLLABORATIONS

*I. E. My Life, Sort of, with Mickey Rooney* (1964)

*My Story, with Pete Rose* (1989)

EDITED

*The World of John Lardner* (1961)

*The Mutual Baseball Almanac* (1954, 1955, 1956)

# Memories of Summer

When Baseball Was an Art,
and Writing about It a Game

## ROGER KAHN

New York

Library of Congress Cataloging-in-Publication Data

Kahn, Roger.
    Memories of summer : when baseball was an art, and writing about it a game : a memoir / by Roger Kahn. — 1st ed.
        p. cm.
    Includes index.
    ISBN 0-7868-6190-8
    1. Kahn, Roger.   2. Sportswriters—United States—Biography.   3. Baseball—United States—History.   4. Baseball in literature.
    I. Title.
    GV742.42.K35A3 1997
    070.4'49796'092—dc21
    [B]                                                                                          96–48711
                                                                                                   CIP

Paperback ISBN: 0-7868-8316-2

Book designed by C. Linda Dingler

FIRST PAPERBACK EDITION

10 9 8 7 6 5 4 3 2 1

To Katy, for her love
To Pee Wee, for his friendship
To Willie, for his trust

And to a pair of aces,
Gordon Kahn, my father,
and Gordon Kahn, my son

# Contents

# Acknowledgments

SOMEWHERE THE ENGLISH NOVELIST Evelyn Waugh wrote, "These memories, which are my life, for we possess nothing surely except our memories . . ."

Who then is an author to thank for all the tumult of memories crushed into that busy, irrepressible four-letter word . . . life . . . LIFE!

Everyone. I thank almost everyone who has crossed my ken, past and present.

I thank Homer for teaching me synecdoche and Dr. Harry E. Wedeck for requiring me to sight-translate the Aeneid, and Yevygeny Yevtushenko for the poem *Babi Yar*, which always renews my pride in being a writer. And King David for his Song of Solomon and a few characters I think I encountered at midnight once in a Dublin pub—Tinbad the Tailor, Whinbad the Whaler, and Finbad the Failer.

I also thank Sir John Gielgud for the way he pronounces the word "borne" in the Hamlet soliloquy and Jack Dempsey for going easy when we sparred and Orel Hershisher and Carl Erskine for sliders, curves, and kindness and, oh, yes, I thank Margaret Sanger for making the diaphragm popular, which just happens to remind me that a short form of *Memories of Summer* could be Ms.

So many aspects of this book reverberate from so many sources, there just doesn't seem to be space enough to acknowledge everyone. I particularly thank Otto Friedrich for the afternoon in Locust Valley when he made the martinis and went to the piano and played the Hammerklavier Sonata for an audience of one. I thank Harold Rosenthal for forty-six years of randy humor and sometimes grumpy, always most touching affection. I thank Robert Frost for swapping baseball stories with me in Ripton, Vermont, and showing me, when he was eighty-six years old, the courage to be new.

Brian DeFiore, the editor-in-chief at Hyperion, first articulated the idea that became *Memories of Summer*. Henry Dunow of Harold Ober Associates, literary agent and father of small, enchanting twins, served as virile midwife. The delivery table—to run this conceit into sodden earth—was an IBM desktop computer named ValuePoint, loaded with Windows 3.1 and WordPerfect 6.1. I entered the computer cosmos in December 1994 and like every other newcomer I grow preachy about word processing. As I heartily thank Messrs. DeFiore and Dunow, I am also grateful to Dr. G. S. Ohm and Professor Allesandro Volta, without whose researches I would have had to set down this work on a manual typewriter without Spell Checker, QuickCorrect, or even a mouse. My first mouse, out of Taiwan, died quietly in mid-passage. I thank Jack Simons of IBM for supplying me with Mouse II, out of the People's Republic of China. (I would probably mention all this even if my publisher were *not* a division of the Disney Corporation, which, as we all know, rode to grandeur on the back of a 100-percent American mouse, originally known as Steamboat Willie.)

Bill James, the sometimes prickly, always interesting baseball statistician, devastated one recent popular sports book for its inaccuracies. He then accused the author of substituting memory for research. I concur in his indictment, but with a caveat. Unlike Ohm, who precisely measured electrical resistance, or Volta, who gauged the exact pressure of electrical current, or James, who creates numerical formulae, the author of a memoir works amid imprecision. Ask two people about their two-way conversation yesterday, and divergent versions spring forward. No one is lying. We simply hear variations on a theme. To set down scenes from distant decades you had better begin with an eidetic memory. Fortunately my father left me that. Remembrance soon becomes a frame for research, and the finished work grows as a function of both memory *and* research.

To limit the number of errors in *Memories of Summer*, I enlisted assistants, whom I here thank: Mary Donnery and Martha Campbell at the Croton Free Library; Tim Wiles at the National Baseball Library in Cooperstown; B. Peter

Carry, executive editor, and Angel R. Morales, research assistant, at *Sports Illustrated*; John Rawlings, editor-in-chief, and Steven P. Gietschier, archivist, at *The Sporting News*; May Stone and Miriam Touba at the New-York Historical Society Library; Ronald E. Wilson of the *Newsweek* library; Bill Deane, the squire of Fly Creek; Paul Susman, doctor of psychology and professor of Mickey Mantle; and my dear and gifted friends, Mark Allen Reese, of Louisville, Kentucky, and Enil J. Bavasi, the grasshopper master, of La Jolla, California.

But I no more guarantee an absence of errors than an immunologist guarantees a flu vaccine. Risk appends the human condition.

"You know," Ronald Reagan said over coffee at the White House on a late summer afternoon in 1988, "three things bother me about getting older."

"What might those be?" I said.

Reagan's intense gaze began to twinkle. I had supplied the proper straight line.

"First," said the President of the United States, "your memory goes." He paused, looked about the sunlit room and continued with perfect timing, "I seem to have forgotten the other two."

Which reminds me, since politics inevitably has elbowed into our pages, I thank Eugene R. McCarthy, a onetime first baseman in the Great Soo League, for standing up against the Vietnam War in the winter cold of New Hampshire, 1968, and giving peace a voice. It cost the Senator his political career.

*These memories, which are my life . . .*

R.K.

# Memories of
# Summer

# CHAPTER ONE

# Clarence at the Bat

*We are talking of summer evenings . . . in the time that I lived so*
*successfully, disguised to myself as a child.*
—JAMES AGEE,
*A Death in the Family*

I SAW MY FIRST WORLD SERIES GAME in 1920, seven years before I was born. The viewing instrument was my father, who relished baseball and had so vivid a memory that friends called him, somewhat laboriously it now seems to me, the Walking Encyclopedia.

We were indeed walking, along Prospect Avenue, a quiet Brooklyn street, under sycamore trees with peeling, patchy bark, and fruit clusters abrim with itching powder. Far back from the bluestone sidewalk, large homes sprawled behind shields of hydrangea bushes and spiked, iron fences—immobile vigilantes in a neighborhood without crime.

My mother had banished us into the springtime for violating a rule: no ballplaying in the house. All mothers in that generation said no ballplaying in the house. All mothers also said, "Take off those sneakers. Take them off at once! Don't you know that sneakers are bad for your feet?"

My father had decided to show me how to spin a breaking ball, and winding up in a long hallway—I wore Buster Brown oxfords, not sneakers—I turned out to have more wrist snap than control. The gray

rubber ball slipped off my fingers and slammed into one wall, rico-
cheted into the other and went crashing along the hardwood floor. All
that machine-gun racket summoned my mother from her book, which
I believe was *Leaves of Grass*. A covey of Brooklyn mothers was rediscovering Walt Whitman that season, and homes like ours resounded with
the poet's sometimes mournful tread. Grass, I knew, because my
mother recited the lines, is the beautiful uncut hair of graves.

Outside I was not certain if my father had decided on a destina-
tion. (One particular dream seemed too extravagant.) More immediately, I had no idea what conversational paths my father, the walking
encyclopedia, would navigate this sunlit afternoon.

Ginkgo trees. That was his topic on the previous Saturday. Ginkgo
trees grew in Brooklyn, but did not originate there. They were found
first in Eastern China. They had vanished from the forests but
remained on the grounds of temples. These odd trees, with fan-shaped
leaves, right here on Prospect Place, probably had religious significance
in old Cathay, during the time of Marco Polo, and what did I think
about that?

Nothing, really, except that ginkgo was a funny-sounding name. I
was seven years old. It was nice to walk with Dad, and I wanted to
make an effort to show that I shared his interest in natural wonders.

"If you put a grizzly bear and a Bengal tiger in the same cage at the
Prospect Park Zoo, and they got into a fight, which one would win,
the grizzly bear or the Bengal tiger?"

My father was short, green-eyed, bald, mustached, powerful, and
he smiled and looked into the distance. "Nature," he said, "is red in
tooth and claw." Then he began to tell me about the sycamores.

I seem to remember a great deal about the trees of Brooklyn, but I
merely tolerated the arboreal lectures, if a seven-year-old can be said to
tolerate a parent, in the hope that my father would veer away from
botany. He played third base for City College, covering, he said, "a
dime, or on a good day a quarter." The coach valued him for his bat, I
suppose. Whenever I watched my father play weekend baseball, he walloped long drives over and beyond left center field that thrilled and
awed me. At some point, when I was very young, I decided that there
was nothing I wanted to do in life as much as I wanted to hit long,

high drives over and beyond left center field, like my father. Through six decades—births and deaths, bonanzas and busts, wars, divorce, and even the absurdity of major league labor strikes—that part of me has never changed.

Squealing with the steel wheels rolling on steel tracks, the Nostrand Avenue trolley rattled across our path. Unlike the trolleys in Manhattan that rode over submerged electrical lines, Brooklyn trolley cars drew power from an overhead cable. A sort of crane rose from the top of the Brooklyn trolleys, maintaining contact with the high cable unless the trolley swung around a turn too rapidly. Then the crane broke away from the high cable, losing contact in a crackle of sparks. The motorman had to dismount and reposition the crane, a delicate process, often conducted over a background of "godammit," and worse.

"Wee Willie Keeler drove a trolley car," my father said. We were crossing Nostrand in the wake of the trolley. "Little bit of a fellow, Keeler, but he almost always hit .300. If you put a gray derby upside down on the green grass in right field, Keeler could slap a line drive into the hat. Quite a batsman, but when he was finished he had to go to work as a trolley motorman."

My heart leaped up. This was not going to be another ginkgo tree perambulation. This walk would shine with baseball talk. My father's strides became urgent. Periodically, I had to shift from walk to canter matching his lurching pace. I would happily have sustained a full gallop to talk baseball with my father. That part of me never changed either, for as long as he was on the earth. There was nobody I enjoyed talking baseball with, as much as this green-eyed, strong-armed, gentle, fierce, mustached, long-ball hitting, walking encyclopedia who was my father.

Touches of sad far-off days still linger. Diffident and soft-spoken men approached my father on our walks and offered him boxes of pencils for a dime. His green eyes softened and he found the dime, but he never accepted the pencils. Every Sunday the *New York Times* published a sepia picture section called the rotogravure, after a particular printing process, and from time to time momentous photographs appeared:

Benito Mussolini, the jet-jawed "Sawdust Caesar"; pipe-smoking, avuncular, oddly ominous Joseph Stalin; a sort of landscape—smoke rising from a Chinese village after Japanese soldiers had ravaged the houses and the people. The Depression reigned and the dictators were rising.

One day a deferential baldheaded man came to the door selling paper flowers cleverly folded in brightly colored little pots. He told my father that he had been a businessman in Germany and that he had opposed the Nazis and one day the Brownshirts came and broke his shop windows and struck him with clubs and terrorized his wife. My father bought a dozen of the little pots with paper flowers. It was natural to miss your homeland, my father said to the refugee flower salesman, but his decision to leave Nazi Germany might in the end turn out to be a good one. America was the land of opportunity.

The salesman said, in a confessional tone, "But I am Jewish."

My father blinked. "Even so," he said, "this is the land of opportunity."

I mention such matters to suggest aspects of the world in which my father and I lived when I was seven. I listened as hard as I could to geopolitical conversations, but my ability to contribute was nonexistent, except for certain questions.

"Why didn't you take the poor man's pencils, Dad?"

"Because now he can sell them to someone who really needs them."

"What are Brownshirts?"

"Hooligans. German hooligans. A bad lot."

I wanted to do more than ask questions. I wanted to understand the world around me and to be respected as a person capable of understanding. My father understood everything. That was why people called him The Walking Encyclopedia. I wanted to be like my father. I wanted to enter the world of men. Baseball became my magic portal.

A game of catch is a complicated communication. The father has the stronger arm, the surer hands. The child has the enthusiasm, a passionate hope that his ballplaying will improve, and something immediate to find out. The first time a baseball bounces against your shin, or pops out of your glove into your cheekbone, you learn the presiding reality of the sport. The ball is hard. After that, you make a decision. Is the pain the ball inflicts worth the pleasure of playing the game? Pain and pleasure, the stuff of love and life, runs strong in baseball.

I don't remember consciously deciding to play ball, but I knew boys who made decisions *not* to play. "Baseball is boring," one said. I sensed that it was not boredom at all, but fright, dominating hard-ball terror, that led him to choose kick-the-can, or stoop tag, or other city games where pain did not lurk disguised as a one-hop grounder.

In childhood I suffered on Ferris wheels, particularly in the jiggling cars that swung on rails high over Coney Island and threatened to launch you into the Atlantic. Large Airedales alarmed me. But I was not afraid of a baseball. The passion to play dominated my spirit, that and the distinct but overlapping passion to win the good opinion of my father. He hit grounders at me in a dozen sandlots, ten thousand grounders in dusty, city fields. The governing discipline was severe. To subdue a grounder you have to watch the ball, watch it from the bat, watch it skim and bounce, watch it right into your glove. But that exposes your face and a baseball can glance off a pebble and zoom into your teeth, like a micro version of one of today's smart bombs. You see it suddenly, mouth-high, and feel the ball at the same instant. The baseball feels like a concrete punch. After a few of these blows, you may want to lift your face as a grounder approaches. Except . . . *except* . . . that way you lose sight of the ball. You'll miss it then, sure as the ball is round. You have to keep your glove low and you have to look the zipping baseball into your glove, or else you'll hear the teasing cry: "You played every bounce right except the last one." You need equal measures of concentration and courage. When I stayed with a nasty grounder—and my father saw me stay with its final, hostile hop—I felt I had achieved something worthy of pride.

The fly ball was another kind of dragon. A child's first tendency is to run at a ball in the air; the heartless baseball then sails over his head. Although this causes no physical pain, it can raise another cry, "How come you're standing over *here*, when the ball bounced over *there*?" The psyche grimaces.

My father began fly-ball drills with soft, arcing tosses, gradually increasing height and range. Then he took a bat and tapped gentle fungos, explaining with great formality that "fungo" is one English word whose origin not even Noah Webster knew. When a baseball carries long, you want to turn. You should not run backwards; that is both awkward and slow. You spot the ball and turn and run to the point where it will descend.

*If* you can determine where it will descend. That is a tricky business, and one of the wonders of major league ball is the way outfielders run down 350-foot drives and make the play seem easy. I possessed no native gift for judging fly balls, but when I did succeed in running down a long one and taking it over my shoulder, my father beamed and said, "Good catch." The praise spoke banners; I worked harder to win those words, "Good catch," than I ever worked at homework or piano lessons. My mother noticed and she never forgot nor, until almost the end of a long life, did she ever entirely forgive my father, myself, or baseball.

We crossed Franklin Avenue and my father abruptly turned left, stirring in me a thrill of hope. "The records say that Keeler batted .432 in the 1890s," he said, "but the game was played differently then. The ball was dead. Batters poked instead of swinging from the heels. Just about the only way you hit a home run was when one of the outfielders fell down."

"Running backwards," I said, "instead of turning and taking the ball over your shoulder can make you fall down in the outfield."

"Conceivably," my father said. He pressed his lips together to suppress a grin, and I could see that he was pleased. "The most solid Brooklyn hitter in the modern game was Zack Wheat, who came from Missouri. He's a motorcycle cop in the Midwest these days. He was a terrific lefthand-hitting outfielder who had a singular trait. Waiting for the pitch, Buck—we called Zack Wheat 'Buck'—waggled his back leg. Then he'd wallop a line drive off the right-field wall."

Zack Wheat was Buck Wheat. How bountiful is the trove of baseball nicknames.

"There were two pretty fair first basemen with French backgrounds," my father said. "Jake Daubert came first, around 1910. He scooped bad throws and ran down long, foul pops. A joy to watch. Jacques Fournier arrived in the 1920s. Only an average fielder, but just about the best power hitter Brooklyn ever had."

We passed St. John's Place and Lincoln Place, walking alongside four-story apartments, tenements really, with street-level shops selling fish and stationery and toys. At length we reached Eastern Parkway, a broad avenue with six lanes of traffic and two access roads, set behind pedestrian pathways and green benches and rows of newly pruned sycamores. This distinctive boulevard was patterned after the Champs-Élysées, including at its font, Grand Army Plaza, an imposing monument for the Union war dead, modeled on the Arc de Triomphe.

"Brooklyn had a pitcher once," my father said, "a lefthander named Nap Rucker. Nap stood for Napoleon. He threw the slowest slowball in the world."

"If his pitches were so slow, why didn't everybody hit them? If he threw that slowly, *I* could have hit him, right?"

"Wrong. Nap Rucker had a deceptive windup. He made the batters think he was rearing back for a fastball. Then, after all that motion, he threw the slow one. Everybody missed the slowball because they had been completely and utterly fooled. Missed the slowball or popped it up."

I needed half an Eastern Parkway block to assimilate that. Pitching was more than throwing fast and accurately. You were also trying to confuse the hitters. You made it look as though you were going to throw fast and then you threw a slowball. You could make it look as though you were going to throw slow and fire the fastball. I got the idea. I didn't actually have a fastball when I was seven years old, but I believed one would appear in time through an unusual mix—practice and spontaneous generation. Then I'd like to try that deception stuff, fooling the hitters with crafty slow ones, and blowing them out of town with my unborn fastball.

"Dazzy Vance in his prime had a different trick," my father said. "For seven years he was the best strikeout pitcher in the league. Vance wore a long undershirt and he took a scissors and cut slits in the right sleeve. It ran clear down to the wrist. When Vance pitched, the long sleeve flapped. It was a white sleeve and the hitters had one heck of a

time seeing that white baseball coming out of that white sleeve. Before
they knew it, the fastball was in the catcher's mitt. Strike three."

"He's out," I said.

We reached the busy intersection of Eastern Parkway and Bedford
Avenue, a street that ran almost the entire length of Brooklyn, from the
cramped treeless blocks of Williamsburg into affluent Flatbush, before
coming to its end near the fishing boats that docked at Sheepshead
Bay. "If the Dodgers had all these good players," I said. I paused to
savor the ballplayers' names:

Wee Willie Keeler.
Zack Wheat. Buckwheat.
Nap Rucker.
Dazzy Vance.

"If the Dodgers had all these good players, why is it that Brooklyn
never wins the World Series, like the Giants and the Yankees?"

My father slowed his stride. "That's quite a long story," he said.

I had asked a defining question about an era. *Cartago delenda est.*
Carthage must be destroyed. As I would later learn in a tower class-
room at Erasmus Hall, Cato's repeated declaration defined an era in
Rome. Why can't the Dodgers win the World Series? That question
spoke to the core of early- and mid-twentieth-century life in Brooklyn.

Brooklyn was settled in 1636 by adventurous Dutch farmers, whose
descendants named their academy after the reformation scholar,
Desiderius Erasmus. The English seized Brooklyn in 1664 and Brooklyn was the site, in August 1776, of the Battle of Long Island, a vital
defensive action in one of George Washington's strategic retreats.

By 1890, the population exceeded 835,000 and Brooklyn had
become a boomtown, storing grain, milling coffee, and manufacturing
barrels, shoes, machine tools, chemicals, and paints. Then on January 1,
1898, a date of limited infamy, the leaders of Brooklyn forgot the
legacy of Washington and surrendered their independence. Brooklyn
became a borough, nothing more, in New York City. Ridicule followed. Brooklynites were said to talk funny, or in the patois tawk
funny. They pronounced "earl" as "oil." They pronounced "oil" as

"earl." And how, down by the Gowanus Canal, did people say, "The Earl just changed his oil?"

The humor was relentlessly denigrating, and largely unfair. You heard the so-called Brooklyn accent in spades, strident spades, mouthed in Hell's Kitchen, on the west side of Manhattan. The real Brooklyn was a place of wooded parks and white sand beaches, neighborhoods, libraries, and decidedly preppy schools. The perceived Brooklyn was a group of stumpy characters, *tawkin'* funny and *trowin'* nickel cigars into an open manhole. At best, some said, Brooklyn was Manhattan's bedroom. Brooklynites were born, lived, slept, made love, and died in the figurative shadow cast by the towers of Manhattan. The denigration nurtured paranoia in the Brooklyn psyche. Presently, the focus for a grand assortment of paranoid anxieties became a baseball team peopled by athletes as splendid as Zack Wheat and Dazzy Vance, that still, somehow, *how long, oh, Lord, how long,* could never win the World Series.

My father turned left at Bedford Avenue. Anticipation gave me a clutch in the throat.

"Could we?"

"If you don't tell your mother."

"I promise. Why can't I tell her?"

"She doesn't want you being spoiled."

"Who's pitching?"

"Mungo."

I knew a bit about the mighty righthander with the name from an ancient Mongol court. Mungo. Van Lingle Mungo. I loved to roll that name along my tongue. With his huge kick and his mighty fast ball, Mungo could strike out anybody, anybody at all, Mel Ott or "Ducky-Wucky" Medwick. Strike out anybody at all, if he didn't walk him.

"Boston is starting Fred Frankhouse. His specialty is the old roundhouse curve. We have an interesting matchup—a big strong fastball pitcher against a man with a sweeping roundhouse curve."

We were walking downhill. The street was paved with cobblestones. I could see, from my walking trot, the roof of Ebbets Field and, atop the roof, the flags, the many-colored flags, the flapping flags that meant Ball Game Today.

Mungo was a glowering six-foot two-inch righthander. We sat close to the field alongside first base and I truly saw Van Mungo glower. When he wound up, he reared back so far that his left toe pointed toward the sky. Then he came over, a mighty pinwheel, throwing the finest fastball in the league. Ray Berres warmed up Mungo. When Mungo's fastball hit Ray Berres's glove, sound exploded through the ballpark. Smoke and thunder lurked in Mungo's arm.

Sadly, this day, Mungo was wild. He walked two in the first inning, another two in the third. Hits by Buck Jordan and Wally Berger put the Braves ahead by five and Casey Stengel, who was managing Brooklyn, replaced Mungo with Les Munns in the sixth. "No more runs. We got Munns," said a man in a tweed cap who was sitting next to my father.

"How come they knocked out Mungo, Dad?"

"Speed alone is not enough," my father said.

"You gotta throw strikes, son," said the man in the tweed cap.

"Tough strikes," my father said. "Nothing belt-high down the middle."

"Yer right," said the tweed cap. "Ya musta played some ball."

I had not before heard my father conversing with a stranger, let alone with a tough-looking fellow in a cap, whose pronunciation was shaky. They fell into easy, informed conversation and at length the stranger said, "Shame they don't draw more."

My father's customary reserve vanished. "If they had a decent team," he said, "they'd draw a million."

"You sura that?" the tweed cap said.

"Absolutely. With a decent team the Dodgers would draw a million at the very least."

Les Munns shut down the Braves, but Freddy Frankhouse's roundhouse, the Frankhouse Roundhouse, silenced the good Dodger bats—Sam Leslie, Len Koenecke, Jersey Joe Stripp. The roundhouse curve is not usually effective in the major leagues because the slow break is easy to follow. But this afternoon, my father and the fellow in the tweed cap agreed, if you put a matchbook on the outside corner of the plate, Frankhouse would break his curve over it.

"How about a match?" I said. "If you put just one match on the outside corner, could Frankhouse break his roundhouse over *that?*"

The men looked at each other and nodded. Yes, he could. "Ya gotta smart one," said the man.

"Thank you," my father said.

"And, son," the stranger said, "I hope you kin hit."

In the eighth inning, after Hack Wilson played a fly ball into a double, the man in the tweed cap rose to leave. "Buncha bums," he said. "That's all they are. A buncha bums."

We stayed until the final out. My father always bought me a Stahl-Meyer all-beef frankfurter, which cost ten cents, in the fifth inning. He always bought me a good hot dog, and we always stayed until the last man made out.

"That fellow who called the team 'bums' was way off base," my father said, as we walked down a cement runway, tramping over crushed green packs of Lucky Strikes. "You'll see mistakes once in a while. Hack Wilson was never a great fielder. But none of these fellows is a bum. Everybody in the major leagues is at the least a very good ballplayer. If you aren't very good, you don't make the major leagues. 'Bums' is a crude word. I never cared for the sound of it. Worse than that, when you call a major leaguer a bum, you aren't accurate."

A wind sprang up and whipped across the sidewalk beside the empty ball park. The April afternoon stung suddenly with cold. "We'll take the Tompkins Avenue trolley home," my father said.

"You were going to tell me," I said after a bit, "why the Dodgers haven't ever won the Series."

The trolley, running east on Empire Boulevard, started with a cacophony of grunts and squeals. The motorman worked two levers, and watching him I began to imagine that he was Wee Willie Keeler, who could hit a line drive into your hat. It would be great fun, I thought, to drive a trolley car, working the big levers, clanging around curves as fast as you could go, then braking so hard the wheels threw sparks up from the rails. That would be wonderful, I knew, but not nearly so wonderful as it would be to be a ballplayer.

A major league ballplayer.

A Brooklyn Dodger.

• • •

My father was born in 1901, the year Queen Victoria died and when, closer to home, the Brooklyn ballclub finished third in the National League. From 1903 through 1914, the years that surely shaped my father as a baseball person, Brooklyn finished in the second division every time. Even with Daubert and Stengel, Rucker and Wheat, Brooklyn could not become a contending club. My father's approach to the Dodgers seemed scholarly and restrained. I suppose he learned how to bury his emotions during those early years when his team played mediocre ball, day after day, month after month, season after sorrowful season.

"The Dodgers won the pennant in 1916," my father said, "but they were no match for the Boston Red Sox. They had a lot of trouble with a young fastball pitcher named Babe Ruth. Then they won again in 1920." A few sitting near us on the cane trolley benches stopped chattering. My father's deep voice and assured manner commanded attention. "They split the first four games in that Series with the Cleveland Indians. We thought the fifth game would be very important and it was. The Dodgers fell behind, but they started a nice rally in the fifth inning. Pete Kilduff, the second baseman, and Otto Miller, the catcher, both got on with nobody out. Clarence Mitchell, the pitcher, was up next, and Mitchell was one pitcher who could hit."

"Babe Ruth," I said, "was another pitcher who could hit."

"Right," my father said. "Don't interrupt. Mitchell walloped a terrific line drive up the middle and the Cleveland second baseman, Bill Wambsganss, ran and jumped and caught that terrific smash backhand. One out. When he came down, he was just a step from second base. He put his spikes on the bag and doubled up Pete Kilduff, who thought the line drive would be a base hit. Two out. Otto Miller thought the same thing and he ran right into Bill Wambsganss's tag. Three out. That was the only unassisted triple play in the history of the World Series."

I tried to imagine the busy scene. Wambsganss jumping. Kilduff stumbling. Miller running with his head down. Why hadn't Miller turned around or at least ducked? Why did it have to be a *Dodger* who hit into an unassisted triple play?

"Next time Mitchell came to bat," my father said, "he grounded into a double play. Two swings. Five outs. Hard to do.

"In the last two games—this Series was best five out of nine—the Dodgers didn't score a run. But what can you expect after a good hitter like Clarence Mitchell makes five outs with two swings?

"I was starting to play college ball and Big Bill Hyman was doing some pitching. When we talked about Wambsganss and the Cleveland Series, we said, like other young people in Brooklyn, 'Wait till next year.'"

"What happened next year, Dad?"

"In 1921 the Dodgers finished fourth."

I looked around the trolley. A placard advertising shaving cream proclaimed:

*In this Vail*
*Of toil and sin,*
*Your head grows bald,*
*But not your chin.*

My father followed my eyes and touched his bald head briefly. "As you grow up," he said, "you learn to live with disappointments."

There had been no disappointment for me this April day. I had seen Van Mungo's windup and Freddy Frankhouse's roundhouse curve. I had watched a major league ballgame with my father and now, on the Tompkins Avenue trolley, I had heard him describe a most amazing World Series. Still, I would have to be careful when we reached home.

"Let's tell Mom we went to the library," I said. "She'd really like it if we told her that."

"The Botanic Gardens," my father said, speaking quietly. "We took a long, healthy walk through the Botanic Gardens. We walked a long way beside a babbling brook."

"Right," I said, "and we saw an unassisted triple play."

My father and I smiled together. We would indeed walk through the Botanic Gardens, beside a babbling brook, but on another day.

# The Plains of Heaven

*There never was a piece of writing ever,*
*anywhere that was too good to appear in a newspaper.*
—FRANKLIN PIERCE ADAMS (FPA)
of the *New York World.*

*I*t WAS NOT 40 YEARS IN THE WILDERNESS between Brooklyn Dodger pennants—not 40 years, just 21. But amid baseball's unique clocks and calendars, 21 seasons is an eternity. Players appear as bright rookies at the age of 23 and enter midlife, with all its joys and crises, at 28. By the time they reach the age of 30, when professionals in other fields are approaching maturity, ballplayers become "grizzled veterans" in the phrase of sportswriters, who may be 20 years older, portly and bald, but still flourish. Ten years is a long lifespan for a ballplayer, in the quickpace of the major leagues, where fame and senility come early. Twenty-one years between pennants is a very long, very dark age.

By 1937, the team I saw lose to Boston, only three years before on the spring afternoon when Fred Frankhouse outpitched Van Lingle Mungo, had already become medieval history. Mungo could have been a great pitcher, should have been a great pitcher, but when Dodger fielders dropped fly balls and dodged grounders, he abandoned himself to fury. Afterwards he brooded and drank. In 1936 Mungo "jumped" the Dodgers, announcing that he was "damn sick and tired of pitching for a bunch of semipros." He returned, of course. Jobs were hard to come by near his home in the tobacco and turnip country around Pageland, South Carolina. But he hurt his arm during the 1937 All-Star game and never could fire his wondrous fastball after that. Many said he threw harder than Dizzy Dean or even Lefty Grove, but the Van Lingle Mungo story, like Brooklyn baseball of Van Lingle Mungo's time, played out as a broken dream.

While the Yankees and Giants grappled in the 1936 World Series, with stars dazzling to consider—Larrupin' Lou Gehrig, "The Iron Horse"; King Carl Hubbell, "The Meal Ticket"—the Dodgers celebrated October by firing their manager, Casey Stengel. The charge: Stengel was a "Merry Andrew," doomed, to use someone else's phrase, for a certain time to walk the night. Stengel's successor, a former spitball pitcher from Wisconsin, bore the manor-house name of Burleigh Arland Grimes, but baseball people called him Ol' Stubblebeard. On the sunniest of Flatbush days, Grimes was dour as a hangover.

Between 1918 and 1926, Grimes pitched 158 victories for the Dodgers. That is a fine accomplishment, but Grimes was not an unalloyed winner. During the infamous fifth game of the 1920 World Series, he threw a home-run ball in the first inning. The bases were loaded; Grimes became the first person to yield a grand slam in any World Series. Clarence Mitchell relieved in the fourth inning, but Grimes remained pitcher of record. The new Dodger manager of 1937 was the losing pitcher in the unassisted triple-play game of 1920. Further, on September 22, 1925, Grimes spent an afternoon with the Dodgers, in which he hit into two double plays and one triple play during a single game. Clarence Mitchell, by this time with the Phillies, surely smiled.

During Ol' Stubblebeard's first managerial year, 1937, the Dodgers finished a remote sixth. Fans could walk across Ebbets Field after games in those days and one twelve-year-old rooter watched the Cubs beat Brooklyn by seven runs, then hurried out of the grandstand to ask Grimes for an autograph. Ol' Stubblebeard shot a right into the child's stomach.

That October the Dodgers swapped four players to the St. Louis Cardinals for "Lippy" Leo Durocher, who was rumored to replace Grimes as manager even before he put on a Brooklyn uniform. In January a banker named George V. McLaughlin, who held the mortgage on Ebbets Field, forced the torporous Dodger management to hire Leland Stanford "Larry" MacPhail, an executive of phenomenal gifts. While trying to assemble a respectable Brooklyn team, MacPhail hired Babe Ruth to coach first base and wallop home runs off not very fast pitches during batting practice. At forty-three, Ruth still had more power than Dodger regulars twenty years his junior. Who would succeed Grimes, Brooklynites wondered with considerable passion? Would it be the streetwise, card-sharp, crap-shooting shortstop from St. Louis? Or the bumbling, lovable, not exactly cerebral, Great Bambino?

All Brooklyn wondered merrily about the future. In the brutal present, now 1938, the Dodgers finished seventh.

Durocher knocked Ruth out of work by demonstrating late in the 1938 season that Ruth could not or would not learn the signs for hit and run, bunt, swing, and other big-league basics. Durocher, whose conversational tone was mezzo-forte, told Ruth in the clubhouse: "Ya missed a sign, ya big bum, because ya don't know the signs. Admit it." After the shouting match Durocher, sixty pounds lighter than Ruth, literally stuffed the big man into a locker. "I knew," Durocher said years later, "that if he came out of that locker and got his damn hands on me, I'd be a goner. But we were in the clubhouse and by the time he scrambled back to his feet, I figured there'd be twenty or thirty guys breaking it up. Which is what happened." Durocher outpointed the big man and humiliated him.

On October 12, 1939, MacPhail hired Durocher as Dodger manager. When Babe Ruth heard the news, he broke into tears. Ruth never again held a big-league job.

MacPhail, now called The Roarin' Redhead, began to broker astounding deals. He borrowed more money from Banker McLaughlin and bought a slick and slugging first baseman, Dolph Camilli, from the impoverished Philadelphia Phillies. He snookered Pee Wee Reese away from the Red Sox, stole Pistol Pete Reiser from the Cardinals and found two stalwart underachievers in the American League—Whitlow Wyatt, a righthander with great pitching sense and a mean slider, and Dixie Walker, an outfielder who would become the team's best clutch hitter and most popular hero. New York writers noted Walker's success in a patronizing way. Typing a Manhattan version of a Brooklyn accent, they called him The People's Cherce. MacPhail pried the great second baseman, William Jennings Bryan "Billy" Herman, away from Chicago during a drinking bout with the Cubs' general manager, and solidified his starting rotation by dispatching $100,000 more to the Phillies and gaining the gifted and bibulous righthander, Kirby Higbe. "I'm gonna do great with the Brooklyns," Higbe predicted in a burst of clairvoyance. "I'm as strong as a bull and twice as smart."

In the season of 1941, Higbe won 22 games. So did Whit Wyatt, who pitched 7 shutouts. Camilli hit 34 homers. Pistol Pete Reiser won the batting championship and led the league in triples, doubles, total bases, and runs scored. After twenty-one seasons, the Brooklyn ball club leaped off its treadmill to oblivion and won a pennant.

The team clinched in Boston and the road secretary arranged for a private train, *The Dodger Special*, to carry the ballplayers home in splendor. On orders from MacPhail, broadcaster Red Barber announced over and over again on radio station WHN: "The boys will be pulling into Grand Central about ten P.M., heah? And I know they'd 'ppreciate a real royal Dodger welcome from their fans." Some ten thousand rooters postponed dinner and made their way to Grand Central Terminal. MacPhail, who had been concentrating on World Series preparations at his office, caught a taxi to 125th Street so he could board *The Dodger Special* and lead the victory procession. But *The Dodger Special* rolled through the 125th Station without stopping. MacPhail stood stranded on the platform. Durocher, and Durocher alone, led the march toward exultant rooters in Grand Central. Some bore banners urging Leo for President.

MacPhail drank Scotch, then caught up with Durocher and said, "Who in the hell gave the order not to stop at 125th street?"

"I did," Durocher said. "I wanted to be sure the team stayed together."

"You did?" MacPhail said. "You told the conductor not to stop?"

"Yup."

"You're fired," MacPhail shouted at the manager who had brought Brooklyn its first pennant in twenty-one years.

• • •

By morning the firing was forgotten and on September 29, the day after the season ended, MacPhail and Durocher were the closest of colleagues, the most admiring of friends. Exhorted by the *Brooklyn Eagle*, which had not enjoyed such a heady time since Walt Whitman resigned as its editor ninety-four years earlier, a madding crowd assembled about Grand Army Plaza and its imitation Arc de Triomphe, for a pennant parade down Flatbush Avenue. The *Eagle* estimated those riding, tramping, and roistering in the parade at sixty thousand. Up front, in the backseat of a handsome Packard convertible, Durocher and MacPhail smiled and waved all the way to Borough Hall. According to the *Eagle*, the multitudes along the sidewalks, watching and bellowing acclaim, "numbered a million people—at least."

Someone remarked that at last the meek had inherited the earth.

"Meek?" said Eddie Murphy, on hand from the *New York Sun*. "This doesn't seem meek to me. Durocher and MacPhail are a reign of terror."

Across a handful of afternoons, the World Series spun itself into a Brooklyn nightmare. The teams split the first two games at Yankee Stadium. Newspapermen had been pointing out what was all too common knowledge in Brooklyn: the Dodgers had never won a World Series. Now came murmurs of hope. For Whit Wyatt not only turned back the Yankees in the second game, 3-2, he rattled the household god, Joe DiMaggio, with a fastball at the chin. Knocked away from the plate, DiMaggio started toward Wyatt. The pitcher, the most courtly of men off the playing field, was ready to brawl. Beyond some shouting, nothing actually happened, but beating the Yankees and unnerving their star was a stronger potion than Trommers' beer and a shot of rye, the boilermaker, popular in saloons along Flatbush Avenue. Some Brooklynites suggested that the Yankees, who had won five pennants in six years, were overrated and that their long-striding, toothy, charismatic center fielder couldn't take it when the chips were down. ("And draw me another one just like the first, Michael, me boy.")

For the third game Durocher started an intriguing forty-year-old knuckleball pitcher, "Fat Freddie" Fitzsimmons. Thirteen seasons earlier, Fitzsimmons won twenty games for John McGraw and the New

York Giants. He did not become a Dodger until he was almost thirty-eight and the Giant management concluded that he was finished. But Fitzsimmons prospered in Brooklyn, winning sixteen of eighteen decisions in 1940. His competitive nature and his unusual pitching motion made him such a favorite that he soon was able to open a bowling alley on Empire Boulevard. (Dixie Walker opened a liquor store on Long Island.)

Fitzsimmons's windup was a curious whirl. He pivoted on his left foot so that at one point he was facing second base. Then unwind, spin, and toss. There was method to this seeming eccentricity. Fitzsimmons sometimes added a gentle fastball or a quite ordinary curve to his repertoire. The success of these pitches depended on surprise and Fat Freddie whirled to conceal the way he gripped the baseball. Since the batters could not see the grip, they could only guess what was coming. In the 1941 pennant race, guileful old Fred Fitzsimmons needed so much rest that he started only twelve games. But given suitable off time, he was simply splendid, winning six and losing only one in his antiquity, and posting an earned run average of 2.07.

With that dizzying whirl wasn't he vulnerable to bunts and naked to sharp drives? Not at all, or so we thought in Brooklyn. Fitzsimmons was an agile round man, widely regarded as the best fielding pitcher extant. Or the best forty-year-old fielding pitcher, anyway.

Matched against the strong Yankee lefthander, Marius Russo, Fitzsimmons scattered four hits across six innings. Neither team could score. Russo came up against Fitzsimmons with two out and a man on first in the seventh. Fitzsimmons whirled and threw and Russo cracked a rocket of a line drive smack into Fitzsimmons's left knee. The ball caromed high into the air. Pee Wee Reese caught it for the third out. Fitzsimmons staggered to the dugout in great pain, cursing with each limping step.

Hugh Casey, a premier relief pitcher, replaced Fitzsimmons in the eighth inning and the Yankees pounded him for four hits and defeated the Dodgers, 2-1. "That damn Durocher blew it," Larry MacPhail told reporters well into the cocktail hour. "He wanted Fitzsimmons to stay in the game. We all did. But the feller couldn't pitch after he took that shot in the knee. Durocher was concentrating so hard on Fitzsimmons that he forgot to tell Casey to warm up. Casey comes in cold and we get beat." Retelling this years later, Durocher exonerated himself and blamed Casey for "choking." (By then, Casey could not mount a defense. Distraught over a broken love affair, he had killed himself at the age of thirty-seven.)

The following afternoon, October 5, 1941, brought a game with yet a stranger denouement. The Dodgers carried a 4-3 lead into the ninth, with Casey throwing four innings of brilliant relief. He retired two Yankees and got two strikes on Tommy Henrich, a formidable slugger. Casey snapped off a huge overhand curve for a swinging third strike and the victory that tied the World Series. Except—as generations of Brooklyn children would hear—"Catcher Mickey Owen dropped the ball!" In point of fact the big curve skidded off the side of Owen's glove. Henrich ran to first, while Owen pursued the spinning baseball toward the Dodger dugout. There was no play. Joe DiMaggio singled. Charley "King Kong" Keller doubled home Henrich with the tying run and DiMaggio scored the run that gave his team the lead. The Yankees won, 7-4, after the strikeout that should have ended the game. Tommy Holmes, a columnist for the *Brooklyn Eagle*, cried out in the press box: "The condemned have jumped out of the chair and executed the warden." The Yankees clinched the Series the next afternoon by winning a well-played, undramatic ball game, 3-1.

To my father, the Brooklyn debacles must have seemed like Wambsganss Redux. The Dodgers seemed doomed always to lose, albeit in interesting ways. The Boston Braves had won the World Series. The Pirates had won the World Series. The Reds had won the World Series. The Phillies hadn't, but they were a caricature of a ballclub, called by baseball writers the Phutile Phils. The St. Louis Browns hadn't, mostly because they had never gotten into a World Series. But why on earth were the Brooklyn Dodgers, with their great tradition and their outstanding 1941 team, that appealing mix, so to speak, of Vance and Wheat, Wyatt and Reese, bracketed with the Phutiles and the Brownies?

To myself—I was thirteen years old in October 1941—the Series remained mythic as an Olympiad. Tickets came only in strips. If you wanted to see Game Three at Ebbets Field, you had to buy tickets for Games Four and Five as well. This meant that the cost of a good pair ran to $36. My father was comfortably fixed, but trying to smuggle $36 past my mother for ballgames was, as he put it, "out of the question."

"Even for World Series ballgames?" I said.

"Your mother feels there are many things more important than the World Series."

"Such as?"

"Such as the siege of Leningrad. If the Nazis win the war, we all go to the hot place in a handbasket."

Juxtaposing the fate of mankind with the World Series may now appear bizarre. It may even *be* bizarre. But that truly was the way things were. The year 1941 provided great triumphs for the Axis powers. The Luftwaffe bombed London with devastating effect. On May 11 a single raid killed 1,436 civilians. Nazi troops conquered Yugoslavia and overcame Greece. The swastika was flying above the Acropolis and storm troopers marched through the marketplace of Socrates. Germany invaded Stalin's Soviet Union on June 22 and on October 3, with Wehrmacht troops and tanks advancing into the suburbs of Moscow, Hitler announced that Russia had been defeated and would not rise again. This news shared front pages in New York with the Wyatt-DiMaggio encounter.

By 1941 my family had moved into a large sunbright apartment near Grand Army Plaza, which placed me within hearing distance of Ebbets Field. Handsome French doors opened from the living room and dining room. Sunlight poured through them and so, from time to time, did the sounds of cheering crowds at Ebbets Field. Red Barber spoke to me through my black Air King radio in a cultured southern drawl that was finely polished and calm, interlaced with urgent bursts.

"Camilli up. Passeau throws. There's a long, high drive to right. Nicholson going back. He's looking up. He's looking up. But he's not going to catch this one. No, suh!"

By rushing away from my bedroom radio, I could reach the dining room in time to hear the cheers, the real cheers, not the broadcast cheers, carrying over the rooftops from the ballpark.

"Camilli hit one, Dad."

"What about homework?"

Back in my bedroom, Barber was saying, "That's number twenty-six for Big Dolph. A real Old-Goldie. An' we're rolling a carton of his favorite smokes down the screen for Dolph. We know he'll 'ppreciate 'em. An' listen, why don't you light up a rich-tastin' Old Gold yourself? A new tobacco, Latakia, makes 'em tastier yet. Medwick's the hitter."

Near the wide intersection of Eastern Parkway and Washington Avenue the huge neoclassical structure of the Brooklyn Museum rose in Indiana limestone. Entablatures bore memorable names: Herodotus, Plato, Virgil, Pindar, Milton. Fine, I thought. Three cheers for Herodotus and Plato. Behind the museum stretched a wonderful ballfield where—and this was important—the outfield ended against a steep bank. No matter how hard and how high you hit a baseball on that little field, it always came back, rolling down the slope. This eliminated the possibility of the calamity that devastated the day: a lost baseball.

You could buy a baseball in any candy store for ten cents. A chocolate bar cost a nickel and a baseball cost a dime. But there was a problem with the ten-cent baseball. If you hit it hard, you never hit it again. The damn thing split. I once swung enthusiastically and broke a ten-cent ball in two. Several of us rushed up for the autopsy. The cover was a strange, stiff material, stitched together in the standard red. It was the internal construction that startled us. The ball was stuffed with newspaper. Crumpled newspaper, covered with odd symbols. Then we figured out that the newspapers, like the ball itself, came from Japan.

"I would have had a double if the ball hadn't broken," I said. "Maybe a triple."

"It's just junk," said Jerry Shaw, who threw the pitch. "Everything they make in Japan is junk."

"Or maybe even a homer. I caught that one right."

"A real ball," Jerry Shaw said, "doesn't have paper insides. It's supposed to be twine around a cork center. No wonder I couldn't pitch that thing. How can you pitch a Japanese baseball with Japanese newspaper insides?"

The quarter ball was the next grade up. For twenty-five cents, you got something you could use for about a week, until the cover got loose and you had to tape it—wrap black friction tape around the twine. That made the ball heavier than you liked, but still usable. The top of the line in the neighborhood was the fifty-cent ball, available at Horowitz's Stationery & Sporting Goods. You could use a fifty-cent baseball for weeks, although the cover would turn from white to earthen tan, with a spot or two of green. That was the best ball we used—the four-colored fifty-center, changing hues as it aged, white and tan and green and red. We seldom saw, and never played with a major league baseball. They retailed for an astronomical $1.35 each. Steve Packer had gotten one, signed by the entire 1935 Brooklyn team, but that was not a baseball. It was an icon.

The Dodgers played at Ebbets Field and we played behind the museum and war raged through the world, killing the soldiers, killing the pilots, killing the innocents. "I think the war is coming here," my father said. "I'm too old to serve and I hope it's over while you're still too young."

"I'll fight the Nazis, Dad. I'd like to fight them."

"For the time being work on your hitting. Jerk that top hand over when you swing. You want to pull the ball. Work on your hitting, and how's the Latin coming?"

That is a touch of a Brooklyn baseball boyhood, 1941. Then, on December 7, the Japanese attacked Pearl Harbor. What would happen to the country, I wondered? Would Pee Wee Reese and Dolph Camilli and Whit Wyatt and Red Barber have to go into the Army to fight the Japs? What would World War II do to the Brooklyn Dodgers?

A Chicago sportswriter named Warren Brown uttered the wittiest summation of wartime baseball. With such stars as Stan Musial, Joe DiMaggio, and Ted Williams still in service, the mostly wartime Detroit Tigers played the mostly wartime Cubs in the 1945 World Series. By way of working up an advance story, the Associated Press polled sportswriters, looking to establish a favorite. "Who do you like?" the wire service man inquired. Brown paused and then said clearly and slowly, "I don't see how either team can possibly win."

By the end of the war, I had become a good enough athlete to earn a few dollars on weekends, playing pickup games in the Hudson Valley, where my father maintained a modest second home. You put up a dollar and if you were playing, say, third base, you asked the other third baseman to match you. The winner got to keep both dollars. After the game, you passed a cap through the crowd and the two teams split the proceeds. It was possible to earn as much as six dollars on a good weekend. I knew other sports existed—football, tennis, basketball, swimming—but when I was seventeen, no sport but baseball held my bounding heart. There was none that I took as seriously, and certainly none that was as personal and transcendent, and interlaced with young, extravagant dreams.

With our skills growing, my summer buddies and I learned to specialize. I could stay with grounders. Jerry Solovay threw a snapping sidearm curve. Red Pressman could run down a fly ball into the next county. So Jerry pitched and I played infield and Red ran his longlegged way in scruffy outfields. We learned as we grew up that every position, each of the nine, requires particular abilities. The catcher has to spin on fouls and block low curves, and think. The shortstop has to range left and right, throw hard, throw quickly, and think. The third baseman has to crouch and lunge and put his face in front of a ground ball, and think. It is a wonder, nine positions, nine different sets of skills. Where we played, on diamonds long since desecrated into building lots, the most appalling mistake a boy could make was mental. Anybody could butch a grounder occasionally or let a throw go high. Anybody could and everybody did. Worse—and not forgiven—was forgetting the number of outs, or losing track of the count. Boys who muffed *too* many grounders had to ride the bench. Boys who made mental errors had to endure ridicule, not notably witty, but loud. "Hey, feller, it was two out. You were supposed to run on anything. Two out. You know. Like after one comes two."

Being considered a smart ballplayer carried more cachet than being a good physics student. If you threw to the wrong base, neither exalted grades nor an Einstein IQ could save you. You were a rockhead. You were "thinking with your ass." The peer pressure created intense discipline. You learned that to play ball, you had to think ahead. Before each pitch you had to focus.

You had to stay in the present and while doing that you had to contend with the future. What am I going to do if the ball gets hit to me? Baseball is surely a game to dream *about*, but it is no game to play while daydreaming. If you consider a cloud shaped like a camel and wonder if it has come all the way from Araby, then when a grounder suddenly drives toward you and two base runners sprint and somebody shouts, "Here!" you open yourself to panic.

I remember the misery of messing up a play. I crouched at third, holding a base runner close. Another runner was leading off second. The batter swung and topped a spinning roller. I charged in, the base runner rushing beside me. I seized the ball barehanded. Should I lunge and try to tag him? Flip home? Either way the play would be close. Time, like the base runner, hurtled on. "First," bawled the pitcher, a cocky, gifted lefthander called Spike. I was out of position to snap the throw. A run scored. I held the baseball. I could no more throw to first than fly. Spike said two words, "Dumb bastard." That was unpleasant, but less so than the sight of my father, seated near third base, averting his eyes.

The way to make this particular play, or one way to make it, is to think as Spike winds up, "If I get a squibber, and the runner goes, I'm throwing home." With that clear in advance, all you have to do is execute, no easy feat given the spin of the baseball, the hooves of the runner, and the general tension. On a hundred afternoons, across those long-ago summers, the alternative to playing focused baseball became clear. Endure constant humiliation, or switch to Ping-Pong. I liked Ping-Pong. Ping-Pong may have been my best sport. But it lacked panache.

I remember misery in the afternoon, and I exult in the recollection of triumphs. The generation that reached adolescence during World War II put on shows of bravado. We all had buddies whom the Armed Forces were drafting. We read newspaper stories of terrible battles. My closest friend, Frank Wolf, and I knew Alan Seeger's World War I poem:

> *I have a rendezvous with Death*
> *At some disputed barricade,*
> *When Spring comes back with rustling shade*
> *And apple-blossoms fill the air.*

Seeger kept his rendezvous. He died in battle. Sometimes on a summer evening Frank and I wondered if Alan Seeger's fate might be our own. "If I go, I'm taking twenty Nazis with me."

"This isn't a cowboy western," Frank said. "Someone you never see, five miles away, fires an artillery piece and it's over. It's over. This is not like a cowboy western at all."

I thought about that for as long as I cared to. "Let's find some girls, Frank," I said.

"If we only had a car," Frank said.

Nobody had a car, and it wouldn't have mattered if anyone did. Without a ration card, you couldn't buy gasoline and teenagers did not get ration cards. I remember longing for a leggy girl named Laurie, who swam with a smooth, overhand crawl. She wore no bathing cap and as she splashed in sunlight, cinnamon showed in her short, brown hair. But Laurie ignored me. She seemed preoccupied with a scrawny, intense, older sort, who limped and played guitar and sang what he called red-radical songs and taught philosophy at a teachers' college somewhere.

One afternoon I had a decent game at third. I snared some one-hoppers. I doubled to left. Twice I outran long foul flies and, racing full speed, caught them over my shoulder. It was hot. After the game, I hurried to the lake. Laurie was wearing a two-piece bathing suit, with a white floral pattern layered on soft green. She approached me with a feline walk. "I was at the game. Did you see me?"

"Yes."

"I just want to say, 'Hello, third-baseman Kahn.'"

"Oh. Uh, hello."

"Third-baseman Kahn, you were swell."

"Thanks."

Laurie lowered her head and looked at me very seriously. "Would you like to go canoeing? We could go way out to the other side of the island."

I hauled an elderly brown canoe into the lake and with Laurie kneeling near the prow I shoved off, jumping into the stern. The canoe shuddered. "Don't tip us," Laurie said.

"You're a good swimmer."

"But I've *been* swimming, third-baseman Kahn. I don't want to get wet all over again."

I paddled toward the island, near the far side of the lake. Laurie lay on the bottom of the canoe, eyes closed against the sun, legs crossed at the knee. "This is really enjoyable," she said.

"Yes," I said. My throat was curiously dry. I had forgotten my Old Gold cigarettes. Laurie had a bright peony mouth and her body was an even tan. "Let's drift," she said.

I wanted to say something as romantic as a poem, but my mouth felt so damn dry. "I like looking at you, Laurie. I'd like to see you where your suntan ends."

"Well, maybe you can," Laurie said. She opened her eyes. "It's okay now. We're behind the island."

I moved to join her at the bottom of the canoe. She smiled and uncrossed her knees.

I reached to stroke her neck and she made a purr of pleasure. Then, in a quite different tone: "Careful. Watch out! We'll be swamped."

That was how I learned a lesson of the ages. You cannot make out in a canoe. But I learned something else that speaks for baseball.

Even though he may not know what to do with her, the best third baseman gets the prettiest girl.

Wartime big-league ball produced anomalies. The draft took single men first, so that the teams with the most married ballplayers tended to fare best for a while. Hank Greenberg, a bachelor, went into the Army on May 12, 1941. Joe DiMaggio, who was married to an actress named Dorothy Arnold, was not inducted until after the season of 1942. In essence, DiMaggio got to play two more full seasons than Greenberg on the basis of matrimony. Leo Durocher was declared 4-F, physically unfit for military service, when doctors discovered that one of his eardrums had been punctured. "I musta stuck a pencil in the ear when I was a kid," Durocher said. "It could have been his own voice that did it," someone else suggested. We were delighted that Durocher could continue to work in Brooklyn, but the military carried off Pee Wee Reese, Pete Reiser, Kirby Higbe, Billy Herman, and a number of fine prospects. Although Dixie Walker led the National League in hitting at .357, the 1944 Dodgers finished seventh, avoiding the cellar by only a game and a half.

In '44 the St. Louis Browns won the only pennant of their fifty-two-year lifespan, finishing one game ahead of the Detroit Tigers. A season later the Browns signed a long-faced outfielder named Pete Gray, who had lost his right arm in a mining accident. Gray was a fine fielder; he caught the ball, flipped it, discarded his glove and recaught the ball in what appeared to be a single deft motion. He was ready to throw immediately. He swung lefthanded, somewhat in the manner of a tennis player hitting a forehand. This extraordinary athlete was no more than a marginal major-league batter and after that single season—he hit .218—the Browns released him. But numbers of us trekked to the Bronx to see him play and cheered the determined Brownie as if he were a Dodger.

We didn't share Warren Brown's professional cynicism about the quality of the wartime major leagues. In our duality—watching big leaguers perform and playing ball ourselves—major league baseball, even during the war, commanded respect. I saw a wartime Brooklyn first baseman, Ed Stevens, crack a high drive clear to the exit gate at Ebbets Field, 399 feet distant from home plate. After the game, I walked to the gate and stared back toward home plate and wondered how anybody could hit a baseball that hard, that far. My father's good smashes carried 300 feet, mighty wallops on the fields we wandered. But by major league standards, the best of them were fly balls. This fellow Stevens routinely hit the baseball a hundred feet longer. Some sportswriters described Stevens as a wartime replacement, an *ersatz* Camilli. Ersatz rang with a revolting Nazi sound. Looking back from the exit gate, I thought that nothing could be less ersatz than a 399-foot wallop. Nobody I played with or against hit for anywhere near that range. Ersatz Camilli, hell. Big Ed Stevens was the genuine goods, a 105-millimeter made-in-America howitzer.

One afternoon two wartime Yankees, Nick Etten and Bud Metheny, visiting friends near Peekskill, N.Y., decided to take impromptu batting practice at a little field near Lake Mohegan. The diamond ran from lakeside to stands of northern ash that rose eighty feet high beyond the outfield. The two Yankees carried cans of Ruppert's Beer and a sack of well-used big-league balls. While Gene Currivan, the fastest pitcher in the area, warmed up, Etten and Metheny sipped beer. When Currivan was ready, they put away the beer and picked up bats. Then, without much effort, they began to launch drives over the field and clear over the trees beyond the field. I was supposed to shag. That turned out to be impossible. You can't run down fly balls inside a forest. As soon as Etten and Metheny started swinging, everything and everybody else, the field, the rest of us, Gene Currivan, his fastball, even the eighty-foot trees, turned lilliputian. Two fellers from The Bigs had come to town.

In point of fact the 1945 World Series that Warren Brown wittily disparaged turned out to be a dramatic seven-game match, which Detroit won over the Cubs, largely through the efforts of two Hall of Famers, Hal Newhouser, a swift lefthander, and Hank Greenberg, just returned from the China-Burma-India theater of war. Newhouser pitched two complete-game victories. Greenberg slugged two homers and three doubles. Peace was upon us. The good life and the superstars were coming back.

I had been mostly cruising through the war. It had not seemed to matter much what Frank Wolf, or Spike the Lefty, or any of us intended to do with the rest of our lives. We were going to have to go into service and fire Garand Rifles and try to survive Nazi and Japanese attacks. What sense was there in planning beyond that? When peace struck, with shocking suddenness in high summer, we were seventeen. We tried to hold off our confusion by chattering rough-tough jokes.

"What are you gonna do now that the war is over?"

"Oh, I got one helluva job lined up."

"What's that?

"Wiping the bluebird shit off the White Cliffs of Dover."

"I got a better job than that."

"Oh, yeah?"

"I'm gonna be pumpin' ethyl at the gas station."

In truth, we were products of puritan households, and quite frightened by ambient lust. My father brooked no obscenity. Once, when he heard me say "damn" as a chore went badly, he lifted one brow and glared me into silence. No obscenity and no lothario behavior. "If you ever have the temerity to get a young lady pregnant," he warned me in a calm, menacing way, "you'll be out of this household before you know it. I don't care if that means you sleep in the streets. You'll live up to this family's moral standards, by Jupiter."

As I marched toward adulthood, at an uncertain tempo, my relationship with my father became complex and strained. He regretted that he had no business to leave me, he said. He was a history teacher and an editor and a founder of the radio program *Information, Please*, in which an urbane moderator, Clifton Fadiman, posed quiz questions for a panel of experts and celebrity guests such as John Kieran and F. P. A. *Information, Please* radiated my father's passion for the world's wonders. There were questions on poetry and gardening and pottery and history, and to be sure, baseball. Within a few seasons, *Information, Please* became the most popular radio program in the country, surpassing even *The Jack Benny Show*. (I think sometimes today, in naked sentiment, the whole country really liked my dad.)

Among all the gifts that my father was granted, eidetic memory, power to left field, optimism, among all these important gifts, my father was missing one, as vulgar as it was important. Business sense. He never demanded a share of the radio bonanza. Nothing was offered. He made good money for his time, but as an employee, who would have no business to leave his son. This agitated him and, combined with my apparent lack of purpose, drove him to anger. "Where are you going? Do you ask yourself that? What do you intend to do with your life? You have to think through questions like that. You have to take stock. You may not drag this family back to the jungle."

Old marriage records indicated that family forebears in Alsace owned many hectares of vineyards. A vineyard, I thought to say, was not exactly a jungle. I said nothing. My father had fast hands, and he was stronger than I was.

In truth I *had* been taking stock, but I was damned if I was going to admit that to anyone, least of all to my fierce and gentle father. By 1945—I would be eighteen that October—I had come to realize that I would not be following Jersey Joe Stripp and Cookie Lavagetto as starting third baseman for the Dodgers. The recognition came gradually, without a specific instant of shock. I noted, in pickup games, that some others were faster, threw better, hit longer. I was a competent sandlot ballplayer, but not an all-star, not even a sandlot all-star. I confronted certain facts. If there were better ballplayers than I in three little summer towns, Mohegan Lake, Shrub Oak, and Jefferson Valley, what chance did I have to ascend to more demanding levels, say the minor leagues? A very small one. And what chance did I have to reach heaven's gate, to summer in the big time, to play third base at Ebbets Field? None. I had no chance at all.

"What do you want to do, third-baseman Kahn?" Laurie asked. We were alone in starlight, lying in a position of Laurie's creation—her head on my shoulder, mine on hers, our bodies extending away from one another. Intimate and chaste, it was the perfect posture for the time—before the pill, before legal abortion—when premarital pregnancy often shattered lives.

"I told you. Go skinny-dipping."

"We've *been* skinny-dipping. I mean what do you want to do with your life?"

"You sound like my father, Laur. You don't look like my father, but you sound like him."

"Be serious. Why are you always joking with me? Please be serious."

"I don't like to talk about what I want to do."

"Why not?"

"Because it may not work out and I'll look foolish."

"Not to me. You could never look foolish to me. Do you want to be a ballplayer?"

"Did. Don't. If I could hit like Musial, I would, but I can't. I can't hit like Musial or even like Big Ed Stevens."

"What then? You can tell me."

I felt a clutch in the throat. "I like poetry," I said. "Sonnets. There's one by John Keats that begins: *When I have fears that I may cease to be / Before my pen has gleaned my teeming brain.*"

"I'm not sure I know what that means," Laurie said.

"Listen to the sound. Listen to the rhythm and the sound. The meaning comes afterwards, after the music."

"Oh."

"I want to write poetry like Keats. Later on I want to write novels."

Laurie was silent for a time. Then she said, "When we went swimming, did you like the way I looked without my clothes?"

"I'm talking about poetry." I was simultaneously aroused and annoyed. "I wished I'd brought my flashlight, or there was a full moon. But I'm talking about poetry."

"I'm taking a course in poetry at Washington Square next semester. I hear it's very interesting."

"Interesting? Poetry is more than interesting." I rolled away from Laurie and sat up.

"Didn't you tell me that your grandfather was a dentist?" she asked.

"Yes."

"Well, wouldn't that be a little bit more sensible? Becoming a dentist? I mean, my mother is a very practical woman. What do you think she'd say if I told her I was thinking of getting engaged to a boy who wanted to be only a poet?"

Bullfrogs called from the lake; the sky froze and turned the stars to ice.

> Follow the Dodgers
> Follow the Dodgers around
> The infield, the outfield,
> The Dodgers got the best team in town

Across years of drift, this inane song became an anthem. I had lost my dream of playing third for Brooklyn and, after my disastrous conversation with Laurie, it became hard to take the other dream—becoming a writer—seriously. "Sure, you can write," Frank Wolf said, gently. "But what are you going to do for a living?"

"Don't worry about that," I said. "I know how to make money."

I then proceeded to worry about what I was going to do for a living, and how I was going to make money. For cloudy reasons, my parents refused to send me to any of the colleges I wanted, all of which would have placed welcome distance between us.

Colgate?
*You wouldn't like it. It's anti-Semitic.*
Middlebury? I could play for the baseball team there.
*You'd freeze in Vermont.*
Cornell? That's your old school, mom.
*With your study habits? You'll never get in.*
I got their letter today. I have early admission.
*Well, anyway we can't afford Cornell for you. Talk to him, Gordon.*

Everybody rejected Brooklyn College as too plebeian and the Washington Square colleges of NYU as looking too much like hat factories. But NYU did maintain a campus in the west Bronx on a plateau called University Heights. Here one found playing fields, a colonnade, the Hall of Fame for Great Americans, and a few Greek revival buildings that pleased my mother. I was dispatched as a day-tripper to college, riding a train on the Jerome-Woodlawn line, a long voyage through darkness, until the tracks rose out of a tube and the subway, the very same train, became an elevated, behind right field at Yankee Stadium. Not Gehrig, not even Ruth, ever smashed one onto the tracks.

I studied with a marvelous historian, Dr. Theodore Francis Jones, who taught a course that surveyed antique Greece through Charlemagne. The professor loved to ask a devout Catholic student named Melchione, "If Christ were alive today, would he be considered a communist?" No matter how many times he was asked, Melchione's response was always the same. He blushed.

Harway Knox Wilson taught freshman composition and liked my stuff. Soon I was hiring out to premeds: freshman English essays, $5 each. The premeds turned out to be demanding employers. "I mean," a boy named Hershey Marcus complained, "you got an A on your essay. How come you got a lousy B on mine?"

"I wrote mine first. I was a little tired when I got to writing yours."

"What are you pulling? You don't need A's. You aren't trying to get into medical school. You take the lousy B's. I need the A's."

That touched the core of what NYU grandly called the University College of Arts and Pure Science. University Heights was overrun by boys so driven to gain admission to medical school, any med school— Southwestern near Dallas, Zurich in northeastern Switzerland—that Hamlet's last words, *The rest is silence,* were important only if worth five points on a final exam.

In this atmosphere, academic life deteriorated. A biologist named Horace Wesley Stunkard devised a course that he honed into weekly torture. "Protoplasm is a polyphasic, colloidal emulsion," Stunkard began one lecture, "in electrostatic and dynamic equilibrium, the phases of which are reversible." He continued in that vein for twenty minutes, addressing 150 boys, making eye contact with none, in a lecture hall the size of a neighborhood theater. Stunkard was tall, horse-faced, and intense. "I hope you all have taken careful notes," he said, "because my guess is that Friday's quiz may have something to do with the nature of protoplasm." He looked up and I could not tell whether Horace Wesley Stunkard was smiling or leering.

Challenged, I fought back with my best academic weapon—memory. The Friday quiz consisted of one Stunkard command. Describe protoplasm. I responded by setting down verbatim the Stunkard lecture. The quiz-section instructor gave me a C.

"I wrote exactly what Dr. Stunkard said," I complained. "Every word."

"So you did," the instructor said. He was slight and pink-skinned, an albino. "And that's why you got a C. You have to evidence collateral reading for a B. For an A we expect research on your own."

"I'm an English major. You expect me to research into the nature of protoplasm, on the side?"

"You aren't in high school anymore," the little pink man said, "and I don't give a damn what you're majoring in and neither does Dr. Stunkard."

I retreated to the Commons for lunch with two bright premeds. "You don't seem to get the point of Stunkard's course," said Hershey Marcus, my sometime employer. He was a powerful, black-haired boy, a fine athlete, and a Zionist. "It isn't in the curriculum to expand our knowledge, or anyway not primarily. Primarily, it's in there to keep Jews out of medical school."

"Stunkard gives two A's, four B's and a hundred and forty C's," said Red Saypol. "That's the point, giving out all those C's. You get a C in freshman bio, and what medical school will take you if you're Jewish?"

"Stunkard teaches a premed elimination course," Marcus said. "The guy hates Jews."

"Check him out," Saypol said. "He worked for I.G. Farben, the German chemical company, in the summer of 1939."

Reference books in Gould Memorial Library bore that out. Stunkard worked as a consultant to Farben in Nazi Germany just before Adolf Hitler invaded Poland. This was not lost on the overwhelmingly Jewish student body of "NYU Uptown." Nor did the driven, scrambling premeds miss another point. The uptown faculty employed no Jews.

The situation was nasty and confusing. But if NYU Uptown mirrored the lace-curtain anti-Semitism of the time, it also offered a program designed to seduce Jewish premeds and their families into coughing up tuition of as much as one thousand dollars a year. Plenty of bio, math, chemistry, and physics; very little in the humanities; nothing at all on modern British and American poetry. During my unhappy tenure there, NYU Uptown did not recognize the existence of T. S. Eliot, Ezra Pound, W. H. Auden, Robert Frost, A. E. Housman, nor even the towering Irishman, William Butler Yeats. Poetry reached Tennyson and proceeded to Browning. Then, the catalogue insisted, poetry died.

The premeds applauded, concealing smiles. "Yeats's imagery," Hershey Marcus remarked when I showed him "Leda and the Swan," "is as tough to figure out as freshman bio."

"But a lot more beautiful," I said. I quoted slowly and clearly a passage I had discovered in my mother's collected Yeats.

*A shudder in the loins engenders there*
*The broken wall, the burning roof and tower*
*And Agamemnon dead.*

"Isn't that amazing?" I said. "He does the whole Trojan War in three lines. Paris steals Helen and gets her and beds her. They come. That's the shudder in the loins. Then look what happens. An orgasm sets off the Trojan War."

Hershey looked puzzled. After a while he became thoughtful. "It's not that I really want to make medical school," he said. "I'd like to go to Palestine and work there as a chemist and build a country where Jews can be safe. But if I stay here and become a doctor, I'll always make a good living and get some respect, even from the anti-Semites like Stunkard. If I can handle the bio, this place gives me an inside track at getting into Bellevue [the NYU School of Medicine]. That's what I'm doing on the campus in the Bronx. What you're doing there, a fine writer like you, I don't know and I'll bet that you don't, either."

In point of fact, I spent as little time on campus as I could. Years earlier the novelist Thomas Wolfe mocked NYU, where he taught freshman composition, as the "School of Utility Trades." When I matriculated, to use the academic word, I was sixteen years old and adrift between two dreams—playing major league baseball and writing poetry and books. A smaller college, where I could have played varsity ball and indulged myself in reading English poetry and Russian novels—and even in the sacrilegious works of Thomas Wolfe—might have given me direction and confidence. But what might have been is an abstraction. I was enrolled, matriculated, enlisted at NYU Uptown. College, like most things American, is a business. Let the buyer, student, patient, or corpse beware.

Despite its limitations, tribal wars, and utilitarian bent, the University College of Arts and Pure Science helped many young men. But to succeed there, you had to be as dogged and as purposeful as, well, a Jewish premed. Or to put this into a term I learned later, but never dared use in my father's house, you had to be hard-assed. As hard-assed as a hungry ballplayer. A fuckin', hard-assed, hungry ballplayer, as my late friend, Leo Durocher, liked to say.

I took to cutting required courses that bored or baffled me. The consequences, in the midst of the ongoing war of annihilation between the premeds and the faculty, were predictable: D's and an occasional F. When these grades traveled south from the Bronx to Brooklyn, my father said that unless I did something significant in college, he was going to throw me out of the household. "As of now," my mother added, "we can't afford to give you an allowance anymore. Just paying tuition for the grades you're getting is wasteful enough."

That meant, while dodging classes, I had to go to work. I found a part-time job soldering sheet metal at a radio factory called Espey Electronics. That kept me solvent, but the work was hot and nasty. I found easier prospective employment selling fluorescent fixtures. No buyers. I signed on as an electrician's assistant, installing fixtures someone else had sold. In most of the novels I read, blurbs listed the author's past occupations, always a varied list. In a sense I was making progress. I was working not on a novel, but on the jacket copy that would be used with the big book, after I got around to writing it. During infrequent trips to the campus I took over the humor magazine *Medley*, determined to produce a provocative edition. I wrote several forgotten light stories. I clearly recall two cartoons I elected to publish.

One showed naked feet extending from a bush. The pair pointing upward was smaller than the pair pointed toward the ground. The caption read: "She: Isn't it a beautiful moon? He: I am in no position to say."

The other drawing depicted a man wearing a sailor cap as he sat face to face with a woman in a bathtub. Both seemed naked. The man in the sailor cap was perspiring. He said, "And that, Miss Smith, is how the torpedo works."

We sold perhaps a hundred copies of *Medley* in the student bookstore before a posse of assistant deans confiscated the magazine as obscene. Now I was not only a dilatory student but a pornographer. Probably I was also depressed. Then Jackie Robinson came along and began my resurrection.

After the 1942 season, Larry MacPhail left Brooklyn and became a major in the Army. His last Dodger team won 104 games, but finished second to a brilliant Cardinal club that won two more and thumped the Yankees in the World Series. MacPhail had rescued the Brooklyn franchise from the rim of bankruptcy; brought radio broadcasting to New York baseball; introduced night games into darkest Flatbush; and created a splendid panoply of promotions. But he was expensive and flamboyant and alcoholic. When MacPhail said at a board meeting that with a war on, he ought to join the Army, no Dodger stockholder, not one, urged him to stay. MacPhail felt both patriotic and aghast. As he told the press that he was resigning *and* that his resignation had been accepted, he wept. When Dolph Camilli gave him a wristwatch as a team farewell present, MacPhail cried again. One month later dry-eyed Branch Rickey—who had built the world champion Cardinals— signed on as general manager of the Dodgers. He was sixty-one years old and a fountain of youthful innovation.

During World War II, Rickey made speeches anyplace in Brooklyn where he could gather an audience, from windy Canarsie by the sea, to stifling Fort Greene, on a paved-over inland rise. Addressing potential physicists and engineers at Brooklyn Technical High School, Rickey spoke of the world ahead. "Baseball will be more magnificent than it has ever been," he said. "We're going to do surprising things. Undoubtedly, scientists will lead the years to come— young men, very much like yourselves, indeed perhaps your very selves, will be the true rulers of society." As Rickey spoke, he shook a glass jar containing raisins and nuts. The prop made no sense until Rickey reached his peroration. "Those who succeed in baseball and in science will first be keen observers and, gentlemen, I hope you have been observing this little jar. Raisins and nuts, nuts and raisins. No matter how many times I shake this jar, as I trust you have observed and marked well for your future—the nuts always come out on top."

After the laughter subsided, Rickey said, with all the seriousness he employed when considering the future of mankind, "Plenty of good tickets are available for tomorrow's game with the Cubs. General admission is only a dollar ten. Thank you for your attention."

Rickey was building an awareness of baseball, the Dodgers, and, to be sure, Branch Rickey. He was baseball man, scholar, moralist, hustler, and preacher all in one, and a person of great and contradictory profundity. Understatement was anathema to Wesley Branch Rickey but when World War II ended, one of the "surprising things" he mentioned at Brooklyn high schools turned into an extraordinary saga.

Defying the color line, the barrier that had walled organized baseball off from blacks since 1885, Rickey signed Jackie Robinson to a minor league contract for the season of 1946. As a rookie playing for the Montreal Royals in the International League, Robinson hit .349 and stole 40 bases. He was not only black, he was damn good, and Rickey promoted him to the Dodgers in April 1947.

As Robinson remarked years later, when we had become friends, "My demand was modest enough." He was not asking to move into a white neighborhood. He was not busing black children to white schools. He was not joining a white country club. He was not marrying, or even seducing, a blonde. He was simply trying to make a living in the infield. But Robinson's "modest demand" threatened and divided the nation as nothing else in the history of American sport. With the cold war gathering, some thought that the only thing worse than having one of *them* playing for a team in organized baseball would be having a Commie in the White House. Wasn't *anything* sacred anymore?

My various jobs meant that I could afford to buy Dodger tickets whenever I wanted and my father and I were able to put aside our differences when we went to games. He let me pay for my ticket once. After that, tickets, hot dogs, scorecards, were on him. I suppose he was as troubled as I that our relationship had turned harsh. It thrilled us both to escape to Ebbets Field. The place, the team, the ballgames, Jackie Robinson, worked potent magic and there, in a ballpark completed when my father was only eleven years old, we were close again, as father and son should be, close and comfortable with one another, and we were friends.

We studied new Dodgers Rickey lumped together as "the youth movement." Gene Hermanski, twenty-six, was a solid hitter. Ralph Branca, twenty-one, the big righthander up from NYU, possessed great stuff, keen intelligence, boundless promise. Wild enthusiasm colored my judgment. I saw Hermanski as a surefire .350 slugger. (He hit a career .272.) Branca? Absolutely a combination of Dizzy Dean and Bob Feller. (He won fewer than one hundred games in a stunted career.) "I think you're a little too quick to put your favorite players on the Pullman car to Cooperstown," my father said. "This is a game where staying power is important." He was always urging me toward caution, but even my father conceded that Carl Furillo, another twenty-five-year-old, had the best throwing arm on earth. We made it a point to come to the ballpark early, so we could watch Furillo fire in pregame drills. He hurled the baseball three hundred feet from dead center field, low and hard with a swift, skidding bounce, knee-high into the catcher's glove. Furillo was throwing the length of a football field and hitting the pocket of a mitt. With a small smile showing beneath the mustache, my father said, "We're going to have quite a team right here in Brooklyn."

Furillo and Branca and Pee Wee Reese were wonderful in the summer of 1947. But Jackie Robinson was something apart. He was unique, solitary, flawed, noble, a figure of pure courage cast in obsidian.

"There was never anywhere in the world a white so white as the white of the Dodger uniforms," says Larry King, the Brooklyn native who evolved into a television interviewer and reporter, host to movie stars and American presidents. "And that white was an important part of the setting."

When my father and I first watched Robinson on a spring day in 1947, we saw the white home uniform, alabaster as never before, then a black face and beautifully muscled black arms. The impact was astonishing. When you looked at the young black man, wearing number 42, white cloth embracing the dark skin, you suddenly realized that every major leaguer you had ever seen in all your life had been a white man. You thought, or at least *I* thought:

*Sweet land of liberty, what the hell is going on?*

Today we have a word for it. *Apartheid.* Apartheid was going on, the most obvious symptom of our country's sustained, illicit romance with bigotry. Racism ruled America and what I saw at NYU—the biology-laboratory anti-Semitism of Dr. Horace Wesley Stunkard— was just one small piece of a large, loathsome picture. At Ebbets Field, in the summer of '47, American apartheid flashed into view like wicked lightning.

In the rough-and-tumble of the basepaths, white ballplayers were always bumping Robinson. As if to make the gauntlet crueler, Rickey assigned Robinson to play first base, a position at which he was a novice. Watching Robinson scramble through some early fielding plays—he had difficulty with his footwork—I concluded that he was not as smooth as Dolph Camilli, while my father concluded he was not as smooth as Ol' Jake Daubert, dead now since 1924. The uncertain footwork contributed to near collisions at first. But when other ballplayers tried to spike Robinson in the heel, his footwork was not the reason. Whites were trying to stomp the colored guy out of their game.

Growing up with baseball, my father and I accepted knockdown fast balls as inherent to the struggle. My father said that they were a part of the sport and often they put the pitcher in a hole and, he continued, you were struck in the head only if first you froze in terror. My father did not admire men who allowed themselves to be terrorized. Pitches plunked me in the body from time to time, and I once saw a teammate panic and duck into the path of an inside fast ball. The sound of a baseball cracking against a skull was ominous, but in the end everyone survived. I don't remember any serious youthful debates about the morality of throwing a baseball at somebody else's temple. Discussions stopped with the cliché: "You can get hurt worse trying to cross the street." For my father's part, he never went beyond the generality, "If you're afraid of a hard ball, baseball isn't your game."

But the throwing at Robinson was more persistent and more vicious than anything I had seen or my father had seen before me and by that measure, persistent, malevolent viciousness, beanballs hurled by brawny whites at the black recruit appeared new and ugly. One day a rangy Philadelphia righthander named Al Jurisich knocked Robinson down and on the next pitch cracked him with a fastball near the elbow. Jurisich was behind in the count. The pitch made no baseball sense. Its purpose was to injure, and Robinson clutched his right elbow and jumped and spun in pain. My father said in a low, shocked voice: "Jesus H. Christ."

This wasn't baseball; this was abuse. Branch Rickey presently held forth on one result: "The unconscionable behavior, the verbal taunts and the attempts to injure Robinson, created on Jackie's behalf a thing called sympathy, the most unifying word in the world." Rickey had studied Latin and Greek; now the old classicist emerged. "That word has a Greek origin," he said. "It means to suffer. Thus to say I sympathize with you means I suffer with you. That is a result these bigoted ballplayers brought about. They made Robinson's teammates and our fans and even some of the hard-boiled newspaper fellows sympathize with Robinson and suffer with him. Not all. Some of the newspaper fellows remained vitriolic. But what turned the tide for Robinson, really, was the abuse. Fair-minded people everywhere sympathized with this Negro and suffered with him, although when he was spiked it was only the Negro's blood that was shed."

The format of *Information, Please,* required the appearance of a guest panelist, who joined three regulars in answering the canny questions posed by Clifton Fadiman and developed—from ideas that listeners submitted—by my father, often in a great surge of concentration on a single Saturday afternoon. Guest "experts," ranging from Wendell Willkie to Leonard Bernstein, provided fresh energies each week, except on those occasions when a guest expert turned out not to answer anything at all. This being radio, silent guest experts disappeared. Guest experts drew the same fee, one thousand dollars, whether scintillating or mute.

To prevent expensive silence, staff members interviewed guests beforehand to determine "areas of information." My father felt especially pleased when a guest turned out to possess knowledge outside of an obvious specialty. Willkie knew the politics of his time, of course, but he also turned out to be an authority on the Reconstruction Era when radical Republicans sought to impose ruthless peace on the defeated South. Leonard Bernstein knew something about everything, except sports. As an impassioned, if subtle, Dodger fan, my father insisted on interviewing guest expert Jackie Robinson personally. Robinson was wholly cooperative; the *Information, Please* fee, the thousand dollars, for a half-hour appearance, was fully one-fifth of what the Dodgers were paying him for an entire season of major league ball. (He was the game's greatest box-office attraction in 1947 and Rickey paid him $5,000 for that harrowing rookie year.)

Gordon Kahn and Jackie Robinson talked baseball for a while in my father's office at 444 Madison Avenue. What interested him beyond baseball? my father asked.

"Abraham Lincoln," Robinson said. "My mother told me to study up on Lincoln and I have."

"Anything else? Music, poetry, philosophy, perhaps? Any bits of special wisdom you picked up in college?"

"Mr. Kahn," Robinson said. "When I was at UCLA, I had to run track, and play varsity football, basketball, and baseball to protect my athletic scholarship. I got C's, and I was lucky to get them."

Robinson helped answer two of the eleven questions posed by Clifton Fadiman, making him an adequate, but not outstanding, guest. "He didn't do half badly," my father said, clicking off the big RCA radio-console in the living room. "Not half badly at all. The man is living under simply hellish pressure."

"I'd like to do that," I said.

"Do what?"

"Interview people like Jackie Robinson, the way you do."

My mother left us, toting a copy of *The Hudson Review*, in dread of finding herself ambushed by baseball talk. But the talk that followed reached beyond the game. My father and I agreed that Robinson was doing something extremely important and though our admiration of him came from different viewpoints, we agreed that he must be an extraordinary man. As we joined in enthusiasm for him and the integration of baseball, other differences between us narrowed.

"I'm not aware of any jobs that consist of interviewing famous people *per se*," my father said, "but have you ever thought of going into journalism?"

"A little." I'd thought a little bit about a lot of things.

"I have friends at the *Herald Tribune*," my father said. "I could set up an appointment and see if they'd be willing to take you on."

I reacted in a guarded way. At eighteen, I'd had to accept the reality that I was not going to be a good enough ballplayer to make the Dodgers. Not then, not ever. But I was still young enough to dream of writing with the tuneful eloquence of Keats, or anyway Robert Frost, whatever Laurie's mother had said. "I'm not sure I want to write for a newspaper, Dad. I was sort of hoping to do more serious writing than that."

My father lit a Pall Mall and held his formidable temper. "Rudyard Kipling called journalism 'literature in a hurry.' No matter how gifted you are, or think you are, there's nothing wrong with writing for a newspaper. Anyway, I wasn't talking about a writing job. The *Tribune* is the best-written newspaper in the country. The only way you can make their writing staff is to earn your way onto it, the same way Jackie Robinson is earning his way into the major leagues.

"I think I can get you a spot as a copyboy. What happens after that is up to you."

Five months later I proceeded into the newsroom of the *Herald Tribune*, which occupied most of the fifth floor of a hulking high-rise on 41st Street between Seventh and Eighth Avenues. I was two weeks shy of my nineteenth birthday. A receptionist named Ada Hufnagel confirmed my appointment with Joseph G. Herzberg, the city editor, the appointment it had taken almost half a year to arrange. A pale, blond copyboy named Eddie McGrath led me to the city desk. "If you're here for a job," McGrath said, "you're in for a long wait. I was the editor of the campus newspaper at Fordham, and *I* had to wait a year before they hired me, just to put away mail and mix paste."

We proceeded down a corridor, bare green wall to the left and glassed-in cubicles to the right. These were offices for Virgil Thomson, the famous composer who was chief music critic; Geoffrey Parsons, the principal editorial writer; John Crosby, glib, mordant commentator on radio programs, and Red Smith, the sports columnist recently imported from Philadelphia, who was beginning to make an impact in New York. I ignored McGrath; it struck me that I was walking down a journalistic Hall of Fame.

When at length I faced Herzberg, he turned out to be deep-voiced, dark-haired, and preoccupied. He told me to sit and at once began studying a copy of the *New York World-Telegram*. I felt nervous and abruptly offended. Why didn't he look at me when he spoke? I didn't realize that the city editor of the *Herald Tribune*, supervising a staff of perhaps one hundred able and demanding people, did not ordinarily interview prospective candidates for the unexalted position of copyboy, any more than Branch Rickey interviewed prospective Ebbets Field hot dog vendors. My interview was a favor bestowed on Gordon Kahn by his friend Joe Herzberg; the audience was granted to me by accident of birth, not on merit.

"How are you doing in college?" Herzberg began.

My face reddened. "Fine," I lied.

"Very important," Herzberg said to page three of the *World-Telegram*. "Newspaper work is wonderful, but the field is becoming less stable. That's why having a degree, if only for a backup, is important. A degree with honors, if possible."

"Yessir."

He turned a page. "Say, Dick, who do we have covering John L. Lewis's speech tonight? He may rip into Taft-Hartley and after that go after Truman."

"Bob Bedolis," said Dick West, the assistant city editor.

"Better back him up with Don Irwin," Herzberg said. "This may be more politics than labor."

"Laborious politics," West said and winked toward me. I grinned ardently.

Herzberg continued to review his newspaper. Then he said, "What did you think of the World Series?"

Jackie Robinson had given the Dodgers a fine year in 1947. He batted .297 and hit 12 home runs, tying him with Pee Wee Reese for the team lead. He stole 29 bases, more than twice as many as anyone else in the league. Despite beanballs and spikings and the "hellish pressure," he played in all but four of the Dodgers' 155 games. Twenty-one-year-old Ralph Branca, who sympathized with Robinson, won 21 games. Boozy Hugh Casey, who didn't care for *nigras*, won 10 in relief and saved another 18, in what was the last season before his arm, or liver, failed. The Dodgers won the pennant by five games from the all-white Cardinals and came closer than any Brooklyn team ever had to winning the Series. But the deepening Brooklyn tradition—losing in October—persisted.

Branca started the first game at Yankee Stadium and pitched four perfect innings. Then, as he puts it, "I got behind and I started over-throwing." The Yankees scored five in the fifth and won, 5-3. Branca did not get another start. Clearly the team's best pitcher, he worked only two brief relief stints after that. The Yankees won an exciting Series, four games to three.

"I think they should have used Branca more, Mr. Herzberg."

"Your dad says the same thing."

"Fellow wins twenty-one, he deserves more than one start in the Series."

"But he's so young," Herzberg said, rising to conclude the inter-view. "I'm a Giant fan myself. I can't understand how an intelligent man like your dad can root for the Brooklyns."

"Jackie Robinson," I said, "is quite a story."

"Thank you for pointing that out," Herzberg said. "Miss Peterson will telephone, if anything opens up."

That February the *Herald Tribune* hired me as a night copyboy. Four of my shifts ran from four p.m. until midnight; the fifth started at eight and lasted until four a.m. At work I carried stories from reporters' hands to the city desk, sharpened pencils, fetched cigarettes, emptied ash trays and mailboxes and answered an elderly black telephone with the urgent greeting, *Newsroom!* I worked hard at tone and intonation there. I wanted to sound tough, but cultured, deeply virile, but not faux Paul Robeson. Sometimes, when I wandered into the promised land, the sports department, somebody growled, "Make yourself useful, kid, and grab our phone for a change."

"Sports." Skip the culture here; mostly sound tough. "What do you need?"

"Yeah, sports. I gotta question for ya. Who won more ballgames, Christy Mathewson or Walter Johnson? Big Six, that is, or the Big Train?"

I covered the mouthpiece and said timorously to the gigantic, bespectacled sports editor, "Uh, Mister Woodward?"

"Speak up, son. I don't bite before midnight."

"Some reader wants to know whether Mathewson or Walter Johnson won more games."

"Look it up, son. Take *The Little Red Book of Baseball* from that shelf next to the AP ticker. Look it up, and tell the man. He buys our paper."

Look it up? That's what my father liked to say when I tried to use him to shortcut a homework assignment. Look it up. Heck with that, I used to think. *Hell* with that. But this wasn't my father speaking. This was Mr. Woodward, Mr. R. Stanley Woodward, the coach, the best sports editor in New York. I looked up the answer, feeling a rousing sense of authority. Mathewson won 373. "But Walter Johnson did better," I told the caller. "He won 416."

"Great. Now will you repeat what you just said to my friend here? We have a wager."

After I hung up, Woodward said, "I could have told you, but this way you're more likely to remember. And something else. Johnson won all those games pitching for some godawful Washington clubs. A pleasant fellow, with the longest arms you ever saw."

"*Boy!*" The night editor's bray spun me, as if by physical force. "Yes, you, boy. Come out of the toy department over there and fetch me three-eighths of an inch of copy paper immediately!"

Calling sports "the toy department," was a common putdown, but Stanley Woodward had assembled the best writing staff on the paper. He rescued Red Smith from the *Philadelphia Record*, where Smith had been required to produce six columns and five news stories each week. Woodward cut the workload to six columns, Sundays off. That let Smith burnish his style. Typically, when covering a back-and-forth ballgame that became tied in the ninth inning, Smith wrote, "After two hours and forty-three minutes of glorious, pitched battle, status painfully returned to quo." As success hugged him, Smith announced, "My needs are simple. Give me this day my daily plinth." Like most of his readers, I had to look up the last word. A plinth is an architectural term, meaning "a base on which a column is placed."

Then, as now, the columnist was star. But close to Smith came featured players, the baseball writers. Baseball was emperor, challenged only on occasion by a championship fight or the Kentucky Derby.

Woodward assigned a witty young Yale man, Bob Cooke, to the Dodgers. Describing Brooklyn's fast, wild righthander, Rex Barney, Cooke offered a classic comment. "Barney pitched as though the plate were high and outside." Rud Rennie, a Canadian native who understood understatement, covered the Yankees. When Cookie Lavagetto, of the Dodgers, broke up Bill Bevens's bid to pitch the first World Series no-hitter, and won the fourth game of the 1947 World Series with a ninth-inning double, most reporters drained their portable typewriters of superlatives. This was one of the most exciting ballgames ever. Rennie began his *Herald Tribune* story: "Cookie Lavagetto made an important hit yesterday." Another time, after observing a 19-1 rout, Rennie wrote: "The game was not as close as the score indicated." Al Laney, who covered the Giants, had worked in Paris through the 1920s and served as business secretary to James Joyce. He composed long, well-considered and quite beautiful passages about baseball, in a style that is vanished, like the Paris Laney loved.

Having hired the son of a friend, Joe Herzberg set about distancing himself from nepotism. He spurned conversation, even civility, addressing me only when he had something harsh to say about the Dodgers. Through one of the NYU Jewish premeds, I heard about a farm in central New Jersey where young Zionists were learning to drive tractors as basic training in a program that would produce tank commanders for the new, imperiled nation of Israel. I traveled to the training farm and wrote a memorandum suggesting a Sunday feature story. Unasked, I provided a headline:

PROSPECTIVE      TANKERS
TAUGHT IN GARDEN STATE

Herzberg beckoned me with his right index finger. "Good idea," he said. "I'm putting a two-dollar bonus on your next check."

"I'll start writing later tonight, sir," I said.

"You won't have to worry about the writing," Herzberg said. "I've assigned the story to Sy Frieden. A veteran like Sy will know how to handle it." Herzberg extended a palm full of change. "Go out to the machine and bring me two packs of Chesterfields."

On secret orders from the business side, the city staff had been frozen. (No one wanted advertisers, or, worse the *Times*, to discover that financial problems were attacking the *Tribune*.) Powerless to make promotions, Joe Herzberg chose belligerent rudeness as his armor.

Stanley Woodward in sports was braver and more reckless. Looking to control costs, someone in the publisher's office asked Woodward to supply a short firing list, the names of two staff members who could be dismissed, "without weakening the paper." Woodward's brave, reckless answer: Stanley Woodward and Red Smith.

An immensely strong, acutely myopic New Englander, Woodward encouraged me to sit in on his discourses. When he was an Amherst undergraduate, he said, he had enrolled in a course taught by Robert Frost, called "Non-Shakespearean Elizabethan Drama."

"A course with Frost," I said in wonder. "What was it like?"

"We read a lot of plays by Beaumont, Fletcher, and John Ford. I didn't like the stuff much and I don't think Frost did, either. Do you happen to know Hornsby's lifetime batting average?"

"Something like .350," I said. "I don't know the exact number."

"That's fine," Woodward said. "I don't like figure-filberts. You can always look the numbers up. But take a pennant race between mediocre clubs and call that a 'dubious battle.' That's the ticket. Where does it come from, the phrase 'dubious battle'?"

"A novel by John Steinbeck. He took the title from Milton. *In dubious battle on the plains of heaven. Paradise Lost.*"

"You know Milton and you like baseball," Woodward said.

"My mother thinks baseball is my religion."

"Keep answering the telephones and reading poetry," Woodward said. "Something may turn up for you in sports."

Late that spring the *Herald Tribune* fired Woodward. The specific was the publisher's demand that he bestow major coverage on something called The Retail Men's Golf Tournament. The players included executives from large department stores, heavy advertisers, though not outstanding golfers. Woodward announced that duffers wandering in tall grass did not constitute news and that *Tribune* coverage in sports was neither for sale nor lease. He was replaced as sports editor by Bob Cooke, the Dodger writer, a former hockey star at Yale, who had been a college classmate of the publisher, Whitelaw Reid. The *Trib*'s great strength had been a willingness to tolerate curmudgeons, eccentrics, rebels, provided only that they came equipped with talent. Woodward was the most talented sports editor of his era, and when the *Tribune* decided that his independent ways made him intolerable, the paper took the first wrong-headed, wrong-footed step on the path that led to its collapse in 1966.

My reaction as a teenaged copyboy was an acute pang at seeing my Miltonic hero banished from his own plains of heaven. But if Woodward had to go, I was happy Bob Cooke came along. Cooke's baseball writing was a delight—witty, informed, and never self-important. Woodward warned his staff that anyone confusing a ballgame with a Battle of Titans would promptly find himself unemployed, and Cooke covered the Dodgers with brio and enthusiasm. Woodward unearthed details of the St. Louis Cardinals' attempt to foster a players' strike against Jackie Robinson. Cooke focused on the ballgames and vignettes.

I had sought out Cooke once or twice to tell him I liked his stuff. He seemed pleased and after a while invited me to join him on the *Tribune*'s amiable and not very good softball team. Cooke was 6-feet 2-inches, possessed a fine throwing arm, and couldn't hit a lick. Like Woodward, he loved English poetry, particularly Shakespeare and the narratives of Thomas Babington Macaulay.

"Are you finished up at college?" he asked one afternoon in Central Park. He was sandy-haired, square-chinned, and open. I'd hit two doubles; he had gone without a hit. There was nothing intimidating about big Bob Cooke, and I said directly, "I dropped out."

He nodded, unsurprised. "I wouldn't have made it through Yale myself without the help of 'The Man of a Thousand Themes.'" This turned out to be an erudite New Haven character, who ghosted homework assignments at modest rates for undergraduates.

"But you can write, Bob. Why did you hire a ghost?"

"Maybe I could write, but I didn't want to put in the hours. Not then. I didn't get serious about writing until my family got me a job as a runner down on Wall Street. I started in the stock market at nine in the morning and by nine-thirty I knew I wanted to be a writer, covering baseball. I quit the day I started, as soon as the stock market closed."

The ballfield extended camaraderie between the sports editor, now light-hitting shortstop, and the copyboy, playing third base. "I'd like to write some baseball myself."

"You'll never get rich writing baseball," Cooke said. "But if you're serious, I'll give you a tip. Read Heywood Broun. His stuff is in the morgue. If you want to write baseball for me, it's a good idea to find out how Broun wrote it. He was the best."

Late the following night, I retreated to the editorial library, where big, beige envelopes brimmed with stories by Broun. He became a columnist and lecturer and founder of the American Newspaper Guild, but the early Heywood Broun covered ballgames. His baseball stories matched keen reporting and droll commentary. I particularly savored Broun's account of the second game of the 1923 World Series, in which Babe Ruth hit two homers and the Yankees defeated John McGraw and the Giants, 4-2. Before the game Broun asked McGraw if he would intentionally walk Ruth in a tight spot. "Why shouldn't we pitch to Ruth?" McGraw remarked. "I've said before, and I'll say it again, we pitch to better hitters than Ruth in the National League." After the Yankee victory, Broun wrote:

> The Ruth is mighty and shall prevail. He did yesterday . . . Ere the sun had set on McGraw's rash and presumptuous words, the Babe had flashed across the sky fiery portents which should have been sufficient to strike terror and conviction into the hearts of all infidels. But John McGraw clung to his heresy with a courage worthy of a better cause.

Following a vivid account of the game, Broun returned to McGraw's pregame statement and pointed out that, true to his word, McGraw had not once ordered Ruth put on base.

> For that McGraw should receive due credit. His fame deserves to be recorded along with the men who said, "Lay on, Mac-

duff," and "I'll fight it out on this line if it takes all summer." For John McGraw also went down eyes front and his thumb on his nose.

Pulled from the soiled beige envelope in the drab newspaper library at one A.M., Broun's stuff lit up the night. He was quoting Macbeth, and Grant at Spotsylvania in 1864, in a brilliant baseball story. Keats and Robert Frost could wait. It would be something just to write like Heywood Broun.

To write baseball, just like Heywood Broun.

# CHAPTER THREE

# The Virgin in the Press Box

*T*HE MOST EXCITING NIGHT at the *Herald Tribune* came on the first Tuesday after the first Monday in November. As the climax of the sports year, the World Series provided a rousing week, but the night of the famous Presidential election of 1948 simply exploded with energy, with newsroom drama, and with a sense that everyone on hand, from the white-haired strong-jawed lady who owned this newspaper, to the skinny copyboy in dark suspenders who ran his chores in quick-time, was forging history. As a group we felt that we were, in Henry Luce's swaggering phrase, "kings of America's continuous revolution."

During the exuberant seasons of Stanley Woodward, the sports department was the center, the living soul of the *Herald Tribune*. Sports was critical to roaring tabloids, the *Daily News* and *Mirror*, and to such loud and venal papers as the *New York Journal-American*. But it is a measure of Woodward's curious genius, that here on the best-written and most literary of America's daily newspapers, you could usually find the best writing—and the largest number of literary references—in the sports section. This was all the more significant because the *New York*

*Times* had not begun to take sports seriously, and Woodward's sumptuous section was an area in which the *Tribune* outclassed the richer and more encyclopedic *Times* just about every day.

"I also like the *Tribune* better editorially," my father said, "three years out of four." In those days newspapers rode out to meet the public under banners describing their political bias. The *Times* maintained that it was independent. The *Tribune* called itself Independent Republican. But the *Tribune* took positions to the left of the *Times* on a range of issues, except when a Presidential election approached. Then independence and sometimes intelligence fled to the four-winded sky and the *Trib* automatically supported the Republican candidate. A disastrous Republican such as Herbert Hoover. A bland Republican such as Alf Landon. A glorious Republican such as Wendell Willkie. "In fact," my father said, "if Attila got the Republican nomination, the *Tribune* would feel it had to back him, also."

"We can't have a Hun as President," I said. "If the paper backs Attila, I resign."

"I wouldn't," my father said. "The position of copyboy is apolitical and you seem to be having a fine time." He managed to look intensely solemn. "Anyway, your concern is academic. Even Truman would beat Attila."

We shared a distaste for Harry Truman, who lacked Roosevelt's majesty and eloquence. Truman tended to state complex positions in a childlike way, as if convinced that voters were simpletons. Or, perhaps, he drew some sort of comfort in mouthing such superficial utterances as "The Russians don't keep their promises." Truman's failure to maintain the Grand Alliance of Britain, the Soviet Union, and the United States . . . well, grim as Stalin was, a healthy Roosevelt surely would have handled the old scoundrel with more sense and skill.

In our Weltanschauung, 1948, my father and I liked Jackie Robinson, disliked Harry Truman, and regarded Tom Dewey, the Republican Presidential candidate, as a trivial character. My father quoted Harold Ickes on Dewey: "When I was a boy," Ickes said, "my mother told me that anyone could grow up to be President. Now I'm beginning to believe it."

•  •  •

Descendants of Whitelaw Reid, a journalist and diplomat who amassed a fortune from adventures in the Cuban sugar trade, owned the *Tribune*. Reid's son, Ogden, ran the paper for decades, until his death in 1946, after which he was remembered as a baron of kindness. When the first edition closed at nine-thirty P.M., Reid often migrated to the Artist and Writers Restaurant, a former speakeasy and the Official Saloon of the *New York Herald Tribune*. The august publisher drank with the staff, talked politics and policy, and sometimes grew a bit wobbly. "The old boy was too cheap to let me hire John Lardner to write two columns a week for $25,000 a year," Stanley Woodward said, "or I would have had both Smith and Lardner as my columnists. But you have to offer a certain amount of admiration for any general who bellies up to a public bar after a battle and goes martini to martini with the troops."

Wet or dry, Reid clung to an ideology: the Republican party alone could save America. Whatever the merits of individual Democrats, the Democratic party at large, with so many branches rooted down among murderous Southern Klansmen, could not be trusted. Wendell Willkie and later Nelson Rockefeller believed the same thing.

Upon Ogden Reid's death in 1946, control of the *Tribune* passed to his widow, Helen Rogers Reid, who did not drink martinis with the staff. She was a strong-willed lady, who wanted to preserve the paper, if not quite so much as she wanted to preserve the family fortune. In the manner of so many widows, I suppose, she was terrified of losing her inheritance. Helen Reid established her older son, the second Whitelaw Reid, as editor-in-chief, but commandeered for herself the ruling title of publisher. She was petite, jut-jawed, and glacial. Her nickname was the Iron Maiden.

Helen Reid insisted that the election of 1948 was, in the phrase of one of her editorial writers, "not just an election but a crusade." A Democrat had resided at the White House for sixteen years. *Tribune* editorials in 1948 attacked Truman with unbecoming shrillness and championed Tom Dewey as the second coming of Pericles.

Political columnists saw a real chance for a Republican victory. Some forecast a landslide. Truman's doctrinaire anti-Communism had lost him the Democratic left. That vote would go to Henry Wallace.

Championing integration lost Truman the Democratic right. That vote would go to Strom Thurmond. Wallace ran as a Progressive. Thurmond ran on a States' Rights line. In a practical sense three Democrats were running against one Republican. Surely, Republicans everywhere believed, the divided Democrats would at last be conquered.

The Reids gathered most of their editorial forces in the huge fifth-floor newsroom to report and celebrate the great event. Movers appeared on election day, November 2, and rearranged chairs, desks, according to a floor plan devised by Joe Herzberg. The movers swept everything before them. The City Desk itself went from the center of the floor toward a far corner.

Bert Andrews, chief of the Washington Bureau, appeared. He had a hard face; he seemed cracklingly intense. Walter Lippman, who wrote the famous political column "Today and Tomorrow," was slight and soft-voiced. I was seeing these famous journalists up close for the first time.

Returns came clattering in on teletype machines, each printing sixty words a minute. Dewey was faring well in Pennsylvania and New Jersey. Strom Thurmond was sweeping Alabama and South Carolina. Henry Wallace, running against the cold war, showed little strength outside of New York City.

There was little time to chatter. The *Trib* was producing new editions every hour or so, with fresh leads, new headlines, revised tabulations of the vote. The pace was both frantic and controlled.

At eleven-fifteen Bert Andrews, who was writing the front-page lead for the eleven-thirty edition, suddenly shouted, "Copy."

I hurried to his desk. "Get me a ribbon for my Underwood," he said. "This damn thing's snapped."

I brought him the ribbon at full gallop. "Shall I change it for you, Mr. Andrews?"

"Nope. Thanks. Change my own." Which he did with great speed. Then picking up his story, Andrews typed, "Mr. Dewey's early lead was dissipating in certain critical industrial states."

"Copy!" Joe Herzberg held a bulletin aloft. "Get this over to Mr. Andrews immediately. Tell him we need another new lead."

With strong showings in Ohio and Illinois, Truman had just

drawn ahead of Dewey in popular vote. This struggle would rage into the end of the night. Herzberg's hand shook as he handed me the bulletin. Receiving it, Bert Andrews's hands were calm. Andrews's hands didn't shake when I gave him the dramatic bulletin. They didn't shake as he typed. They hadn't shaken when he changed his own typewriter ribbon under the guillotine of a deadline.

I never met Bert Andrews formally, but watching him perform under pressure in the teeming newsroom worked an epiphany within me. I had been thrust into my job, muttering about Keats and Thomas Wolfe. Then I worked among other copyboys, who talked of emerging as a new Twain or another Melville.

No more of that.

I wanted to write baseball as well as Heywood Broun and I wanted to become as good a newspaperman as Bert Andrews. On the night that Harry Truman upset Thomas E. Dewey, I finally realized how hard it was to be that good.

Bob Cooke brought me into the sports department in 1950 as a copyreader at $48 a week, twice my salary as copyboy. He wanted me to learn basic newspaper skills: writing headlines, cutting and editing stories. The promotion thrilled and alarmed me. No longer would I have to mix paste, run errands, and put away other people's mail. But good copyreaders are gems, and if I turned out to be a crackerjack, I might spend the rest of my days on the desk, correcting other people's stories and never experiencing the world beyond the office. I hoped I was not doomed to write headlines like DODGERS TOP PIRATES, 5 TO 3, BEFORE 24,678 at EBBETS FIELD. (If that was a little short, you could pad the head by inserting a word after the crowd figure: FANS or SPECTATORS or WITNESSES.)

Two things worked in my behalf. Cooke regarded me as a potential reporter, not a career deskman. Then, in truth, I wasn't very good at writing headlines to the size and shape some intricate layouts required. That is a high skill, like being a champion at Scrabble, and doesn't have much to do with how you write.

As an ordinary deskman I learned how a newspaper works. Stories came in to a Western Union room, transmitted in Morse Code, and transcribed by fast-typing telegraphers. Copyboys carried them to the chief copyreader, or slotman, who gave each a "slug," or label. Sitting inside a U-shaped arrangement of tables, the slotman distributed stories to his subordinates, who sat around the rim. Slugged and edited stories went down a chute to the composing room, where they were set in type by union printers, who earned more than double my wages. Following hand-drawn layout charts, other printers inserted type into models of pages. Only union members could set and move the type. If an editorial hand—even the jeweled hand of the Iron Maiden—ever touched type, the printers warned that they would shut down the paper with a strike.

The pages were pressed into molds which were then affixed to huge rotary presses, each capable of producing 35,000 copies of the *New York Herald Tribune* every hour. When the presses roared and rolled, vibrations shook the building. Conveyor belts carried the finished newspapers to ground level at Fortieth Street, where fleets of trucks, massed like so many Patton tanks, waited to fan out through the City of New York. Joe Herzberg called this process, the production of the newspaper, "a daily miracle."

A lot has changed. Today, you can write a newspaper story without paper. The old union printers, with their harsh and self-protective shop rules, have gone to their rewards. Most of us get our news first from television or computer networks.

But memory and romance being what they are, the 1948 *Herald Tribune* still seems to me more miraculous than modems and faxes and billions of disciplined electrons marching to the orders of a mouse.

I can't explain expressly why understanding the interiors of the *Herald Tribune* helped me write baseball. When I first went forth to cover the major leagues, Red Smith volunteered forceful advice in his gentle way. "There are only two excuses for a baseball writer's going to the office during the season," Smith said. "One is to drop off an expense account. The other is to pick up a paycheck." But surely the inside newspaper knowledge kept me aware, if only subliminally, that I was a newspaperman, not a Broadway buddy of Leo Durocher, not a coach on the staff of Field Marshal Casey von Stengel and not, whatever my boyhood dreams, a member of the Brooklyn National League Baseball Club, Inc.

In the autumn of 1950 Cooke and his deputy, Irving T. Marsh, appointed me Schoolboy Sports Editor. The title resonated, but that was grandiloquence. I was editor, correspondent, staff, helped only by a few high school students whom I was authorized to engage for a retainer of $3 a month. "Tell them that working for us will look good on their resumés," Marsh said.

"Sure."

"And don't take your own position quite so lightly. People develop newspaper reading habits when they're seventeen years old. If you can get these kids reading the *Trib* today, they'll still be reading the *Trib* in the year 2000."

High school coaches in New York City wanted to be paid extra for coaching. (Most were gym teachers.) The authorities countered that teachers did not earn extra money for supervising a camera club or advising a debating society. What was so different about coaching sports? The coaches walked; that is, they continued their teaching duties but refused to work after classes ended. Since you can't very well have high school teams without coaches, the entire New York City public school athletic program disappeared.

"All right," Marsh said. "Let's use a little ingenuity. Start going to the schools. Find out what's happening to the high school athletes who've lost their teams."

The athletes without teams weren't doing much of anything at DeWitt Clinton or Forest Hills or Thomas Jefferson or Newtown or at the High School of Commerce, where Lou Gehrig played. The series I wrote about their dismay became a rallying point for young athletes, parents, and the coaches. At length the Board of Education capitulated. Coaches would draw modest additional compensation, which simultaneously restored interscholastic sports and made faculty advisers at student newspapers unhappy. Didn't they deserve extra compensation, too? My province ended with sports. Looking at other aspects of the schools was the work of the attractive and energetic education reporter, Judith Crist, who later won renown as a movie critic.

"You've brought back high school sports," Cooke said, with high enthusiasm. "You're too good to waste on those dunderheads at the Board of Education. I'm putting you on general assignment. You'll be covering everything, except, course, major league baseball."

"Thanks. Great. Why not baseball?"

"How old are you?" Irving Marsh said.

"Twenty-two."

"We like our baseball writers to be older than the ballplayers that they write about," Marsh said.

Less than two years after that, in March 1952, Cooke dispatched me to spring training and the Brooklyn Dodgers. Four of the nine starting players on that remarkable team would be elected to the Hall of Fame. On the day that I reached the spring training hotel in Miami, Duke Snider was twenty-five, Roy Campanella was thirty, and Jackie Robinson and Pee Wee Reese were thirty-three. I was twenty-four, younger than every later-day Hall of Famer and indeed younger than any regular on the squad.

Friendship. We could be friends. The ballplayers and I were not walled apart by generations. But first I would have to control my awe and then I would have to gain some trust.

I had seen about seventy major league games, but I had not covered any. Not a single one. To understand the level at which big-league ball was—and often still is—played, you had best get close. Television slows the speed at which the baseball moves and the terrific rapidity at which plays happen. Television tries to put a 450-foot home run onto a 25-inch screen. That creates microbaseball. The real game is swift and high and dangerous and wide. Microbaseball is something else. Virtual unreality.

A good seat at a ballpark is vastly better. But nothing matches being on the field. A few days after I'd joined the team, Vin Scully, a young, redheaded broadcaster, said he was going to do a little shagging during early batting practice and why didn't I go out to left field with him?

I borrowed a glove and jogged past third base and veered and loped until I reached a patch of grass about 300 feet from home plate. Three hundred feet. A football field distant. Far away, Ben Wade, a 6-foot 3-inch righthander, threw zipping fastballs. He was a veteran of a

decade in the minors and he was firing hard, even though this was bat-
ting practice, because he wanted to make the Dodgers. Big, soft-voiced
Gil Hodges was the hitter. Outside breaking stuff bothered Hodges.
Fastballs were his ambrosia.

I was standing in the outfield to run down fly balls during a casual
morning workout. Others standing in the same outfield, also running
down fly balls—but more casually—were Duke Snider and Carl
Furillo. I was the rookie, the rookie writer, and suddenly the rookie in
the outfield, naked alongside of major league all-stars.

Hodges cracked a high line drive and someone, maybe George
Shuba, maybe Andy Pafko, said, "Yours." I moved in, remembering to
stay on the balls of my feet. That way the ball approaches smoothly.
When you run on your heels, the ball comes at you in lurches and the
last lurch will carry it over your head.

I had caught high line drives before. I concentrated on running in a
gliding way, so I'd look competent to these major leaguers. Glide and
follow the ball. That's just what I was doing when the ball accelerated
and climbed, not like a baseball at all, but like a jet-fighter, scrambling
to intercept an incoming raider. Mayday. Mayday. Mayday. Hodges's
liner hurtled over my head. It carried toward the fence, where a pitcher
doing a windsprint paused long enough to catch the baseball with
insolent ease.

I had never seen a drive like that from the daunting level of the
field. It was struck harder than any drive I had ever sought to catch,
and not by a mere subtle increment of power. Hodges smacked a 335-
foot liner that never rose more than ten feet from the ground. A routine, well-hit, catchable drive in the major leagues. But in my experience, the fiercest wallop of all time.

"You'll get the hang of it," Scully said.

"Don't press," George Shuba said.

Hodges slammed another liner that Pafko caught in stride. He
parked two fastballs over the fence. Then Scully caught a fly—the sort
of fly some call lazy—that tumbled out of the roof of the sky, dropping as ominously as a dive bomber. Shuba grabbed another. Now it
was my turn again.

Hodges looked at a high pitch, then cracked yet another line drive.

Damn, I thought, but after all, what was worse, line drives that just kept going or the fly balls driven into the upper firmament? There were no easy plays this bright March morning.

This liner was shorter. It carried over the infield and bounced. The ball came buzzing toward me across the grass, attacking like a speedy snake. The worst thing would be for the ball to zip under my glove, or hit my sneaker, or rush between my legs. I had no fear of getting hurt, but I was terrified lest the baseball make me look like a fool in front of the Brooklyn Dodgers. I approached slowly. The ball was losing speed. Head down. Glove low. Palm soft.

Whew.

I scooped the ball into my right hand and tossed it to the captain and shortstop, Pee Wee Reese.

He called my name.

"Yes, Captain."

"You're supposed to pick up the baseball *before* it stops."

"There is always going to be a bridge," Bob Cooke said, "between the ballplayers and the writers. It a subtle kind of thing, but always there." For the next eight months, I would be reporting on the Dodgers almost every day, and in the everyday real world, neutral reporting does not exist. As you cover your beat, the daily ballgame, you describe good plays and bad, the base hits and strikeouts that shape the outcome. You do that as fairly as you can, but the selection is imprecise. Did the game turn on a messed-up sacrifice in the fifth inning or on a short passed ball in the eighth? You check your scorebook. You talk to the manager. And you decide. Is the outfielder who bunted into a double play, or the catcher who mishandled that good slider, your nominee for loser of the day?

Then as now ballplayers read the papers. They knew when they were being praised or damned and by whom. Raw hostility and cold contempt between ballplayers and sportswriters presently seems to be the norm in many cities. During the gilded era when I started covering baseball, working conditions were too intimate for sustained hostility. The athletes could not hide from the press. Every inch of every clubhouse was open to credentialed journalists. Win or lose, like it or not, the ballplayers had to submit to interviews, at the pleasure of the press. Afterwards writers found themselves nose to nose with muscular ballplayers in railroad dining cars, hotel elevators, saloons, and, to be sure, the clubhouse the next day. That had the effect of keeping press commentary within boundaries in what was really a wonder of checks and balances.

I went forth to cover the team for which I had rooted all my life, players whose names still ring with splendor, and watched baseball every day across seven months, as the 1952 Dodgers managed to win the pennant. Their skills were glorious but so, I learned, were the skills of other major leaguers. The best home-run hitter in the league was Ralph Kiner of the Pittsburgh Pirates. The best pitcher was Robin Roberts, who won 28 for the Philadelphia Phillies. The best all-around batter was Stan Musial of the St. Louis Cardinals. The team with the knack of giving the Dodgers nervous fits was the New York Giants, under their brilliant, crap-shooting, charming, hooligan of a manager, Leo Durocher, who has made the Hall of Fame, but posthumously.

These Dodgers played under the burden of a troubled recent history. In 1949 they won the pennant, but the Yankees wiped them out in the World Series, four games to one. In 1950, the Dodgers finished second, missing a tie for the pennant when they lost to the Phillies in the tenth inning of a game played at Ebbets Field on the last day of the season. In 1951 the Dodgers finished second again, missing the pennant when they lost to the Giants in the ninth inning of the final game of a playoff, when Bobby Thomson lined his famous home run into the lower left field stands at the Polo Grounds. No one questioned the Brooklyn club's ability, but many, in other dugouts and in press boxes, questioned the team's courage. "The Dodgers have developed a unique formula," said an acerbic old baseball writer named Harold C. Burr. "In the big games they play just well enough to lose."

This was a dominant team but profoundly vulnerable. "Losing the way we did over that stretch," Pee Wee Reese remarks, "gets to go deeper than the ballgames. It makes you wonder what kind of a person you really are."

Here then were the Dodgers: divinely talented, but haunted by self doubt. Integrated in a still largely and passionately segregated country.

Playing noble and sophisticated baseball in a borough, a corner of New York City, that many regarded as a provincial joke. Although this is difficult to prove, I believe that the only people who rooted against these flawed, magnificent Dodgers were descendants of those who championed Torquemada and the grandchildren of those who sold lists of secret trade unionists to nineteenth century robber barons. You could pull for favorite players in St. Louis, the Bronx, or even Washington, D.C., but if part of your heart did not go out to the Jackie Robinson Dodgers, then part of your heart was granite, dead as a tombstone.

Close-up and in person, the Dodgers were open and varied. They were not as forbidding as the New York Yankees—"the lordly Yankees," sportswriters used to call them, as in "Casey Stengel's lordly Yankees yesterday put to rout the Washington Senators, 14-4, before 56,918 witnesses at Yankee Stadium." The Yankees had been winning for a long time; they had won fourteen World Series since Babe Ruth's breakthrough October of 1923. All those victories created a manner that was, at least in the beginning, quite intimidating. The Yankees swaggered and didn't seem to want to chatter with the press.

The first time I had to cover a Yankee game during spring training, 1952, I asked Stengel about his pitching rotation. He had two power righthanders, Allie Reynolds and Vic Raschi, and a gifted lefthander, Ed Lopat. But Whitey Ford was in the army. Whom did he intend to use as his fourth starting pitcher? I was asking Stengel the question and covering a Yankee-Dodger exhibition because Rud Rennie, the regular Yankee writer, had suffered a coronary.

"Well, I don't know ya," Stengel said, "and I don't like to talk to guys I don't know, but the other feller on your paper got sick, so I will help you, since the other feller, who I do know, is a good man."

I was standing in front of the Yankee dugout at Al Lang Field in St. Petersburg, Florida. As it happened, Reynolds and Raschi were seated on either side of Stengel, chewing tobacco. "We don't do things here like the Brooklyns do things," Stengel began. Over the next ten minutes, he told me that he could use his starting pitchers as relievers and his relief pitchers as starters, and what did I think about that?

That was sophisticated thinking for 1952—Stengel's handling of pitchers would be dazzling even today—and I had some trouble grasp-ing Stengel's point. I was used to baseball where starters started and relievers relieved and managers did not interchange stalwarts, unless the pennant was on the line. Stengel was giving me a lot to grasp in a hurry and on top of that, I had trouble focusing. While Stengel spoke and I scrawled notes on folded sheets of yellow paper, Reynolds and Raschi silently spat tobacco juice around my shoes. On good days, each was a fine control pitcher. This Florida afternoon they were control spitters. "Now take the man from the country with the good curve," Stengel said, referring to Johnny Sain of Arkansas. "He won more than twenty starting in the other league. But he has good experience and has been a Navy test pilot, so if I need him to relieve, he may not be nervous, which is important in that particular situation, if you catch my drift."

I looked down. Muddy blobs ringed the front of my black oxfords. Reynolds and Raschi, not looking up, were spitting juice, by way of punctuating Stengel's complex sentences. Big men. Strong men. Spitting men. Twin cobras. After a while, I retreated to the Dodgers' side of the field.

Years later, I asked Reynolds about his behavior. "We knew who you were," he said, "and it was nothing personal. We were just making sure that you knew who *we* were. The New York Yankees." The style of the grand Yankee teams, the ballclubs of Ruth and Gehrig and DiMaggio and Mickey Mantle, proceeded from intimidation. Kind-ness—Reynolds did me a significant favor in 1954—could only come later, after the Yankees had displayed their rugged ways. Humanists will criticize the intimidation approach, but as white-haired, soft-voiced Jim Turner, the Yankee pitching coach, told me one afternoon: "You have to keep this in mind, kid: Big-league baseball is not a fuck-ing tea party." Intimidation was the way the old Yankees conducted each day's business. As all those won-and-lost records proclaim, it worked.

The Dodgers were infinitely more approachable. The Dodgers hadn't won fourteen World Series. They hadn't won any. Good as they often were, they had never been the best. As a result the Dodgers lived with self-doubt. They had a touching need to explain. Swaggering teams and redneck teams and brooding teams and drinking teams all played in the major leagues during the years when baseball was the unchallenged national game. Variousness was a baseball wonder years ago when all the ballparks were distinct and all the hotels looked different and nobody had yet tried to homogenize hamburgers, highways, America.

Among the swaggerers and the drinkers and the rest, the Dodgers led the major leagues in nouns. They were the most verbal ballclub in the annals. If you spent some effort getting to know the Dodger cast, you found a wonderful assortment of characters, happy to share their experiences with a young sportswriter who appeared to be at least reasonably trustworthy and showed a decent respect for their big-league skills.

I talked pitching with Preacher Roe and Carl Erskine. Roe, a rural doctor's son, disguised his ferocious intelligence behind a hillbilly manner. "Even when ah do strike out Musial," Roe said, "the wind from his swing plumb blows me off the mound." After the droll comments, Roe held forth on the subtleties of his art, as we rode trains or ate bacon and eggs in coffee shops around a league that extended from Boston to St. Louis. In 1952 baseball had not yet recognized California. "Sometimes when I'm gunning for a hitter I can get with a slow curve down low," Roe said, "I set him up with a fastball around the eyes. That's a ball, fer sure, and he won't swing, but like it or not he picks up the speed of that pitch. And that clicks somewhere in his head. Now, when I throw the slow one, he's still reacting to the fast pitch up around his eyes. He swings too soon. I got my man. He makes out on a pitch in the strike zone, but he gets thrown off by the pitch around his eyes. When I hear someone sayin' the high fast one was a bad pitch because it was a ball, I got to wonder what they might be talking about. This game is not as simple as it seems." Nor was Roe himself. To supplement his Dodger salary of about $25,000, he taught geometry winters in a Missouri high school. "Angles," he said, with a quick, little grin. "It must come natural to me figuring out angles."

Erskine, trim and serious, threw a strong overhand curve and had a change of pace that was always surprising the hitters. As he released the change, Erskine pulled hard, as though drawing down a window shade. This had the effect of imparting terrific spin. "The hitters," Erskine said, "pick up this ball that's spinning like the dickens, rotating like a fastball. They react to the rotation and when they first pick up the pitch, they think they see a fastball. That spoils their timing. They get off balance. They shift their weight forward and start their swing too soon. By the time they adjust—all this takes place in less than half a second—it's too late. That's why a lot of changes get popped up, or sometimes even get a hitter so paralyzed that he can't swing the bat at all." Erskine spoke about his work with passion and eloquence. He was a lover of narrative poetry and sometimes in those distant days he recited from memory long works by Robert W. Service. These people fascinated me. The craft of Roe and Erskine was not the sort of stuff one learned playing weekend sandlot games at Lake Mohegan.

Gil Hodges, strong and quiet, liked riddles and puzzles. Duke Snider, the sometimes melancholy prince, never drew as much happiness from his great gifts as he might have. Carl Furillo followed a solitary star. He had quit school after the eighth grade and, he told me on one train ride, "I don't like hanging out with fancy guys, who try to make me think I'm fucking dumb." Hugely popular Roy Campanella spun out minstrel-show stories. "In the old colored leagues, I sometimes had to catch a triple-header. That's right. Three games on a hot Sunday afternoon. They didn't pay me much for playin' the three, but I didn't mind because"—pause, soulful look, wink—"they was giving me fifty cents a day meal money! Hey, that's true. Ask anybody that was there."

Jackie Robinson was a gentle, thoughtful, loving man, disguised as a firebrand. As the first black to play in the major leagues, Robinson was the first target of bigots on the field, in the grandstands, in the press box. His defense was to put forth a bristling personality, needling and jockeying in sharp and sometimes nasty ways. "It's like I've got antennae," he said. "I can tell who's an *anti* before they even speak." By 1952 few of Robinson's *antis* dared argue against the right of blacks to make a living in the major leagues. But most of the sportswriters complained that Robinson was "uppity." I marveled at a curious thing: the same qualities that made a white ballplayer a battler, a competitor, a hard-nosed son-of-a-buck, those very same qualities made Jackie Robinson an uppity coon. Prejudice, particularly among the newspapermen, came in tiers. Ol' Minstrel Show Campy was a terrific fellow, they thought, *just because* he resembled an end-man in not-very-dark black face. Robinson exuded an air of complete independence, and that was not acceptable in a Negro. Like Robinson, I found this thinking outrageous. As soon as Jack realized that I shared his outrage—his antennae truly were quick—we became fast friends.

Presiding over this Continental Congress of a baseball team was Harold "Pee Wee" Reese, the shortstop and captain. Raised amid the racism of Kentucky, he had exorcized his own demons and worked quietly to get others to do the same. He didn't lecture on civil rights. Reese disliked drawing attention to himself. He simply accepted Robinson as a buddy. At a time when a third of the country's schools were still segregated, Reese and Robinson went to the racetracks together, played cards together and warmed each other up with a thousand games of catch. Once the games began, they played hit and run and executed double plays with something close to genius.

Reese knew that reporters and photographers and Pullman porters and bellhops had jobs to do that were important to them and significant to their sense of dignity. As team captain, he insisted, usually with success, that the other ballplayers act thoughtfully toward the people around them. Simplistically, Reese was the older brother everyone always wanted to have. In the words of Heywood Hale Broun—Heywood Broun's greatly gifted son—he was both a gentleman and a gentle man. Which is not to say he didn't play rugged, competitive baseball. He was a wonder.

The 1952 Dodgers lost their strongest pitcher, strapping twenty-six-year-old Don Newcombe, to the military draft, which lingered along with the punishing war in Korea. Ralph Branca suffered a bizarre injury during spring training. A canvas beach chair gave way under Branca's 220 pounds and he crashed—coccyx first—against an upright bottle of soda pop. After that, back pains destroyed his effectiveness. (Branca says the accident—rather than psychological aftershock from Thomson's home run—was his undoing.) This left the team without a classic strong-armed righthander, and, it developed, any pitcher who could come close to twenty victories. The draft was impartial. In May the Giants lost Willie Mays, no less, to the Army of the United States. But Charlie Dressen, the stumpy character who managed the Dodgers, argued that big pitchers were more important than any other players. "If they was gonna do it right," Dressen said, summoning his unusual gift for phraseology, "to make up for the pitcher they got from me, the Army woulda took two Mayses from the Giants."

The Dodgers played a scrambling sort of season, strong, courageous but not overpowering. To general surprise, a twenty-eight-year-old righthander named Joe Black emerged from the obscurity of the Negro Leagues and a minor league season in which he lost more games than he won and became the best pressure pitcher extant. Black threw just two pitches, a high, hopping 95-mile-an-hour fastball and a small, snapping curve, knee high at the outside corner. Black discouraged batters from leaning toward that corner by directing an occasional fastball at the chin. He had minored in psychology at Morgan State College and when he achieved success as a reliever, he possessed the good sense to play things down. "It's not that complicated," Black told reporters. "When they tell me to throw high, I throw high. When they tell me to throw low, I throw low." Black spoke gently and sometimes polysyllabically but when it was time to go to work, he parked gentleness beside his warmup jacket in the dugout. I saw him once loosen a Giant pinch hitter named George Washington Wilson with a fastball that sent Wilson diving toward earth so frantically that Wilson ducked out from under his cap. That is, his cap hung briefly in the air. Black's knockdown passed between Wilson's cap and head, white lightning. Wilson then struck out in haste.

Black won fifteen games and saved another fifteen, and would have been selected Most Valuable Player in the league, except that a block of white baseball writers from the Midwest voted en masse for a white Chicago outfielder named Hank Sauer, who hit 37 home runs but batted only .270. Sauer fielded marginally and was so slow afoot that in 151 games that season he stole exactly one base. With Sauer the Cubs finished fifth. Black pitched the Dodgers to a pennant. He played a critical role in almost a third of the team's victories.

Joe and I struck up a pleasant, unself-conscious relationship. He told me that the Dodgers were paying him $7,500 for the season, a higher salary than anyone in his family had ever made. "It was hard in my hometown, Plainfield, New Jersey, you know. The Depression. And if you were a colored person, the Depression hit you extra hard. My father was an intelligent man and the best work he could find was sweeping out an auto factory."

"You went to college," I said.

"Scholarship," Black said. "I could play sports. But, see, when I got to college, I didn't *just* play sports. I read Shakespeare. I took a minor in psychology. I studied public speaking. And then, after all that, it turned out the best living I could make, as an educated colored man, was as a pitcher."

"In the colored leagues."

"We had to wait for Jack. Satchel Paige and Monte Irvin and Campy and all the rest of us, we had to wait for Jack. Sure I pitched in the colored leagues. In the winters I went down to the Caribbean and pitched there. Pitched close to twelve months a year to make a living. But anyway my Spanish improved. I can order a first-class meal in two languages."

The Dodgers did not get around to signing Black until 1951, when he was twenty-seven years old, positively geriatric for a prospect. Then they sent him to the minor leagues "for seasoning." Across 1951, he won 11 and lost 12 in Triple A, not a record that demanded a promotion to Brooklyn. But Billy Herman, once a great infielder, now a Dodger coach, saw something special in Black—fire, intensity, guts. On Herman's recommendation the Dodgers added Black to their roster so that now, at the age of twenty-eight, he was finally playing in the major leagues. His color had walled him out for at least five years.

"I would be bitter," I said.

"I don't have that luxury. The way things are," Joe Black said, "colored people can't afford to be bitter."

The Dodgers won 96 games and the pennant. Actually, it took them 92 victories to clinch. Out of that total, Black won fifteen and saved fifteen, recording an earned run average of 2.15, the lowest in the league. He was a third of a pennant, all by himself, and I exulted in his triumph. He had beaten so much, against terrible odds and, as we would later learn, at very great cost. (His arm would never again be quite as lively.)

I exulted for my native borough, where I had walked with my father in the afternoons of boyhood, where I had dreamed of playing baseball and doing high deeds. I exulted for my new friends, Jackie and Pee Wee and Carl Erskine and the Duke. I exulted for myself, a rookie baseball writer, a virgin, covering a pennant-winning team. But in my secret heart, I exulted most for Joe Black's victory over the armies of bigotry—the Klan, of course, and the foul-tongued baseball people and the patronizing press. Joe Black's accomplishment reached beyond baseball. His victory in the summer of 1952 set back all those heroes in business and law and medicine and academia and politics, who said, in smooth-tongued ways, that a person could not truly stand tall, or even stand among the best, if he was born a Negro.

What a fine season.

Come on.

Let's start the Series.

# CHAPTER FOUR

# Neutral for Brooklyn

*I*N THE PANELED, ODDLY SHODDY living room of the hotel suite where he resided, along with Ruth, his little, fierce, blonde wife, and a white poodle she addressed as Foo-Foo, Charlie Dressen convened a council of war. He gazed hotly at his lieutenants, Jake Pitler and William Jennings Bryan "Billy" Herman, and moved to set the strongest possible agenda. "We gotta win the fucker," Dressen said. "Who we gonna trun?"

Charles Walter Dressen, of Decatur, Illinois; Cincinnati, Ohio; Oakland, California; and the Bronx and Brooklyn, New York, was a smallish, thick-necked character, 5-feet 5-inches tall, who regarded himself as a brilliant baseball strategist, a master psychologist and a consummate orator. In truth, Dressen could be all these things, but a need to discourse on his own acumen put off people. As Tommy Lasorda, a later, loud Dodger manager remarked, "You never had to wonder if Charlie was a genius. Right up front Charlie cleared that one up. He told you that he was a genius. Told you so himself."

Another problem for both admirers and detractors was comprehending Dressen's strain of English. "Trun," for example, meant throw or sometimes threw. You needed fast reflexes to keep up with Dressen's tenses. "Fucker" was a catch-all. It could mean a difficult, wind-blown fly ball, or a grounder that took a bad hop. It could also mean a cruel person, an aggressive umpire, a hostile newspaperman or a bad clam. In the 1952 Dodger council of war, "fucker" meant the World Series. When Dressen was asking who to trun in the fucker, he was saying, "Since we don't have a twenty-game winner, or anybody even close, who's the best man on this flawed pitching staff to start the first game of this World Series against the Yankees?" Translating Dressen, while not easy, could be rewarding. A boil of ideas bubbled within his swampy grammar.

In the climate of the 1990s, Dressen would be acclaimed as the sort of American Original baseball needs, a shrewd and motivated primitive, like Dan'l Boone or Sitting Bull. Although his expletives would make him a risky talk-show guest, Dressen would certainly draw approving profiles from such establishment organs as *Sports Illustrated* and the *New York Times Magazine*. (Jolly Cholly Dressen May Talk Funny/But Jolly Cholly Makes Serious Sense.)

Dressen's misfortune, or one of them, was to manage in darkest Brooklyn during the early 1950s, while Leo Durocher and Casey Stengel were managing in the sunburst of New York. The establishment columnists, Red Smith and Jimmy Cannon, ran, or rather taxied, with a New York crowd. A long cab ride to Brooklyn jarred their ganglia. Worse yet, once you were done with your work out there in Brooklyn, would you ever find another cab to carry you back to civilization? The columnists didn't like the odds; they seldom made the trip to Ebbets Field. So Dressen, described by Jackie Robinson as the best and smartest manager "I ever played for," labored in semiobscurity, his glories celebrated in limited ways. "There's tricks to this game, kid," he told me, "and I'll learn you a lot of them. All of them, if you listen good to what I say. I ain't no Ned in the third reader."

The Dodgers sometimes played a variation of charades. I watched once as Ralph Branca placed an index finger near one of his eyes. Three or four teammates instantly cried out, "Dressen." This was charades with a pun. The indication "eye" signified Dressen's favorite pronoun. But it was a mistake to confuse a lack of high style with any lack of substance.

Dressen came out of southern Illinois, armed with a grade school education and enough courage to play in the backfield of the Chicago Staleys, the forerunner of the Chicago Bears. He weighed 140 pounds. Switching to baseball, he played parts of eight seasons in the major leagues, mostly at third. Once, in 1927, when he was twenty-nine years old, Dressen batted .292 across 144 games for the Cincinnati Reds. He even hit two home runs that year and led all National League third basemen in assists. I don't denigrate his baseball skill; for a 5-foot-5 inch, 140-pounder to make the major leagues at all represents accomplishment. But to the cold eye, Dressen emerges as a marginal performer. His forte, less tangible than slugging homers, was a grasp of the science and tactics of baseball.

Dressen studied other players and memorized their strengths and weaknesses. As a third baseman, he knew that Max Carey was a dangerous bunter and Sunny Jim Bottomley, about the same size and strength, preferred to swing for the fences. He played them differently. He knew which pitcher threw what particular pitch in a clutch and he had an extraordinary knack for picking up another team's signs. He was, in brief, a brainy ball player, which is why the Reds hired him to manage in 1934. He held the Cincinnati job for four years, never bringing the team out of the second division. His Reds finished last twice. Manager Dressen was a small Cincinnati catastrophe.

But when Durocher took over the Dodgers in 1939, he immediately engaged Dressen as a coach. "I don't care what happened in Cincinnati," Durocher said. "This guy knows baseball. He knows it a ton."

Dressen helped Durocher and Larry MacPhail revive the Dodgers and in 1946 after MacPhail bought the Yankees, he hired Dressen to coach for him again. Charlie's belief in his own powers promptly tripped him. After studying American League pitchers, Dressen decided he had found a flaw in the delivery of Fred Hutchinson, who threw hard fastballs for the Detroit Tigers. "When he's gonna trun the curve, he cocks his glove," Dressen informed Joe DiMaggio. "I can tip ya." DiMaggio, struggling to regain his prewar batting stroke, listened receptively.

"We gotta wait for our spot," Dressen said, "but at the right time, with guys on base, I'll pick it up. Then I'll whistle, good and loud. That means curve."

DiMaggio nodded. In the fifth inning, with two men on base, Dressen, coaching at third, spotted Hutchinson's telltale mannerism and loosed his loudest whistle.

"That's how the little son of a bitch almost got me killed," DiMaggio explained afterwards. "I heard the whistle. The pitch started toward my head. I hung in, waiting for it to break. It never broke an inch. I barely got my head out of the way. I told Dressen, 'No more help. I intend to stay alive. I'll go back to hitting by myself.' My language may have been a little stronger than that. A *lot* stronger." DiMaggio liked telling this story to the New York columnists who drank with him at Toots Shor's restaurant on Fifty-second Street. Dressen's reputation shriveled and the Yankees dropped him. He had to go to work managing the Oakland Oaks, in the Pacific Coast League.

Immediately after the Dodgers lost a chance to tie for the pennant with the Philadelphia Phillies in the last inning of the last game of the 1950 season, Walter O'Malley seized control of the team. Remembering the shrewd assistant to Durocher, rather than the man who blundered in the Bronx, O'Malley hired Dressen to manage. He gave Dressen a one-year contract and told him, "You have to win the pennant. I've studied the history of the franchise. In Brooklyn you're either first or you're bankrupt. Charlie, I'm giving you a fine job, $35,000 a year and expenses. If you want to keep the job, you have to win."

"I'm a winner, Mr. O'Malley," Charlie said. "You can bet on that."

"I'm an investor, not a gambler," O'Malley said. "You have to win."

For almost five months during 1951, Dressen, who was fifty-three, lived out a dream. Gil Hodges, Duke Snider, and Roy Campanella pounded home runs at a record Brooklyn pace. Carl Furillo hit solidly and threw out twice as many baserunners as any other outfielder in the league. Jackie Robinson was batting .350. The pitching—Don Newcombe, Preacher Roe, Carl Erskine, Ralph Branca—while not as dominant as the hitting and defense, stayed solid. The Dodgers moved thirteen-and-a-half games ahead of the Giants. The date was August 11. From that point forward, the Giants began the most extraordinary pursuit in baseball history. Across the balance of August and through September, the Giants, fired by Durocher and the magical rookie, Willie Howard Mays, won 37 and lost 7, a phenomenal pace, .841, under phenomenal pressure.

Dressen had trouble keeping his poise. In August the Dodgers brought up Clem Labine, a bright, twenty-five-year-old righthander, with a snapping curve ball and a buzzing sinker. Labine won his first four starts. On September 16 Dressen started him against the Philadelphia Phillies in Ebbets Field and Labine struggled. The Phillies loaded the bases in the first inning, and Willie Jones, their leading power hitter, worked the count full, three balls, two strikes.

Dressen whistled for timeout. That dangerous whistle again. Dressen's whistle seized attention, like a siren at midnight. He walked to the mound, jut-jawed, right hand in back pocket, scratching. Labine waited. "Don't walk him," Dressen said.

"I know that," Labine said. "Did you come all the way out here to tell me that?" Jones hit Labine's next pitch into the left-field stands and soon the Phillies put the game out of reach.

Dressen raged, but held his tongue when four reporters from afternoon newspapers—"the four pall-bearers," he called them—entered his office beneath the right-field stands. It was a tough loss, he said, but *sheeyit*, we'll get 'em tomorrow.

"*Sheeyit*," Dressen told his friend, a character known as Red the Florist, "we shudda got them fuckers today." Worse, the kid pitcher had sassed him. *You come all the way out here to tell me that?* Well, the hell with that smart-assed kid pitcher. We'll win the thing without him, Dressen decided. No rookie sasses me like that.

Dressen did not give Labine another start until the Giants had caught the Dodgers, and forced the pennant race into a playoff, best two of three, and won the first game. Then, finally, desperate, on the brink, Dressen put his ego aside and let the gifted rookie work. Labine pitched a shutout.

But the next afternoon belonged to Bobby Thomson.

In a hotel elevator a fan cursed Ralph Branca, the losing pitcher. "Why are you calling Branca all those terrible names?" Walter O'Malley asked.

"I bet a hundred bucks," the man said. He did not recognize the president of the Dodgers. "Branca cost me a hundred bucks."

O'Malley had been calculating on his own. Nice long World Series. Attendance close to 350,000 for seven games. Receipts from all those hot dogs, beers, and scorecards. A million-dollar week, a million at the very least. Plus advance ticket sales for next year and a richer television contract. Not a million. A two-million-dollar week, two million dollars, gone with the wind that scatters torn-up ticket stubs in twilight ballparks, after the crowds have milled back into darkening streets.

*"I'm* not cursing Ralph," O'Malley told the stranger in the elevator. "He did the best he could. But he cost me considerably more."

O'Malley did not curse, nor did he fire the manager, but it was a narrow decision. "I was never as impressed with Charlie as Charlie was," he told me, twenty years later, "but I didn't want to be seen as someone who fired a manager a year. So I signed him for another season, with certain reservations that I successfully kept to myself."

It is hardly fair to say, as many have, that the 1951 Dodgers collapsed. They simply played six weeks of ordinary ball, while the Giants played like gods. But if Dressen had benched his ego and continued starting Labine, his hottest September pitcher, the Dodgers would have won a game or two more in the regular season and baseball history would have been changed.

No tied pennant race. No playoff. A Brooklyn pennant. And instead of hitting the most famous home run in baseball history, on October 3, 1951, Bobby Thomson would have played golf. Or so people at the top of the Dodger organization maintained.

When the *Herald Tribune* sent me out to cover the Dodgers the following spring, I had little sense of the politics of professional baseball. I thought a ballclub was a mostly amiable entity, like my old Lake Mohegan Nine, where everyone pulled together, trying to win. Confusing the major leagues and the sandlots is naive. The demands and rewards—like the skills and the egos—are not comparable. But confusing the majors and the sandlots is an understandable error, particularly when you are young and you can sidle up to Pee Wee Reese and say, "You know I used to play a little infield myself."

• • •

Walter O'Malley had become chairman of the Board of Trustees at Froebel Academy, the Brooklyn day school I attended, a decidedly preppy and conservative Protestant institution. (O'Malley was Roman Catholic. His interest in Froebel seems to have sprung from a desire, on some level, to enter the Protestant establishment, which dissipated as he grew more wealthy.) When I joined the eight other newspapermen covering the Dodgers, O'Malley summoned me for a private audience in his spring-training office at Vero Beach, Florida. We sat on wicker chairs in the pleasant March heat and he said that he was proud that "a Froebel boy" had gotten this wonderful position, covering the Dodgers, at this very early age, and for this very fine newspaper, the *Herald Tribune*. He didn't care for the tabloids, himself, and how were my dad and mom, and would I send them his personal regards, and anytime either of them wanted to see a game, I had only to ask, and he would be happy to welcome them as his guests at Ebbets Field. His *personal* guests. It was a heady greeting and the beginning of a complicated and rewarding relationship that had tugs and pulls and bumps and bruises, but lasted for a quarter century, until O'Malley's death at the Mayo Clinic in high summer, 1979.

O'Malley was a consummate autocrat. If he was happy to greet me in the spring of 1952, so was Emil J. "Buzzie" Bavasi, his first vice-president, and so was Lafayette Fresco Thompson, his second vice-president, and so, of course, was Charlie Dressen, whose job depended on his performance, his press ratings, and O'Malley's whims. Bavasi, wealthy and charming, introduced me to the cocktail called a grasshopper—brandy, green crème de menthe, clear crème de cacao, and cream, whipped with shaved ice into a froth. "A green malted milk," I pronounced.

"No malted ever had a kick like a grasshopper," Bavasi said. "Drink 'em slow."

"I'd better take your word for that."

Bavasi, vice-president and bartender, smiled. "I'm glad you're with the club," he said. "I need somebody I can really talk to. Talk to and trust."

Fresco Thompson offered me his treasury of baseball stories.

When he was traded to the Dodgers in 1931, Thompson, a 5-foot 8-inch infielder who hit without much power, drew the locker adjacent to Babe Herman, a towering outfielder, who once batted .393. Babe Herman was also renowned for misplaying fly balls, one of which landed on his right shoulder in the late inning of a close game. Still, Herman was proud of his slugging. He glared down at Thompson, and grumbled, "I don't like gettin' dressed next to a .250 hitter."

"And I," Thompson snapped, "don't like getting dressed next to a .250 fielder."

Across my first long season, there was humor and camaraderie, baseball lore, and first-class travel, in private Pullmans, and dining cars with white tablecloths and shrimp cocktails and steaks and apple pie, and then a club car and lounge chairs, brandy and cigars, for hours of easy talk. In this setting Dick Young, the gifted, contentious reporter from the *Daily News,* said over and over: "I don't want to be a millionaire. I just want to live like one. Which is what I'm doin'. Millionaires would love to have my job."

The manager was always available, telling me what he had said in a private team meeting, telling me what he intended to say at the next and even more private team meeting, telling me what he had done, telling me what he would do, an unlettered Doctor Johnson searching for Boswell and—who can blame him?—for a little job security as well. "What ya gotta understand," Dressen said, "is my team is hated more than any other team is hated, because we give the guy a chance."

"Robinson?"

Dressen nodded a curt, little nod. "Robe-is-on," he said. He pronounced the name as a blend of Robinson and Robeson. "It makes 'em madder that he's so good. He's the best fucking player I ever managed."

I mention coming to the majors "close-up" because, as the shade of Clarence Mitchell insists, I had come to major league ball long before, through my father. It was that way also for Bob Feller and Mickey Mantle and for ten or twenty or fifty million men who grew up and became faces in the crowd. Baseball and summer afternoons, fathers and sons, are threads in a long American story. The tale runs throughout this century, and it has roots in the days when baseball was the dominant American sport, the game fathers and sons played in hot Carolina mill towns and dusty California valleys and crowded Brooklyn sandlots, in Iowa and Alabama and Oklahoma and Rogers Park, Chicago, a city game, a country game, a summer, spring and fall game, the dominant game, as much as any sport can be, a universal.

Growing as it did in the seasons after World War II, baseball triggered a change in American life quite above and beyond the field. Put succinctly, before there was a Martin Luther King, there was a Jackie Robinson. Before public schools were integrated, the Dodgers were integrated. The great divide, between blacks and whites, disappeared on the old Brooklyn Dodger team. That consideration aroused passions, transcending the cheers for balls and strikes. With a varied, verbal, integrated cast, the Dodgers became America's team, loved in baseball and beyond, but also, as shrewd, illiterate Charlie Dressen recognized, despised in baseball and beyond. As they were a vision of an integrated nation, an America still waiting to be born, so the Dodgers were traitors to hallowed White Supremacy, our own native American-made apartheid.

Now, in my first season of big-league ball, the integrated Dodgers had triumphed in a league where five of the eight teams still fielded all-white lineups and they were next going forth to play a World Series against the all-white Yankees, the defiantly all-white Yankees, the most triumphant and arrogant and possibly greatest ballclub on earth.

This was easily the best team in Brooklyn big-league history, which dated from the nineteenth century and the championship squad of 1890, nicknamed, following spasms of nuptial activity, the Bridegrooms.

The Brooklyn Bridegrooms won the 1890 National League pennant by six games, but the modern World Series had not yet come into being. After it did, Brooklyn teams won five pennants, played in five Series and lost all five. In the argot this phenomenon—Brooklyn losing in October—acquired a denigrating nickname.

The Flatbush Folderoo. That concept, and with it a vague sense that even the best of Dodger teams would somehow find a way to choke up, was the crown of thorns Charlie Dressen shared with his intelligent and integrated team.

• • •

With support from Billy Herman during the council of war at his suite in the shabby Hotel Granada, Charlie Dressen decided to start Joe Black in the first game of the 1952 Series. Negro pitchers had appeared in the World Series before, but without success. Satchel Paige relieved for Cleveland 1948, helping mop up a lost game. Don Newcombe started twice for the 1949 Dodgers and the Yankees beat him both times. In designating Black as point man, Dressen was defying the developing belief that black pitchers lacked the guts to win under pressure. On top of that, he was starting a reliever. "I told ya there was tricks to this game, kid," Charlie began, when I cornered him at the hotel, "and, kid, I know 'em all. I'm gonna give the Yankees what they ain't expecting." He made a sound—whfff—and a quick, sideways gesture. "The big Indian [Allie Reynolds] likes to throw at my guys' heads. Well, now I got a big guy [Black] who ain't afraid to throw at *their* guys' heads. They know it. They've scouted him. So maybe he won't *have* to knock anybody down. Just knowing he can do it, that's what makes the difference. But don't quote me or I'll get in trouble. Me and Black, too. I'm not supposed to talk about the knockdowns. If I do, it's oops, wham, Goodbye, Dolly Gray."

"What about the racial stuff, Charlie? What about starting a Negro in the Series?"

"You mean prejudice? I know about prejudice. I know *all* about prejudice. I don't go to church, but my parents was Catholics and when I was a kid in Decatur, the Klan come by one night and set fire to a cross on the front lawn. I looked out the window and all I could see was fire.

"Fuckers burned a cross on a little kid's lawn. That's all you have to know about prejudice.

"My best player is colored and my big pitcher is colored.

"I'm glad I got 'em both."

In 1952 the World Series was the climax of the sporting year, as it had been for much of the century. (The rival Super Bowl did not appear until 1967.) Baseball people looked forward to the Series, of course. So did the sportswriters and the broadcasters and the public, even people who followed the game only casually in early season. With every October came a collective, voluptuous, national surrender to the charms and excesses and glories of what Jack Keefe, Ring Lardner's archetypical ball player, called in his earnest, phonetic way, the World Serious. Sensible businessmen scaled down work schedules Series week. You just couldn't get much done. Portable radios appeared in every office. "Here's the pitch," shouted Mel Allen or Red Barber or Vince Scully, "and there goes a long high drive . . . !"

The radio voices ruled the streets. You walked down a sidewalk and if the day was warm and windows remained open, you followed the Series from one apartment to the next, from one radio to the next, Emerson, RCA, Admiral, Air King, Zenith, Motorola, Philco. "This one," cried Allen or Barber or Scully, "could be outta here . . . !"

Summer was gone, and we didn't want it to be gone. Winter was threatening but now, for this week, we had the Series, our last leaf. Let the Germans drink dark beer and drown their sins in Munich. Let the Frenchmen roll peasant maids in Bordeaux. The World Series was our Oktoberfest, our Vendage, our festival before the cold length of another winter descended.

Come on, we said.

What are you waiting for?

Play ball!

My father wanted to talk baseball and two days before the Series began we met in the bar and restaurant on West 40th Street, under the Herald Tribune building. The Artist and Writers Restaurant featured hearty German fare at prices newspapermen could afford, and a sixty-foot darkwood bar where pellucid martinis ruled. Scotch was a vigorous runner-up. A large stuffed fish that J.P. Morgan hooked in 1908 dominated a barroom wall. A tarnished suit of armor guarded the entrance to the dining room. The Artist and Writers was clubbish, masculine, and crowded at the cocktail hour by writers from the *Tribune*, *Newsweek*, the *New Yorker*, and the *New York Times*. Later, toward eleven o'clock, tuxedos entered. The old Metropolitan Opera House, with its "diamond horseshoe"—box seats for the wealthy—stood a block away.

I was comfortable in the restaurant, a regular of two years standing, and my shortcoming, raw youth, was counterweighed by my job. I was one of the few patrons who knew Allie Reynolds and Jackie Robinson by their first names. Occasionally middle-aged strangers asked me to arbitrate arguments. "Who's a better pitcher, Erskine or Roe?" (I stopped settling arguments after remarking that this season Erskine seemed better by a hair. The stranger responded, "Yer fulla shit. What the hell do you know about baseball, anyway?" The man was shouting and the bartender, Leo Corcoran, directed him to leave.)

My father looked drawn, but as he sipped a Manhattan cocktail, he brightened. I drank a Scotch. "How can you swallow that stuff, Dad, with the fruit salad and the sugar and the cherry?"

"During prohibition," my father said, "the whisky was so poor we all starting drinking cocktails to disguise the taste. And in the words of Artistotle, man is a creature of habit."

Florid, stocky Dick West, the day city editor, moved past. "Who do you like?" he said in a conspiratorial tone.

"The Brooklyns in seven, Dick."

"Are you handicapping or rooting?" West winked a great, red-faced, drinking man's friendly wink.

"A little of each, sire," I said.

*Sire.* I had picked that up from Red Smith. When first we met, I called Smith "sir." By way of indicating that formality was unnecessary and even a bit distasteful, he called me "sire." Smith liked the word or thought in his extraordinary way that it suited me. Whatever, Smith called me "sire" often during a friendship that lasted thirty years.

I wanted to introduce my father to Dick West and Duke Snider and Pee Wee Reese and Red Smith and Allie Reynolds and Casey Stengel and all the wondrous people who had suddenly entered my life. My father, I suppose, wanted to talk baseball the way we always had. He was fifty-one and suffering from episodic chest pains; the past must have seemed a safe, consoling place.

"This could be a most interesting Series," he said. "The Yankees have a remarkable pitcher in Allie Reynolds. Vic Raschi, behind him, is darn near as good." Before writing a story called "Series Prospects" that afternoon, I had studied Reynolds's records, supplied in a blizzard of numbers by the Yankees publicity office. "The Superchief," Red Patterson's press release began, "led all American League hurlers in

1952 with an earned run average of 2.06. The Superchief believes in finishing what he starts. He opened 29 games for Manager Casey Stengel's Bronx Bombers this season and completed 24. That is a completion percentage of .828, tops not only in the northernmost borough, but in all of baseball.

"He plays a terrific end game, too. Casey used Reynolds in relief six times and Allie posted a perfect performance record with six saves. Six for six! You could also call him Big Chief Whiff-in-the-Face. Reynolds topped all rival A.L. moundsmen with 160 strikeouts.

"Not bad for a Creek Indian, who started life on a Reservation."

My father said Reynolds had a fine fastball that he threw toward the uniform letters. Speed and the rotation caused the baseball to rise. "That's the high, hard one," Gordon said. "It bothers anybody, even big leaguers. Even if you hit the high, hard one, you tend to pop it up."

This was exactly the kind of magical baseball knowledge that made my father the thunder and the cannon of my early life. "Actually, Dad," I said, "the guys don't call it the high, hard one anymore. They call that hopping fastball the hummer."

Gordon Kahn blinked and sipped his drink. I ordered another round.

"Who is 'they'?" Gordon said.

"The fellers. Pee Wee. Preach. When Campy wants a pitcher to throw harder, he tells him: 'Hum that pea.' The ball is the pea. The fast one is the hummer."

My father assimilated my words and remarked that the language of the game was always in flux. "When I started," he said, "they didn't call the feller alongside third a coach. He was a coacher."

"Reynolds will probably give Gil Hodges fits," I said. "Dressen wants Gil to start going with the outside stuff, driving it to right, and he's had Billy Herman working on that for weeks. But without much success. Hodges hits thirty or forty homers a season trying to pull everything."

"You can't change a slugger's style in a matter of weeks," my father said.

"I guess, but the point is that Hodges does most of his damage against second-rate pitching. Reese, Billy Cox, hit the good pitchers and bad about the same. Hodges murders weak pitching, but he can't touch tough righthanders who paint the outside corner. So if he's going to get to Reynolds, he simply has to change his style."

Traveling for a season in the major leagues, listening, studying, taking notes, writing as many as 3,000 words of baseball every day, I had developed a sophisticated understanding of the game. This came easily because my father had provided me with a solid grounding in basics. But now, as the Series dawned, I had developed to a point where I knew more about the intricate patterns and subtleties of major league baseball than my father. We both recognized this—a profound changing of the guard—and it made us uncomfortable.

"Tickets, Dad," I said. "I can get you tickets."

The day before Buzzie Bavasi had asked me to come to the Dodger office at 215 Montague Street. He took my arm, led me to his desk and opened the center drawer. Twenty or thirty strips of Series tickets rested in stacks. "Some of these are great and some are ordinary," Bavasi said. "Tell me the truth now. Tell me how many you need for the grocer and the butcher and I'll take care of you with the ordinary tickets. Tell me how many you need for your dad, and I'll give you the best in the ballpark. Home plate. First or third. But don't take any more of the good ones than you really need for your family. Okay?"

At the bar my father insisted that he had important work to do and could not possibly get away for the opening game of the World Series. Or any other game until the weekend, for that matter.

"The weekend games are at Yankee Stadium. I won't get the terrific tickets there that Buzzie sold me for Ebbets Field."

"The weekend," my father said. "I can't get away for a game until the weekend. But then I'll be happy to accept your offer. How much do I owe you for a Sunday ticket?"

"My treat," I said.

"Nonsense." My father thrust a ten-dollar bill into my hand. He had four dollars change coming, but wouldn't accept it.

Captains of the old guard do not easily relinquish command.

That was on Monday. Tuesday brought more intense conversation.

"You worried, Joe?" I said.

"You trying psychology on me?"

"No. Just asking a reasonable question. You're starting the first game. If I were starting, I'd be worried."

"You're not a pitcher." We sat in the front room of Joe Black's apartment on Decatur Avenue, in a middle-class black Brooklyn neighborhood. His baseball career, in the Negro leagues and organized ball, had imposed a vagabond lifestyle, forcing Black to travel America, Cuba, and the Caribbean rim eleven months a year to make a living. Now that he had achieved stardom and, he hoped, stability at the age of twenty-eight, Black wanted roots. His wife, Doris, passed a licensing examination and began teaching in a Brooklyn elementary school. The Blacks liked the community where the Dodgers played. They moved there; they intended to stay there.

"If you don't mess yourself up with mind games," Black said, "pitching is pitching in the colored leagues or in the World Series. I mean on the one hand, the hitters are better up here, Stan Musial, Eddie Mathews, Ted Kluszewski. And coming up Berra, Mantle, Woodling. But, hey, look, I got a lot going for me that I never had before. Camp [Roy Campanella] calls a great game, like he knows what I want to throw before I do. You see that team behind me. You see them every day, same as me. Cox, Reese, Robinson. Can they pluck ground balls? Duke and Skoonj [Carl Furillo] and Pafko. The best outfield arms in the league and they don't make errors. Hodges. He could field great without a glove. Everybody talks about the Dodgers' hitting, but this is the best *fielding* team I ever saw." Black paused, counting blessings. Then he said, "How about you? Are you worried?"

"Why should I be worried?"

"Doesn't the *Tribune* put the World Series on the front page? You ever had your byline on the front page before?"

"Not so's I remember. I'll tell you something else. I've never been to a World Series game before."

"Me, neither," said the first game's starting pitcher. "But wait a minute. Playing ball all the time and growing up in Brooklyn and coming from a family with money, how come you never went to the Series? Where were you in forty-one, forty-seven, forty-nine?"

"My mother hates baseball," I said, "and she had the checkbook."

"Be careful with the mind games, man. They're bad enough in baseball, but the worst mind games of all go on in families."

"Of course, I'm nervous, Joe. The Series story goes through a set of additional editors on the night desk, and I have my own style, and maybe they won't like it, and the story has got to be long, very long, eight to ten pages. I have to write that much and make it good and get it done in about an hour."

"Think of the money you're making,"

"The *Trib* pays me $72.50 a week."

"Let's see," Black said, "that comes out to around $3,800. But looka here. The Dodgers pay me $7,500. That comes out to $125 a game.

"But we're both rookies, and that's the way it is."

In truth, Bob Cooke felt concern that writing the lead on the first World Series game I had ever seen could prove overwhelming. He submerged his doubts underneath a brief pep talk. "Don't get fancy. You can handle this. You've handled everything all season. A ballgame is a ballgame. [An echo of Black's pitching is pitching.] I'll be in the office backing you up. Just remember: Begin your story with the most important things that happen.

"I'll see you later for a cocktail over at press headquarters."

Wildly nervous, I repeated, "Begin with the most important things. Right. Important things. Begin."

Cooke grinned thinly. "Better relax. If you enjoy the game, so will your readers."

Charlie Dressen, after deciding to start a rookie relief pitcher, went into a panic, which he tried to wash away with words. Dressen gathered his mighty Dodger squad for meetings on Monday and Tuesday—the Series began on Wednesday, October 1—and issued a curious call to arms. Twice. Like most great teams, the Dodgers had beaten up the second division, the bottom four clubs in the National League, notably embarrassing the Pittsburgh Pirates, a franchise run by an increasingly desperate Branch Rickey. The Dodgers defeated the Pirates 19 times in 22 games, a winning percentage of .864. That is a barely plausible figure in competition between major league clubs.

"You guys are gonna win this Series if you keep your heads on right," Dressen said, "like you kept your heads on right against the Pirates. They don't change no rules because you're playing in October. [Pitching is pitching and a ballgame is a ballgame. All these protestations actually underscored that the Series was indeed something special.] Three strikes is still out. Four balls is a walk. The rules they got in Forbes Field all season is the same rules they got in the Series. They don't change nothing.

"Now here is what you're gonna do. Just forget you're playing the Yankees. You're playing the Pirates."

The ballplayers sat in silence and surprise. "Just do it," Dressen said. "I'm the manager. Do what I'm telling ya."

"But Charlie," somebody said. "How can we? It says the name of the team right on their shirts."

"I know that," Dressen said. "Don't you think I know that? I'm trying to get you guys to use your heads.

"Now when you look at their uniforms, I don't want you to see NEW YORK on the front."

"But it says NEW YORK," someone interrupted.

"I don't care what it says," Dressen shouted. "I want all you guys to see another word.

"PITTSBURGH. When you look at them shirts, I want you to see PITTSBURGH on the front."

That is how, on the cool afternoon of October 1, 1952, the Brooklyn Dodgers marched from their clubhouse at Ebbets Field, to do battle against the Pittsburgh Yankees.

Six hundred of the best and most popular sportswriters in the country would cover every inning of every game. The ranks included Red Smith of the *Trib*, Jimmy Cannon of the *Post*, and John Lardner of *Newsweek*—the New York stars; Shirley Povich of Washington, Walter Stewart of Memphis, and such assorted other celebrated writer-columnists as Roy Stockton of St. Louis, Fred Russell of Nashville, and Vincent X. Flaherty of San Francisco. The closest major league stadium, Sportsman's Park in St. Louis, stood 2,140 miles east of Flaherty's home base, but the old World Series transcended geography. It was a front-page story across the country, especially exotic to people who lived thousands of miles away. Few Americans had seen anything more of a World Series than patchy black-and-white scenes worked into newsreels. Those glimpses left imagination free to roam. Today each inning of every game is televised in luminescent color into every hamlet, sports bar, and hollow on the continent. The televised World Series is now as available as soap opera, and the television directors rerun every close play five times. The weight of all the replays crushes the romance of the game under a sort of pseudo-realism that is pressed upon us as relentlessly as all those commercials that distort the natural flow of a ballgame.

The night before the 1952 Series was to begin at one-thirty in the afternoon at Ebbets Field, the night before the game to which my father had declined a perfect ticket, the night before Joe Black would try to defeat the great Allie Reynolds and the Pittsburgh Yankees, Bob Cooke led me into a festive hall at the Hotel Bossert in Brooklyn Heights. This was the Hospitality Room for baseball people and sportswriters covering the Series. Here buffet tables beckoned, with roast chicken, baked ham, and prime ribs of beef. Four bars offered a dozen different drinks. There was a carton of Camel cigarettes on every table. All this bounty was offered up for free, it was utterly free, to every accredited sportswriter and baseball man. In the large hall, six hundred people milled about, gulping free food, drinking free drinks, smoking free cigarettes, and talking baseball.

"Hello, Dolph."

"Hi-ya, Bob, How's the family?"

Hallelujah. This broad-shouldered, soft-voiced man was Dolph Camilli, 1941 National League home-run champion and Most Valuable Player. Big Dolph (smaller up close than I had imagined) led the Dodgers to a pennant across the summer when I was thirteen years old.

"I used to watch you play, Mr. Camilli."

"Call me Dolph. A lot of people used to watch me play."

"Now," Cooke said, "I pay him to watch the Dodgers."

"I know," Camilli said. He smiled quickly. "I hear you're writing good stuff, son. Let's get a drink."

I was being welcomed into a restricted club. It was elitist, all-male, almost entirely white, an avatar of what has become Politically Incorrect. I was thrilled to join. (That is not to say that I didn't start knocking down walls as soon as I got my bearings.) Baseball was *The Game* and everyone knew it was the game and its elitism was deeply grained. Football? A nice exercise for college *boys*. Basketball? John Kieran, who launched the famous column, "Sports of the Times," said, "Basketball doesn't write."

Tennis? Clubby.

Hockey? Canadian.

Golf? "Listen," said Burt Shotton, the Dodger manager who preceded Dressen. "Any game where a fifty-year-old man can beat a thirty-year-old man, ain't a sport. Argue with that."

"I wanted to ask you about pulling all those homers to right," I said to my old hero and new friend, Dolph Camilli.

"Look for the fastball," Camilli said. "If you get a curve or a change of pace, you'll be able to adjust. But if you look for the curve and then you get the fastball, it's by you. It's gone. In the catcher's glove. So if you want to pull home runs, always be ready for the fastest stuff the pitcher throws."

Billy Herman joined us. "So you're going with the rookie," Camilli said.

"He's a good rookie," Herman said.

"So far," Camilli said. "Maybe we'll find out how good tomorrow."

I lingered in the big room very late, talking baseball with professionals who truly knew the game, a roomful of heroes sprung fully formed from mythology to life.

On game day the place looked different, rather grand for Brooklyn. I had been going to Ebbets Field since 1934, and I had never seen it so brightly groomed. Red, white, and blue bunting hung from the railings of the lower deck. Work crews had scrubbed the aisles clean of every shred of debris, including last week's chewing gum. A military band tooted John Philip Sousa marches. The weather was mild, in the high sixties, and a fresh breeze stirred a dozen flags atop the roof. Something was up. The World Series was up; and the bunting and the band and, indeed, the very air proclaimed that this was no ordinary day.

At twelve-fifteen news photographers posed Charlie Dressen with his head sticking through a horseshoe of posies. They also did that with horses that won at Aqueduct. "You're a winner, Charlie," shouted bald Herbie Scharfman of Hearst's International News Service. Scharfman aimed his bulky Speed Graphic, the big, square press camera of the day, and ordered, "Smile." Dressen obliged with a horsey grin.

The photographers took pictures of Yogi Berra pumping his bat. They prevailed upon Casey Stengel to pose with an arm around fierce little Ruth Dressen, who touched her tinted hair. The military band subsided. Gladys Goodding, the house organist, played "Casey Would Waltz with the Strawberry Blonde." Newspapermen, hundreds of newspapermen, swarmed over the Brooklyn grass behind home plate. The players took batting practice, rushing in and out of the cage, and yet more hordes of reporters studied every swing. Other sportswriting cadres massed in each dugout. It was difficult to interview the ballplayers in the middle of the mob scenes. Anyway, the players were nervous. They made little nods, by way of being courteous, but they didn't want to be interviewed. They had to get ready to play a game.

"What are all those writers doing?" I said, indicating the mass in the Dodger dugout on the first base side. "There aren't any ballplayers in there right now."

"The writers," Red Smith said, "are interviewing each other. "That's an October tradition. The writers interview each other before the game. Afterwards, in their stories, they quote each other."

Joe Black moved toward us on the way to practice swings. He looked solemn, winked gravely, kept walking.

"A very good feller," I said. Smith was still adjusting to the reality of blacks in major-league uniforms, and had complained that Jackie Robinson was too loud for his taste. On behalf of the seven blacks then employed in the National League, I became self-appointed propagandist to the most widely read of sportswriters.

"A very *large* feller," Smith said. "Can he hit?"

"About like me, Red. He batted .139. But can he pitch? That's the question. And the answer is: Boy, can he pitch."

"But now," Smith said, "he has to pitch against the Yankees." He sighed. To Smith, the Yankees embodied the major leagues. By contrast, the Brooklyn Bucolics were highly talented, excessively talkative minor leaguers. "Follow me," Smith said. "I understand there's food and drink available in the ad hoc restaurant they've set up way out there under the right field stands."

"Drink?" I said. "I don't think I ought to drink before I write."

"There's no reason why you should," Smith said. "I may have a drink or two myself, but I've been to this sort of thing every season for twenty years. It becomes just another bunting and throwing party when your eyes grow as jaded as mine. This is the first Series you've covered. You are about to lose your maidenhood. For that event, sobriety may be appropriate."

"This will be the first World Series game I've ever seen. And I'll be watching from the press box. Isn't that something?"

Smith had done some homework. "Your friend Joe Black will be watching his first World Series game from the middle of the diamond. We have twenty-five minutes until he throws the first pitch."

It was a fastball, letter high, on the inside corner. Hank Bauer, the Yankees rugged right fielder, a powerful fellow with the merciless features of a bordello bouncer, took the hummer for a strike. No radar guns existed in the 1950s, but a complicated electric-eye device had measured Black's hard stuff at 95 miles an hour. You could see right away he had a good fastball this October day.

Reynolds, the best pitcher on earth, was slightly off his game. In addition to hard stuff, Reynolds threw a nasty, sweeping curve, which he mixed in with an occasional 100-mile-an-hour knockdown. Batters earned their pay—some said combat ribbons—when Reynolds pitched. But this afternoon his curve broke wide and low. You can't spot knockdown pitches when you keep falling behind in the count. You have to come in with fastballs for strikes. Reynolds customarily throttled the opposition, but you cannot throttle good hitters when you are pitching from behind. They know you have to come in with a fastball and they prepare.

Opening the second inning of a scoreless game Jackie Robinson cracked a fastball into the lower left-field grandstand for a Dodger run. The Brooklyn crowd applauded sedately, as though fearful noise would enrage the Yankees. Reynolds walked around the pitching rubber in a tight, angry circle. He believed profoundly that knockdown pitches subdued black batters. "They just don't get up swinging like the white guys do. I don't know why, but they don't. When I go against Cleveland I knock down [Larry] Doby and [Luke] Easter and after that they don't want to hit against me. That's the way it is with colored batters."

"Chief," I said. "They throw at Robinson and Campanella all the time."

"I don't know about *they*," Reynolds said. "I know what works for me."

Very quickly, in the top of the third, Gil McDougald, the Yankees' twenty-four-year-old third baseman, pulled a home run to left and tied the score. McDougald's batting posture was unusual. He stood with legs spread wide, the left foot pointing toward third base and the right toe pointed toward first. The bat drooped over his right shoulder. Today a dozen coaches would assault him. *Move your feet closer together. Hold that bat up, as though you meant to do some damage. We got a system here. Everybody's gotta learn it.* Casey Stengel had the good sense to leave McDougald alone. "However he looks," Stengel said. "The kid can hit." That was, in fact, the Stengel system. Go with what works. All we want to do is win. This ain't ballet and it ain't a beauty contest, neither, which is a good thing for you writers, if you catch my drift.

Suddenly, the game felt tense at Ebbets Field. The Yankees' number-seven hitter had tied the score with nobody out. Now came Billy Martin, the raucous banana-nose from Berkeley, who took over second base after quiet, gentlemanly Jerry Coleman was called back into the Air Force to fly fighter missions over Korea.

Black looked fidgety. He threw three straight balls to Martin. He wiped his forehead with a white uniform sleeve. Then he struck out Martin, and Reynolds, on a full count, and rough Hank Bauer with a curve at the knees. He had fanned the side. The rookie was not getting rattled. Smith put a yellow sheet of Western Union copy paper into his portable typewriter and began to write the middle of his column. The Herald Tribune syndicate, which distributed Smith's work and paid him half of every dollar it collected—a total of about $30,000 a year—insisted that he compose early matter on each World Series game, to satisfy the mix of deadlines across the country. Some afternoon newspapers bought Smith's column and rushed his running commentary into print. All Smith's World Series columns in the 1950s were written middle first, then end, then lead. Somehow, the good ones came out seamless.

Phil Rizzuto and Mickey Mantle singled in the Yankee fourth. Then Joe Collins, the Yankees' first baseman, drove a hard liner toward right center. Rizzuto tagged up with the run that would put the Yankees ahead. Furillo, the greatest arm on earth, caught the Collins drive and threw home. His throw looked even harder than the liner. Rizzuto, a shrewd baserunner, stopped in his tracks and slid back to third. A ground out to Robinson ended the threat.

The Yankees charged again in the fifth. This was a driving and relentless ball club. McDougald, up for the first time since his homer, walked. Martin lined a single to left center. McDougald raced to third where he slid into the tag of skinny, horse-faced Billy Cox. Andy Pafko's throw had nailed McDougald—yet another potential go-ahead run—on a very close play. Smith looked up from his typewriter. "Something happening every minute," he said. "This is a ballgame."

With two out in the sixth inning, Pee Wee Reese lined an outside fastball safely to right. Duke Snider was the batter, a batter at last coming into his own. In his first World Series, three years earlier, Snider found himself outmatched by Yankee pitching and struck out eight times in five games. Now, at twenty-six, he had learned to lay off bad pitches. Reynolds tried to tempt Snider with a wide curve. Snider looked. The ball bounced into the dirt and spun away from Yogi Berra. Reese ran to second. Reynolds walked another tight circle. The count went to two balls and one strike. Reynolds came in with a fastball and Snider lifted a long drive, high over the scoreboard in right centerfield. The baseball bounced on the cobblestones of Bedford Avenue, where reckless children pursued it among honking Plymouths and Chevrolets. This was Snider's first World Series home run. (He hit ten more on an eventful journey to the Hall of Fame.) The Dodgers led by a score of 3-1.

The Yankees charged yet once again in the seventh. Irv Noren walked. Gil McDougald slapped a grounder into the hole on the left side. Billy Cox, the best third baseman of his time, lunged and speared the ball and started a snappy double play. Jackie Robinson at second was the unshakable pivot man. Billy Martin lashed a hard drive up the line. Cox wore a cheap, black, shabby glove. Shabby and magical. He stabbed backhand and trapped the drive between his black glove and the brown infield earth. Martin strained toward first, hoping to beat out a hit. Cox waited and looked at the baseball. It was signed by Warren Giles. Hope swelled in Martin's breast. Cox gunned down the young Yankee by half a step.

Things brightened for the Yankees in the eighth. Gene Woodling, a solid .300 hitter, batted for Reynolds and cracked a high smash against the screen in right center field. The carom eluded Carl Furillo and kicked past Snider. Woodling, a squat, barrel-chested character, rumbled into third. Bauer flied to center and Woodling scored easily when Snider's throw sailed up the first-base line. Black retired Rizzuto, but it was a one-run game again, a one-run game in a small ballpark. With two shaky outfield plays, the great Dodger defense seemed to be wavering.

Ray Scarborough relieved Reynolds and got two quick outs. Then Reese lined a fastball into the lower stands in left. He had hit a homer in the Dodgers' disappointing 1949 Series and now, with this crucial eighth-inning drive, Reese became the first Dodger ever to have walloped two World Series home runs. Ever. From the Series of 1916, in the time of Woodrow Wilson, until this one in the time of Truman, Eisenhower, and Nixon, no Dodger had hit more than one home run in a World Series career. Babe Ruth hit fifteen in ten Series. Mel Ott hit four in three. You had to concede that Brooklyn's recurrent autumn disasters amounted to more than wretched luck. The element of powder-puff hitting persisted.

History aside, the 1952 Dodgers had regained their two-run margin. In the ninth inning, the visiting team has to play for a victory, not a tie, and now the Yankees stood three runs away from taking a lead.

Snider ran down Yogi Berra's long fly to right center. Robinson moved smartly toward second and threw out Joe Collins. Black dug deep and struck out Irv Noren. That gave the Dodgers the victory, 4-2. In five previous World Series, no Brooklyn team had ever won the opening game. The big relief pitcher walked off the mound in a cheerful, businesslike manner and extended his hand to Roy Campanella.

Other Dodgers congratulated Black with enthusiasm, but there was no leaping, no whooping, nothing close to hysteria.

You'd have thought they had won a game from the Pittsburgh Pirates.

"A splendid game of rounders," Red Smith remarked. Rounders is an English ballgame, bearing some resemblance to baseball, popular with girls in the prep schools of Sussex and Devonshire.

"Not bad for baseball, either," I said. Smith looked up from his portable typewriter and his brutal deadline and offered the benediction of a smile. Then, unsmiling, he resumed typing a segment of his "Views of Sport." I broke decorum with a glance over his left shoulder. Smith wrote:

> Charlie Dressen, Brooklyn's resident Djinn, had Snider, Robinson and Reese hit home runs, inspired Cox to feats of dazzling legerdemain at third base and called for the best in the throwing arms of Pafko and Furillo. It was a brilliant managerial performance, as perhaps it should have been since thanks to one Bobby Thomson, Dressen had an extra year for laying his intelligent plans. It was also a very good game of rounders.

It wasn't rounders and it wasn't a semicool *not bad for baseball*, either. It was simply and directly one hell of a ballgame. Now I had to write a three-thousand word story that would start on page one and continue inside, adjacent to Smith's droll, polished prose. Voices echoed. Hurry up. The first edition is waiting. We have deadlines at the *Herald Tribune*. This isn't the *Encyclopaedia Britannica*. We publish every day. Hurry up, but show a civil respect for your native language. Bob Cooke would be reading my story and Red Smith and Jackie Robinson. And my father.

A good game offers a half dozen angles. A good *story* begins with the writer selecting the right angle, the element or elements that determined the outcome of the game. This selection is the underlying basis for a strong lead. If a writer makes the wrong selection, and begins with tangential matter, nothing, not even eloquence, will save his story. A misconceived lead ruins everything.

Good writing is critical to a great sports section, but writing has to proceed from informed, accurate reporting. I remember John Lardner making this point about his father, Ring. "In my father's stuff," John said, "if he wrote that right field was the sun field, then it was, and second base was always right where it belonged." A good sportswriter is also a good reporter; the one presuming, encompassing the other.

Grasping the key factor in a complex game, and doing it quickly, is not as simple as it may appear. The best of baseball writers, the two Lardners, Smith, Cannon, and the Dick Young of the 1950s understood baseball from their marrow. The poetry or noise they made proceeded first from deep understanding. My job in the Ebbets Field press box after the Dodgers' great victory on October 1, 1952, was to find the right angle and—just about as important—get the score in the first paragraph. Competent baseball writing does the same today.

What? Announce the score in the first paragraph? It already appears in the headline. Before turning to a newspaper, most fans have heard the score on radio or TV. Indeed. But getting the score in the first paragraph inflicts an appropriate discipline on a baseball writer. It lessens the chance that he or she will write a maundering, self-indulgent essay. Besides, the score is the point of every game. On the *Tribune*, if you did not get the score in the first paragraph, the copydesk bounced your story back to you. Today, as in the 1950s, if the score is not contained in the first paragraph, chances are that the writer is stumbling. "I hate those wordy bastards who keep trying to write poetry, when all the reader wants to know is who won and why." That was Dick Young, of the *Daily News*, holding forth in his customary manner.

Here was an extraordinary—and dare I say, poetic—game, dumping a basket of angles into the press box. One angle was the Dodger defense. It excelled, wavered briefly, but in the ninth, with Snider running down a long fly and Robinson moving swiftly to his right, defensive skill forged Brooklyn's victory. There was the quiet excellence of

Pee Wee Reese, who had played every inning of every Dodger World Series game since 1941. Two hits for Reese and he scored half the Brooklyn runs. There was the clawing drive of a Yankee team, unwilling to concede the permissibility of defeat and clearly raging for another chance tomorrow. Racial aspects ran through the game: Allie Reynolds's harsh theory about Negroes as hitters and Joe Black's journey through bigotry from obscurity to triumph.

For my purposes, the racial material lay out of bounds. Bob Cooke didn't approve of integrated major league baseball and his deputy, who ruled the copydesk and scrutinized every important story, maintained a Gatling-gun chatter of prejudice. "Hey," he liked to tell me, knowing my fondness for Robinson and Black, "maybe we'll assign you to the Yankees next year. We wanna find out if you can cover ballplayers who are *white*."

Many marvelous aspects illuminated baseball writing in the 1950s, but sensitivity to the condition of blacks was not among them. No editor pressed for pieces about which ballplayer behaved badly in what bar, as happens today, but neither did the sports editors or the baseball writers—or the thinkers who composed editorials, for that matter—express outrage when the Chase Hotel in St. Louis accepted twenty-two Dodgers and turned away Black, Robinson, and Campanella. "You have to know the background," one renowned sportswriter, who had worked in St. Louis, informed me. "The owner of the Chase had one of his nieces raped by a Negro."

I asked what that had to do with where Jackie Robinson slept.

"You should be more accepting of things," the columnist said.

I channeled my anger into a brief piece: INTEGRATED DODGERS AGAIN SEGREGATED BY HOTEL MAN. I wish I had thought to check out of the Chase and check into the Hotel Adams with Black and Robinson. But I did not, and, worse, my story never made the paper. The deputy sports editor informed me, with an angry long-distance call, that I was being paid to write baseball, not race relations, and as long as he was running the copydesk, I was damn well gonna write what I was supposed to write. Was he gonna have to send me a Western Union telegram, or did I get the message?

I got the message; when I began to write about baseball bigotry, I had to publish in small magazines, *SPORT* and the *Nation* and a forgotten journal for blacks called *Our Sport*.

My story on the first game began: "Home runs and Joe Black, the combination that brought Brooklyn the National League pennant, brought the Dodgers the opening decision in their quest for their first World Series championship yesterday. Jackie Robinson, Duke Snider, and Pee Wee Reese slammed in all the Brooklyn runs with homers. Black made the hitting stand up with good speed and great control and while a record Ebbets Field crowd of 34,861 watched quietly, the Dodgers whipped the Yankees, 4-2."

Serviceable. Clear. Conservative. Not dashing. But in my double debut—the World Series and the front page—I wasn't ready to be dashing. I had put the most important things up top, chosen the right angle and recorded the score in the first paragraph. After that the story moved at a decent pace. I wrote quickly and hard; as I typed, peanut shells popped from my Smith-Corona. Toward the end I tried a bit of commentary.

For a fellow who was the last man on an uncertain pitching staff last spring, Black hasn't done badly.

Neither did any of the players. The crowd poured $209,892 into the coffers and the athletes get a good share of the receipts from the first four games.

Today Carl Erskine will try to prove that Black isn't the only Dodger pitcher who can beat the Yankees in October. In his first Series start, Erskine draws a formidable opponent. Vic Raschi, the big, black-haired righthander has started five Series games for the Yankees across the last four autumns. Erskine has been the Dodgers' most effective starter all season. He pitched a no-hitter against the Cubs on June 19, a performance complicated by a 40-minute rain delay. "Actually," Erskine said, "the delay turned out to be encouraging. I played bridge to pass time in the clubhouse and when I made four no-trump, I figured that a no-hitter was possible, too."

He has a soft wit and a gentle manner, but there is no grittier competitor in baseball than Carl Daniel Erskine of the suddenly sister communities, Anderson, Indiana, and Brooklyn, New York, where the Dodgers won an important ball game yesterday.

I was rooting. Rooting silently in the press box. Rooting visibly in my story. Rooting wildly in my heart.

I never knew a worthy baseball writer, who wasn't—at the core—a rooting fan. Of course, you want to mask that a bit.

Root? Me? Sir, I am a reporter. (*Come on, Carl. Come on, Oisk, baby. Let's nail these Yankees to a wall.*)

# Turning Professional

A N AUTUMN SHOWER FELL ON Brooklyn Thursday morning, making
puddles in the sidewalks along Sullivan Place and sending little
rivers running down the cobblestone gutters of Bedford Avenue
toward Empire Boulevard and Fred Fitzsimmons' Bowling Lanes.
Around a gray tarpaulin unrolled across the infield, rain soaked the
hallowed soil of Ebbets Field, where the Yankees and Dodgers were
scheduled to meet again at one o'clock. The pitching would match Vic
Raschi, thirty-three, a rugged veteran from West Springfield, Massachusetts, once called The Springfield Rifle, against Carl Erskine, an
earnest Indiana son of the middle border, whom the Brooklyn come-
dian, Phil Foster, nicknamed Oisk.

At twenty-five, Erskine seemed rather an unlikely major-league
pitcher. He stood barely more than 5-feet 9-inches tall and his frame
had none of the intimidating bulk you saw in Raschi or in glowering
Allie Reynolds. Erskine's features were regular, chiseled but not gross.
He was a trim, handsome fellow with quiet passions for classical
music, of which he knew just enough to want to know more, and nar-

rative poetry, which he had memorized by the volume. Erskine was thoughtful, temperate, and devoted to his wife and children. His idea of a wild day on the road consisted of a visit to the natural history museum in Pittsburgh. He refused on moral grounds to throw at batters' heads. He neither drank nor indulged in the raucous obscenities that were, and are, part of baseball lingo. I sometimes called Erskine, after a gentle Protestant hymn we sang at Froebel Academy, "Lead, Kindly Light."

The pitcher as intelligent gentleman traces at least to Christy Mathewson, the great New York Giant righthander, fl. 1910, and extends through Tom Seaver and Orel Hershiser in the modern era. Pitchers seem to belong to a more literate genus than, say, right fielders. Perhaps this is because, as Warren Spahn, who won 363 games, phrased it, "Every pitch I threw had an idea behind it." Great pitchers exercise intelligence as well as muscles in their constant quest to retire hitters. The 120 pitches that spin out a complete game are a wonder of changing speeds, changing locations, changing rotations. The successful pitcher seeks always to serve exactly what the batter is *not* expecting. After hours, he probably excels at the shell game or cards. (Mathewson, in fact, was a champion checkers player, who took on as many as eight opponents simultaneously and beat them all, while blindfolded. He was a hard thrower and also a calculating thinker.)

After each demanding start, pitchers have three or four days for rest and contemplation before climbing the mound again to go to work. Some use the down time to raise hell. Others, in Mathewson's time and Erskine's time and today, read and think deep thoughts.

But for both the hard-drinking brawler and the aesthete, big-league pitching is a rugged task. You had better be bearing stout tools when you mount that little knoll that rises in the center of the diamond. Erskine had big hands, with powerful fingers, and an extraordinarily supple wrist. Branch Rickey routinely asked prospects to throw a baseball as far as they could, just moving the wrist, not the arm, and holding the pitching hand palm up. As far as anyone recalls, Erskine held the distance record for this curious and daunting event. The strong, supple wrist enabled him to throw an overhand curve that sank like a stone on the sea. He could put so much backspin on his change-of-pace that the floater looked like a fastball as it left his hand. Erskine also fired a lively fast one and he had developed excellent control. In 1952 he was breaking through to stardom.

"Still raining, Doc?" Erskine asked the question of Dr. Harold Wendler, an osteopath who was the Dodgers' trainer. If the game was on, Wendler would work to loosen Erskine's tight right shoulder.

"I do believe it's let up," Wendler said. "I think we'll have a ball-game."

"I want to see for myself," Erskine said, and that was the beginning of a small disaster.

Windows in the trainer's room and the adjoining clubhouse at Ebbets Field were crescents of frosted glass placed near the ceiling. They provided ventilation and privacy. Fans milling about on Sullivan Place could hardly peer in through windows nine feet above the sidewalk. ("Where else but Brooklyn," Harold Rosenthal remarked later, "do you climb a ladder to look out a window?")

Erskine fetched a stepladder, climbed up and worked a window open. The rain had stopped. There was going to be a game for him to pitch.

As Erskine clambered down, his foot slipped and his right knee slammed against a metal radiator cover. Erskine had torn up the same knee playing high school basketball. Pain and nausea assaulted him and he sat down on the nearest object, a black equipment trunk. His head sagged forward and he banged his forehead just over the right eye on the same metal edge that had pounded his knee. My Lord, what a morning.

Charlie Dressen came running from his office. "It's all right, dammit, Carl. You take another day. I'm gonna warm up Loes." Billy Loes, a twenty-two-year-old righthander from Queens, had won thir-teen games that season.

"I'm okay," Erskine said, a bit grimly. "I just need a few minutes. Anyway, my dad's come all the way from Indiana to see me pitch in the World Series. I'm not letting everybody down."

Shaken, determined, Erskine lasted into the sixth inning. In every one the Yankee lead-off man reached base. In four of the six, the Yankee number-two batter got on base as well. In the first inning Roy

Campanella threw out Hank Bauer and then Phil Rizzuto, trying to steal. Erskine struck out two Yankees in the second. The Dodgers bunched three singles in the third inning—one a push bunt by Duke Snider—and Roy Campanella batted in Pee Wee Reese with the Brooklyn run. But Erskine was scrambling to throw strikes, and to focus past his aching knee. "He ain't pitching like Erskine," Dressen said after a while,

"No, he ain't," said Coach Jake Pitler.

Still he was pitching with grand and gritty determination.

The Yankees tied the score in the fourth, went ahead by a run in the fifth and when they loaded the bases with nobody out in the sixth, Dressen bowed to the inevitable, told Erskine to ice his knee and summoned Billy Loes. A run scored when the Dodgers botched a double play. Then Billy Martin, the street kid from Oakland, stared down Billy Loes, the street kid from Queens, and hit a three-run homer into the left field seats. The Yankees won, 7–1. Red Smith, who loved watching baseball, looked toward me in the eighth inning and said, "Interminable."

"I better start my lead," I said.

"Write one for me," said Smith, who again had to start his World Series column in the middle. ("Carl Erskine qualified for a Purple Heart before the shooting started," Smith began what ultimately became the fifth paragraph of his piece.)

Rud Rennie, the Yankee beat writer, said from time to time, "The Dodgers aren't playing the Pirates today. They're playing *like* the Pirates." He was going to start off his piece—notes and commentary—with an observation along that line. Harold Rosenthal, the so-called swingman, commandeered Erskine and the radiator cover. What angle did that leave the youthful lead writer, myself, after a sloppy and finally one-sided game? I wrote:

> The Yankees settled down at Ebbets Field yesterday and with a crushing 7–1 victory evened the World Series at one-game apiece. While the crowd of 33,792 fans watched gravely, Vic Raschi, the heavy-chested righthander, overpowered Brooklyn with a three-hitter, and Billy Martin, the skinny second baseman, buried the vestiges of Brooklyn's hope with a three-run homer in the sixth inning when the Yankees scored five times.

Martin, 24, a pinch runner in last year's Series, has matured rapidly. So has Mickey Mantle, who won't reach his twenty-first birthday for two more weeks. The Kid from Commerce, Oklahoma, slammed three of New York's ten hits.

What elixir has Casey Stengel been feeding his young warriors? Pure Flatbush water?

While I typed, Pee Wee Reese was working to enliven the Brooklyn clubhouse. "Where are all the interviewers we had yesterday?" he asked. "What's going on? Come on. I'm ready. Someone ask questions."

"How about that Raschi?" Rosenthal began. "Was he as fast today as the last Series you saw him in, umm, 1949?"

"Gosh, no," Reese said, "but he was just as impressive. He used to have the big fastball and the good curve. Now it's different, change-ups and a good slider. Not the same pitcher at all, but still a very good one."

"What about *your* pitcher and the radiator cover?"

"I guarantee you this," Reese said. "That radiator cover will not be in this clubhouse next season."

After the two games in Brooklyn, the Series moved without interruption to Yankee Stadium, the most majestic and renowned baseball ballpark on earth. Three tiers of seats surrounded much of the playing field. The triple-tiered stands rose steeply and rather darkly. Ballplayers, trained to ignore their surroundings and concentrate on the ground ball at hand, admitted feeling overwhelmed by the magnitude of the place. From the roof of the topmost desk, a filigreed facade—trademark of an architectural style and the New York Yankees—commanded the eye. Municipal Stadium in Cleveland held more fans. Fenway Park in Boston and Ebbets Field placed spectators closer to the action. But huge, idiosyncratic Yankee Stadium was the great Coliseum of Baseball, as the Yankees were the Imperial rulers of the game.

At Ebbets Field one tiny corner in left centerfield stretched 399 feet from home plate. The similar spot at the Stadium was 466 feet. Closer to the left-field foul line the power alley in Brooklyn extended 350 feet. The Stadium alley ran 415. Of course, the Stadium had been constructed with Babe Ruth's lefthanded power in mind, so here in this Dakota grassland in the Bronx, the right-field foul pole stood only a popgun shoot away from home: 296 feet. There was no fence, only a low railing in front of box seats.

Vast field. Short right. Grandiose facade. Uncomfortable benches without backs in the bleachers that ran behind the outfield. A positive avatar of eclecticism. Nothing like the old Stadium exists today, including the current Yankee ballpark where the playing field has been reshaped many times and the entire structure has been remodeled, very expensively, with uneven results.

When the Series moved north for three days, my responsibilities eased. As the reporter assigned to the Dodgers, I had drawn the job of writing the lead on games in Brooklyn. Now the lead assignment passed on to Rud Rennie, the Yankee beat man. I had only to cover the familiar Dodger dressing room, which let me sit back and enjoy a game without the dread of having to type all those words in all that hurry for the front page.

Lefthanded pitching was the order of this Friday afternoon. Stengel started Ed Lopat, born Edmund Lopatynski, nicknamed Steady Eddie, a stocky native New Yorker, once a movie usher, thirty-four years old, who threw off-speed stuff. Since seven Dodger regulars batted righthanded, Lopat was embarking on perilous seas. "But in our ballpark," Stengel said, "them righthanders can hit them long flies to left center all day, and my excellent outfielders will run and catch them."

Dressen chose tall, angular Elwin Charles Roe, called Preacher, who was born in Ash Flat, Arkansas, the son of an Ozark doctor and who pretty much embodied the Arkansas country slicker. Roe mixed four or five pitches, including a spitball, which he spotted in clutch situations. He had shut out the Yankees in the 1949 World Series, baffling even the Bronx household god, Joe DiMaggio.

"How did you get DiMaggio out like that?" a reporter asked afterward.

"Ah kinda fooled him with muh forkball," Roe replied.

"I didn't know you threw a forkball," the reporter said.

"Yep," Roe said. "The forkball is one of muh best pitches."

Maybe so, but Roe's forkball possessed more than a sharp downward break. It sailed homeward bearing a high level of humidity. "I caught spitters all the time in the Negro Leagues," Campanella observed years later. "But Preacher threw the best wet one I ever saw."

It came up chilly on Friday and both Roe and Lopat scrambled in the cold. The Yankees got a run in the second; the Dodgers tied the score in the third and went ahead with a run in the fifth. Fidgeting, concentrating on the mound, Roe reminded Red Smith of an underfed and underpaid country school teacher. Lopat, in contrast, "had the prosperous appearance that goes with chubby people, such as venal aldermen from the west side of Chicago."

Robinson opened the eighth with a looping single to center. Campanella singled to left and Robinson slid into third ahead of Gene Woodling's throw. Andy Pakfo's fly to left field scored Robinson. The Dodgers now led, 3–1; they were more than one home run ahead.

Not for long. Berra cracked a line drive into the lower deck in right and Roe kicked a heel against the mound. He threw a fair number of home-run balls, but rarely when the game was close. In tight quarters Roe went with his humid fork ball. Dodger fans perspired in the chill.

Reese singled in the ninth for his third hit and when Robinson followed with another single, Stengel trudged to the mound, and summoned a rookie righthander named Tom Gorman. Lopat had yielded ten hits and four walks. Fifteen baserunners, but he had allowed only three runs. Not much style, but extraordinary grit.

Gorman got two strikes on Andy Pafko. He was concentrating on the batter and as he threw again, Reese broke from second base and Robinson broke from first. A double steal.

The pitch came in hard, low, inside, a sinker, a ball. It struck Berra on the top of the left index finger. Berra caught with that finger outside the glove. Berra blinked in pain, then couldn't find the baseball, which was rolling fifty feet away in foul territory. Reese and Robinson, the best baserunners in baseball, scored. The Dodger lead was comfortable, 5–2.

Johnny Mize pinch hit a home run in the last of the ninth, but the game had slipped out of the Yankees' reach. The Dodgers took a lead in the Series, two games to one, with this 5–3 victory.

In dressing rooms today, sizable areas remain off limits to interviewers. Players who don't want to talk to reporters can find sanctuary in a lounge or trainer's room.

There were no such restrictions in baseball's golden days. All dressing rooms, winners' and losers', were opened within five minutes of a game's end, and inside there was no place to hide. If you were man enough to make the major leagues, you had to be man enough to talk to reporters, win or lose. I went to the Brooklyn dressing room first, giving the Yankees time to compose themselves.

I asked Charlie Dressen what prompted him to risk sending Reese and Robinson to steal in the ninth inning of a one-run Series game. "I didn't get prompted," he said. "They did it on their own. The two of them, I let 'em run whenever they want. They know how to play."

I sought out Reese. He said, through cigarette smoke: "I got the feeling Gorman was bearing down so hard to get the out that he was forgetting about the runners. When I got a good jump, I just took off."

"I was watching Pee Wee," Robinson said, "and the pitcher and the hitter, watching a lot of things at once. Reporters are supposed to be able to do that, aren't they? Watch a lot of things at once."

"And good reporters can, wise guy," I said.

Robinson laughed—a high-pitched laugh. "When I saw Pee Wee move, I was gone. With the lead I had, there was no way Berra could throw me out. So there wasn't that much risk, if you take the time to think over the situation. Pee Wee and I don't run in that spot unless we're damn sure we can make it."

In the Yankee dressing room, platoons of writers asked Berra what happened. He had collected three hits, half the Yankee total, smashed an eighth-inning homer and here he was, wearing goat's horns, because everyone was assuming that the two-run passed ball cost his team the game. "Without it," someone said, "Johnny Mize's homer ties the score."

"Mebbe not," said wise old Preacher Roe, back on the Brooklyn side. "See in that situation, with us ahead by three, I didn't care if Mize hit a homer. I wanted to get him out, sure, but mostly I don't want to walk the big feller. I want bases empty. I want to pitch out of my full windup.

"Now without that passed ball, say Pee Wee and Jack don't score. Then we got what . . . a one-run game?

"You've seen me work all year. You know I wouldn't be pitching the same to Mize if we only had a one-run lead."

It would have been time for the humid fork ball that no one hit well.

The Yankees, with their studied sense of style, established the press playpen—hospitality headquarters—in the Grand Ballroom of the fashionable Hotel Biltmore. "Walter O'Malley can't match this," Red Smith said, "because there aren't any fashionable hotels in Brooklyn." Brooklyn, I thought, my native ground, is the Albania of baseball.

It would be Reynolds against Black again tomorrow. "This is the way the World Series is supposed to be," Smith said. "Uncertain and competitive."

I said, one thing did seem certain; we were going to look at a well-pitched game. But I was thinking about our dinner in the Biltmore, which would be free, and the baseball talk ahead, all in the service of my job, and I remembered the title John Lardner put on a collection of sports columns.

*It Beats Working.*

Allie Pierce Reynolds was thirty-seven years old in 1952, a mature and slab-chested exemplar of the intimidating pitcher. At 6 feet, 195 pounds, he was no giant, but there was a solidity to Reynolds that suggested he could throw a baseball through a redwood tree. He had the high cheekbones and flat features common to some native American groups. Even apart from baseball he was a wealthy man. Through what was probably a mistake in high Federal places, the government had deeded a tract of Oklahoma land back to Reynolds's Creek tribe. "They returned some land they took from us," Reynolds said, "without realizing there was oil underneath. My family gets a healthy share of oil revenue."

"Can I ask how much? Not to write. I'm just curious."

"I'll put it this way," Reynolds said. "I make more from oil than I do from pitching." (The Yankees were paying him about $60,000 a year.)

Wealthy or not, Reynolds was hungry. He always had a huge fast-ball but wildness kept him at such minor league spas as Cedar Rapids and Wilkes-Barre for four seasons. "Looking for the strike zone," he said. "That and confidence. I was strong, but underneath I was just one more scared Indian kid."

Cleveland brought him up to stay in 1943 and Reynolds led a weak wartime American League in strikeouts. But during his four seasons at Cleveland, Reynolds developed a reputation as a phenomenally hard thrower, who tended to tire and lose close games in the late innings. There was even some talk, in baseball's chronic obsession with race, that Native Americans had a sort of ethnic trouble contending with major league pressure. Look at Chief Louis Sockalexis. Didn't he drink himself out of the majors in three seasons? Look at Jim Thorpe. Maybe the greatest all-around athlete in the annals, but no more than a lifetime .252 big-league hitter, a flop. Indians, some said, quit when the baseball wars got nasty. It is a small irony that Reynolds, a victim of such racist babble, himself preached racist nonsense of his own: Black men can't stand up to knockdown pitching.

The Yankees acquired Reynolds from Cleveland at the end of the 1946 season, trading their popular power-hitting second baseman, Joe Gordon, for someone who was then a thirty-one-year-old under-achiever. Stengel landed in the Bronx at about the same time with a brace of theories and some complex new pitching ideas. He told Reynolds not to worry about finishing games. "Start and throw as hard and as long as you can. I got other fellers in the bullpen to finish up." In 1947, his first year with the Yankees, Reynolds led all American League pitchers with a winning percentage of .704.

Used to relieve four times in critical games, Reynolds won one and saved three. As he grew confident, Reynolds evolved into a superstar, who indeed tired in late innings, but also into a reliever, who could overpower the best hitters with that one- or two-inning burst of power pitching so common today. He threw two no-hitters in 1951, one against a strong Cleveland team in July and the other against the hard-hitting Boston Red Sox in late September. The final Red Sox batter was Ted Williams and Reynolds retired him with a high foul pop. Or seemed to. Berra spun under the foul, wavered in the breeze and dropped the ball. Reynolds threw Williams another 100-mile-an-hour fastball and Williams lifted another pop foul. Berra held the ball this time, for the final out, and hugged the reserved Reynolds in triumph and relief.

Allie Reynolds and the Yankees vs. Joe Black and the Dodgers. Yankee Stadium, October 4, 1952. A matchup for the ages, or at least this particular age when the Yankees, Dodgers (and sometimes the New York Giants) ruled the world.

With the Dodgers leading by two games to one, Stengel's choice of Reynolds was automatic. This was a must game for the Yankees and it took little genius to play the ace. But Stengel, as usual, drew up plans on many levels. His best fielding first-baseman was Joe Collins, born Joseph Kollonige in Scranton, a cheerful, friendly man of twenty-nine, a solid .280 hitter in 1952, and a reliable glove. With Reynolds throwing fastballs to (and at) the Dodgers' righthand hitters, there figured to be a lot of action on the right side of the Yankee infield. When the "Superchief" was in form, nobody pulled him.

Stengel's other first baseman, John Robert Mize of Demorest, Georgia, thick-armed, cat-eyed Big Jawn Mize, had hit 51 homers as a New York Giant five years earlier. But Mize was slow. He couldn't range to stab grounders and now, after his thirty-ninth birthday, his home-run power seemed buried in the past. All year, starting and pinch-hitting, Mize had hit only four long ones.

Except . . . except, he hit one yesterday, off the formidable Preacher Roe. Stengel saw something. Or sensed something. Whatever, he started geriatric Johnny Mize at first base against fireballing Joe Black, and batted Mize cleanup, right between Mickey Mantle and Yogi Berra, quite a spot for a refugee from the rocking-chair and horseshoe-pitching set. Wasn't Stengel worried about scorching grounders burning Mize? Stengel had managed the Yankees to three consecutive World Series victories and he contended with questions he regarded as impertinent with short bursts of artillery: "Yer fulla shit to ask that and I ain't gonna tell you why."

The Yankees were an angry bunch. Allie Reynolds warmed up silently, fiercely, determined to prove himself a better pitcher than he had showed when he lost the opening game to a rookie. There was no small talk with his warm-up catcher Charlie Silvera. The Yankees were not in a chattering mood.

Reynolds started the first inning by blowing a fastball past Billy Cox. But Reese caught up with a fastball and singled to center. Reynolds threw a hard curve to Duke Snider who bounced the ball toward Billy Martin at second. Martin went down to gauge the hops; his spikes caught as he fielded the ball and trying to force Reese at second, he threw into left field and Reese sped to third. First and third for Brooklyn, none out and two tremendous hitters coming up. Both, as it happened, were black.

Reynolds brushed Jackie Robinson, then threw three strikes that Robinson took. Robinson batted aggressively. He struck out seldom. It was rare to see him called out and rarer still to see him called out with a runner on third. Something was happening.

Campanella, squat, powerful, a little sumo wrestler of a ballplayer, batted fifth. True to his theory, Reynolds threw the first pitch, a 100-mile-an-hour fastball directly at Campanella's head. Campanella lunged to earth. When he arose, Reynolds struck him out.

Black walked Mantle with two out in the first, then retired Mize. Gene Woodling doubled in the second. He did not advance. Reese, emerging as a star of the Series, singled with two out in the third inning. He had led the National League with 30 steals. Now when he broke for second, Berra threw him out.

The weather was mild and sunny and the Stadium was full, with 71,787 paying customers. Counting the six hundred reporters who looked on without paying, the attendance exceeded 72,000—greater than the 1952 population of Alexandria, Virginia, or Brockton, Massachusetts, or Columbia, South Carolina, or Racine, Wisconsin. As the game unfolded, the throng sat quietly. There was sometimes a sense at the Stadium that you were gathered with a corporate crowd, deal-makers out for a day in the sun, not ardently concerned with baseball. But this crowd was too vast for easy categorization. Probably the silence expressed the nature of the game—very quiet and at the same time very tense.

In the fourth inning Black started Mize with a low, breaking ball.

Then he threw a good fastball, up and in. The Dodger scouting report said that Mize had trouble connecting with high inside fastballs. As though expecting this particular pitch, Mize swung falling away from the plate, and cracked a blazing line drive into the twentieth row of the lower deck in right. He had hit a fine, rising fastball for his second home run in two games. Casey Stengel pumped a fist and shouted, "Yeah!" The Yankees and Casey Stengel and Allie Reynolds led, 1–0.

The Dodgers were not rattled. They were a dogged, contentious team. As the fifth inning began, the Brooklyn bench began cheering sarcastically when Reynolds threw fastballs for strikes. "Faster, Reynolds. Cut loose, Allie. Hey, Big Chief. Is that as hard as you can throw? Hey, Big Cheese, throw harder." This was not mindless trash talk. The idea was to goad Reynolds really to throw harder, ever harder, until at length he threw his arm out, and the Dodgers knocked him out. Robinson, whose tenor carried well, led the Dodger bench jockeys. *Hey, Big Cheese.*

Reynolds glowered. Andy Pafko lined a single. Gil Hodges, having a wretched Series at bat, worked Reynolds for a walk. The Dodger dugout grew louder. "Harder, Big Chief. Woo. Woo. Woo."

Carl Furillo, a relentless fastball hitter, drove an outside pitch deep into right centerfield, where Hank Bauer caught up with it. Pafko advanced to third.

The hitter was Joe Black, a fine all-around athlete. Dressen, coaching at third, clutched his left shoulder. Black touched the blue bill of his cap.

Sign dispatched.

Sign acknowledged.

Suicide squeeze.

Reynolds reared back and fired overhand. Pafko, the tying run, broke for home plate. Black stabbed his bat at a low fastball and missed. Berra tagged out Pafko. Four innings remained, but the game was over.

The Dodger tactic of goading Reynolds to throw harder did half of what was intended. Reynolds did indeed throw harder, ever harder. He struck out ten Dodgers, including Robinson three times and Campanella twice. But he did not throw his arm out. Reynolds faced only thirteen batters over the last four innings. Dressen lifted Black for a pinch hitter in the eighth and the Yankees scored against the relief pitcher, Johnny Rutherford, a slight, skilled righthander, who soon afterwards quit baseball to practice medicine. Mantle hit a long triple off "Doc" Rutherford and scored when the relay from the outfield went wild. Throwing harder, ever harder, Reynolds shut out the Dodgers, 2–0. The Series was tied for a second time.

October Saturdays were important football afternoons for the *Herald Tribune*, and some of my colleagues were banished from Yankee Stadium. Harold Rosenthal had to drive to New Haven, where Yale defeated Brown, 28–0. Ed Sinclair shuttled to Princeton, where the Tigers, still playing single-wing football, won their 24th straight, defeating Rutgers, 61–19. The *Tribune* was loyal to its Ivy League heritage and readership, though neither Yale nor Princeton drew as many as 25,000 fans. This weekend at Yale and Princeton, as in the Bronx and Brooklyn, everyone was talking baseball, talking about this thrilling World Series.

Still, we had only three bodies at the Stadium: Red Smith, Rud Rennie, and myself. My assignment was to write a single "inside baseball" story, covering both the Dodger and Yankee dressing rooms. I trudged out of the sunlight along bare corridors, under the three-tiered grandstand—some called this netherworld "the catacombs"—and walked into the glare of the losing dressing room. Intensity still charged the air.

Shirt off, Jackie Robinson was shouting, "You can't hit what you can't see." No one had asked a question. Robinson looked at the congress of reporters and repeated his shout. It was as if he wanted to disarm the press, shouting down an interview. Batting cleanup, he had been called out on strikes three times.

"Jack," I said, "were those third strikes really strikes or did the umpire blow some calls?"

"I can't bitch," Robinson said. "It's not as if I *saw* those pitches. I didn't know where the ball was, he threw so fucking fast."

Joe Black nearby said, "Listen, that pitch I tried to bunt was the fastest pitch I ever saw. Reynolds just reared back and let go. I'm amazed the cover didn't come flying off the ball."

The Yankees were calmer, but not manic. "Chief," someone shouted at Reynolds, "you sure made that loudmouth Robinson look silly."

Reynolds knew better than to inflame a great opponent. "The man is a good hitter," he said, quietly. "He just had a bad day. We all have 'em."

"You sure didn't."

"My curve was a little better than it was for the first game," Reynolds said, "but it's still not what I want. The fastball was fine."

Stengel sat back in his office chair. "My pitcher was tree-mendous," he said. "He pitched tree-mendous, especially when you figure he had just two days' rest. That was the kind of game you'd look for the other day [Game One] when he had a lot of rest." Already Stengel was focusing on tomorrow. He was going to start Ewell Blackwell, a faded former National League star. "If we lost this one," Stengel said, "I was gonna use the other feller [Vic Raschi]. But we didn't lose this one and now I'd rather give him [Raschi] another day's rest."

"If the Series goes seven games," someone said, "you can start Reynolds again in the big one."

"I can't play the games up until next spring, even if that would help your stories," Stengel said. "One day at a time. Anyway, *this* was a big one. Or wasn't you watching?"

My father thought that all things being equal, Carl Erskine had a fair chance of outlasting a Ewell Blackwell, past his prime. But getting to the next step, actually beating the Yankees at the Stadium, was another matter, entirely. He explained this to me carefully in his rich bass-baritone.

I had picked him up at his apartment, the seven splendid sunlit rooms, French doors and a Hellenic bookcase, with a portico that vaulted above small Doric columns, welcoming all to the family library. (The first book was a green-bound volume on the Greek sage Abaris. The last, clad in burgundy, told the story of Ulrich Zwingli, a sixteenth-century Swiss Protestant reformer who died in a religious war.)

"Write well, now," my mother said, as we left. "The family expects that of you."

My father did not drive. He had purchased a large blue Studebaker sedan for cash in 1936, enrolled in a driving school, and quickly passed his licensing test. Two weeks after that, chauffeuring my mother and two friends, he plowed into a greengrocer's sidewalk display. Asparagus, broccoli, kale, squash, and tomatoes flattened before my father's big Studebaker bumper. No one was hurt. In crisis, as he found himself pointed toward a sidewalk, my father confused the brake pedal with the accelerator. That humiliation—miscoordination under pressure—troubled the old City College third baseman beyond recovery. He never drove again.

"A small pitcher like Erskine is going to have to work very hard," my father said. I pointed my car, a used, blue 1946 Ford Tudor—the *Tudor* was the *two-door* sedan—toward the Brooklyn Bridge. Ahead lay an hour's drive. The car was rattly and steered badly. Still, it was the finest vehicle I could afford. The payments were $26.40 a month.

"It's not just size, Dad. It's where you throw the ball. At the Stadium, you want to keep them hitting toward center. No home runs. You pitch to spots."

"That may be so," my father said, "but I know pitchers and I've watched Erskine. He has to throw every pitch as hard as he can."

"And Reynolds?"

"He doesn't always throw the fastball as hard as he can. Sometimes Reynolds cruises."

I was rolling up the East River Drive. Reynolds threw the strike-out pitches to Jackie Robinson all out. He did the same when Joe Black was trying to bunt. But Reynolds mixed in some 80-percent fastballs, saving his strength. At cruising speed, he could still get good hitters to fly to Mantle. With just the *Tribune* and the *Times* as his eyes, my father had picked that out.

"You're sitting downstairs behind home plate," I said. "You'll see Erskine's stuff up so close, you'll want to grab a bat."

"Not at my age," my father said. "And not with your friend Mr. Erskine's overhand curve ball. I told you, curves troubled me. But I do know fastballs."

• • •

We were driving to a ballgame together on a fine, sunny day, as fifteen years before we walked to ballgames together on fine sunny days. The backdrop then was a world moving toward war, atomic bombs, and Holocaust. The ballplayers then were Mumbling Van Mungo, Roundhouse Frankhouse and Lippy Leo Durocher. Today's players—Robinson, Reese, Rizzuto, Campanella, Mantle, Snider, Berra—were a cut above the oldtimers. Several cuts, at the very least. This day's backdrop was Adlai Stevenson's doomed campaign against Dwight Eisenhower and the antics of the controversial vice-presidential candidate, Senator Richard M. Nixon of California. So much had changed, but not the closeness of a father and a son going to a ballgame together.

Eisenhower had just made a speech at the Milwaukee Arena where he said he "saw eye-to-eye" with Senator Joseph R. McCarthy of Wisconsin, on "subversives in government," but disagreed with McCarthy's "method." From the Democratic camp came word that John J. Wiley, Nixon's old Senate campaign manager in Marin County, and Morris F. Richardson, formerly the Republican mayor of Whittier, Nixon's hometown, both intended to vote for Governor Stevenson and his running mate Senator John Sparkman of Alabama. "I once thought that Nixon was a spirited young man who would not compromise his ideals," John Wiley said. "I've worked with him. Now I know better."

My father, a Democrat who had no use for extremes of right or left, said the Republican strategy was clear and probably effective. Eisenhower held the centrist ground, not approving of "that bounder McCarthy," but not breaking with him, either. The general was running as a statesman, above politics, and leaving "the rough stuff" to Nixon. "It's shaping up as a nasty campaign," my father said.

I said the *Herald Tribune* was leading with Eisenhower's speeches, which were ordinary, over those of Stevenson, often soaring, six days out of every seven. "I keep a record in my scorebook," I said. "And watch the front page tomorrow. Nixon is going to the game."

"The *Tribune* is a wonderful paper except for that automatic right turn before Presidential elections. But it always finds its bearings again. Besides, I don't mean to criticize your employer, and perhaps you

shouldn't either. What are you writing today?" The Series was eclips-
ing politics, at least for us, even in a Presidential year.

"Notes. Whatever I can find. Sort of the flavor of the day, if I'm
being clear." A vague World Series assignment like "notes" would have
alarmed me the week before, but now the freedom to write whatever I
picked up was a nice challenge. I was turning into a professional. "I'll
pick up a lot after what Reynolds did yesterday, Dad, but I have to
point the story at tomorrow, too. I'm watching Game Five, remembering Game Four and looking toward Game Six. It takes some concentration."

"You never worked like this in college."

"College? *That* college and *this* World Series? You're comparing the
inferno with Eden."

"Which poet will it be?' my father said, pleasantly, "Dante or Milton? Make up you mind."

I maintained 45, ten miles over the limit, and the Ford Tudor
jounced along between the East River and Yorkville. The brakes were
uncertain. The car felt topheavy, a rollover waiting to happen. I still
wonder how any of us survived our youth, driving such dangerous
cars.

"I hope you don't mind getting to the Stadium early," I said. "I
need to, so I can look for decent stuff. You want to get, say twenty
items, and use the best eight."

"Early is fine. It's always been. I enjoyed watching batting practice
when you were a boy and I still do. Why don't you ask about that
botched squeeze play? I wonder if the Yankees stole a sign."

"The pitch was low, Dad. Easy to bunt. You don't throw low
when you're anticipating a squeeze."

"I'd still inquire."

"I will. Stay in your seat afterward. I'll write as fast as I can, then
pick you up."

As I walked into the Dodger dugout, George "Shotgun" Shuba called
my name. He had been assigned to play left field and he asked me to
walk out there with him. "This is the hardest left in baseball," Shuba
said. "I want you to see that for yourself."

"I don't know if I should. I mean, I'm not in uniform. It's batting-practice time. And people are in the stands."

"Come on," George said, urgently.

In October at the old Yankee Stadium, the three-tiered grandstands played havoc with the daylight. Standing in left field you looked above the high-facaded roof toward a bright sky. Lower, the stands seemed very dark. Almost everybody smoked in 1952; a smoky haze from ten thousand cigarettes seeped out of the dark grandstands.

"Watch," Shuba said.

Bobby Morgan, the reserve shortstop, stood in the batting cage 300 feet away. I had to stare in hard to make sure it was Morgan. He swung, and for a moment I lost the baseball in haze. Then I saw it climbing against the dark stands. It rose, but suddenly the backdrop was bright sky and I had trouble locating the baseball. As it descended, I picked it up against the stands, but when it bounced, it was thirty feet to my left.

"I lost that one, Shotgun. I lost it two or three times."

"See," Shuba said, fiercely.

"Not really."

"I'm playing here today, my first Series start, and I want you to know how tough it's gonna be. You're not like some of the writers. You played ball. All right. You've seen this left field. Now come on." We walked toward the batting cage, staying in foul territory. Shuba kept his glove shoulder high in case a line drive jumped into our faces.

"I'll tell them, George."

"Who?"

"The other writers. I'll tell them left field here is murder, particularly if you haven't played it before."

"I don't mean for you to do that," Shuba said, "But we're friends. I just want you to know."

At the batting cage, I sought my father in the dark stands. There were so many faces it was dizzying. "You hear about Martin?" said Tommy Holmes, of the *Brooklyn Eagle*. "He says Dressen used the same squeeze sign—grabbing a shoulder—back in Oakland in 1949. Martin says he picked it off yesterday and tipped Reynolds."

"I'll see what I can find out."

"Sure I got the sign," Billy Martin said. "Aren't you always writing that Dressen is a great brain? If he's so smart, how come he doesn't change his steal sign. I mean, don't he remember? I played for him in '49. Yeah, I stole the sign. As Allie was winding up, I shouted, 'There he goes.'"

Dressen was quick. "If they stole the sign, why did they throw the ball low?" He wouldn't go further. "Listen, kid, you start to talk about signs, you give too much away. Stay with what I told you. They didn't steal a fucking thing. The pitch was low."

I found Reynolds cooling out beside his locker. He was drinking a Ballantine's beer. He did not have to work today. "Who told you all this stuff?" Reynolds said.

I filled him in. "Well, you've done some work and I'll straighten you out, if you don't use my name. I mean write it, but don't quote me by name. Is that a deal?"

"Sure."

"Billy did get the sign, and then he shouted, 'There he goes!' Pafko isn't a great runner, but damn, I had to nail him, so I just threw the damnedest fastball of my life."

"Black said it was the fastest pitch he'd ever seen."

"I was trying to throw high, but I missed my spot. Yes, we stole the sign. Billy picked it off. I heard him holler. We'd set that up. Then I missed my spot. But the pitch was so fast, I got away with one. Now leave me be. I'm off today.

"And remember now. You can quote me, but don't use my name."

Small as he was, Carl Erskine looked strong and confident. With one out in the first inning, Phil Rizzuto lined a fastball into left center-field. Shotgun Shuba broke with the crack of the bat, stared through the smoke and the chiaroscuro light and ran down the drive, a fine play. There was a bounce in Shuba's stride as he trotted back toward his position. He had defeated the forces of haze and darkness.

An inning later Gene Woodling smacked another hard line drive, this one toward the seats in right field. Andy Pafko put his right hand on the box seat railing and launched himself toward the ball. He caught it at the top of his leap. What looked like a two-run homer died in the pocket of Pafko's glove. To cold-eyed observers, these two smashes suggested that Erskine was making mistakes. To the more mystical, the catches meant something else. This was Erskine's day. He could make mistakes and get away with them.

His curve was formidable. His fastball was good enough and his change of pace kept the big Yankees hitters off stride. Going into the fifth inning, he was pitching a one-hitter and no Yankee had reached second base. The Dodgers chipped away at Ewell Blackwell and when Snider homered in the top of the fifth inning, Brooklyn moved ahead, 4–0.

Suddenly Erskine lost his touch. He walked Hank Bauer. Martin singled. Irv Noren batted for Blackwell and singled home Bauer. Gil McDougald forced Noren, but Rizzuto singled and Martin scored. Mantle fouled out and when Johnny Mize came to bat, Rud Rennie said, "The deuces are on the table." The Yankees had scored two runs. Two men were out. Two runners were on base.

Erskine got two strikes on Big John Mize. "Four of a kind," Red Smith said. Erskine wasted a breaking ball. Then Mize hit a fastball deep into the lower stands in right. It was his third home run in three days, his third homer in three World Series games. He was having a rebirth at thirty-nine. I made a note to find out why, if Mize was belting high inside fastballs toward distant counties, the Dodgers still were pitching him high and tight.

The Dodger lead and Erskine's mystique suddenly were history. Dressen marched mournfully toward the mound, right hand in the right back pocket of his uniform. Erskine's description of what happened next is splendid:

"I see Dressen coming and I'm thinking, 'Oh, no. I've got good stuff.' I look at Dressen coming closer and I think the numbers are against me. October fifth, it was. That was a wedding anniversary, my *fifth*. The *fifth* inning. I've given the Yankees *five* runs. Forget thirteen. Five must be my unlucky number.

"Charlie says to give him the ball. You weren't allowed to talk when he came out. He was afraid you might argue him into leaving you in, and you had to wait on the mound for the next pitcher, so's you could wish him good luck. Now Charlie has the ball. I'm through. The fives have done me in. Suddenly Dressen says, 'Isn't this your anniversary? Are you gonna take Betty out and celebrate tonight?'

"I can't believe it. There's seventy thousand people watching, more than lived in Anderson [Indiana] where I grew up, and he's asking me what I'm doing that night. I tell him yes, I was planning to take Betty someplace quiet.

"'Well,' Dressen says, 'then see if you can get this game over before it gets dark.'"

Berra followed Mize and drove a fastball into deep right centerfield. Snider, Erskine's roommate, ran hard and leapt prodigiously and caught the ball.

The crowd, 70,536 paying customers, was wildly excited by the events on the field and Richard Nixon decided the time was appropriate for a political walkabout. He grinned persistently and waved. After Nixon passed beneath the press box, Harold Rosenthal announced, "Now I know why I don't like the man. He looks like all those sons of bitches who got the temporary jobs I couldn't get at the Post Office Christmas week when the Depression was bad and everybody starved, except guys who looked like Nixon."

The Bronx in 1952 was still New Deal Democratic, and the walking, waving, grinning politician attracted boos. These were drowned out as soon as Johnny Mize lumbered out to play first base in the sixth inning. Mize drew an ovation.

"The crowd has it right," Smith said. "Mize deserves the applause. He's older than Nixon. Been around longer." I looked that up. John Robert Mize was older than Richard Milhous Nixon, by two days.

Johnny Sain relieved Blackwell in the sixth. Sain was Stengel's best reliever—after the protean Reynolds—and the Yankees, ahead, 5–4, looked in healthy shape. Long John Sain's variety of curves had produced a remarkable career, although he did not become a winner in the major leagues until he was twenty-eight years old. Sain spent six seasons in the minors, then, as Stengel knew, served as a Navy test pilot in World War II, learning aerodynamics, which he said deepened his grasp of pitching. "The stitches on the ball," he said, "like the wings of an airplane are an airfoil. They can provide lift. Hopping fastball. Or sideslip. Curve and slider." Sain was a quiet sort; he did not speculate on whether flying through all those wrenching midair loops and barrel rolls helped him contend with pressure on the ground.

With Blackwell gone, Dressen benched Shuba, switched Pafko to left, and sent Carl Furillo to play right field. Furillo celebrated with a lead-off double in the sixth, but Campanella and Pafko popped up and Hodges struck out. The big first baseman had come to bat twelve times without hitting safely. Erskine, recovered from The Curse of the Fives, retired the Yankees easily in the sixth. Snider tied the game at 5-all in the seventh, singling home Billy Cox. Then it was Sain and Erskine, the test pilot and the choir boy, matching magnificent efforts. Inning after inning, the Yankees went out in order and at the end of nine innings the teams were still tied.

Sain opened the bottom of the tenth with a grounder to Jackie Robinson's right. Robinson threw to the outfield side of first base. Hodges stretched and the umpire, Art Passarella, called Sain out. Bill Dickey, the first base coach, leaped in indignation. The call stood. Erskine then retired McDougald and Rizzuto.

Cox singled in the eleventh. Reese singled him to third. Snider's double to right center sent Cox home. Snider had driven in four runs. The Dodgers led, 6–5.

Mantle rolled back to Erskine. One out in the last of the eleventh. Here came Johnny Mize again. Mize drove another huge liner toward the right field seats. Furillo jumped as though striving for orbit. At the top of his extravagant leap he snared the ball. For the second time a Dodger outfielder had intercepted a home run. Berra stepped up, pumping two bats. A fan shouted, "Hit one like Mize, Yogi, only two feet higher." Erskine fanned Berra and broke into a shining smile. He had retired nineteen men in a row. He had beaten the Yankees, 6–5. The Dodgers were one game away from their grail.

A dramatic report reached the press box as the game ended. An Associated Press photograph showed that in the disputed tenth-inning play, Johnny Sain's left spiked shoe was creasing the first-base bag while Robinson's throw was still a yard away from Hodges. And reaching for the ball, Hodges appeared to have taken his foot off the base. "It looks like Erskine only retired eighteen in a row," said Red

Patterson of the Yankees. [Umpire] Art Passarella retired the nine-teenth. He made two lousy calls on a single play."

In the Yankee clubhouse Stengel said, "They tell me I ain't suppose to say anything against the umpires, but that call in the tenth inning was terrible." He shook his head. "I got no more to say. What's the use of talking, anyways?"

Johnny Mize spoke in a simmering Georgia drawl, "You coulda driven a damn wheel-barrow between Hodges' foot and the bag. The throw was late and Hodges caught it off the bag. With our lead-off man on, there's no telling what we would have done. That call altered the outcome of the game."

When I returned to the press box, Smith reported that the AP was preparing a blow-up of the photo to place on display at press head-quarters.

"It will be lively," Smith said, "when we get down to the Biltmore."

"I was planning to have dinner with my father."

"Some other night," Smith said. "He'll understand. We have more work ahead of us, you and I."

He then began typing with great speed: "Erskine, Snider, Mize, and Nixon—these were the featured actors of the most lurid entertainment yet offered in baseball's big show." Of course, Smith did not really mean lurid. He meant wondrous, amazing, awesome, majestic, astounding. Maybe the best World Series game in the history of the world. But this small bespectacled, urbane, graying man, my most gifted *Herald Tribune* colleague, had a horror that the ten million strangers who read his column every day might think that a ballgame had gotten him excited.

Actually, a great game—and we had watched a very great game—thrills the finest baseball writers with overwhelming fervor. As Heywood Hale Broun put it, "Our excitement at great baseball made bubbles in our blood."

Fervor was a wellspring of the craft.

It took me forty minutes to complete my notes and write a dressing room story. Then I found my father, sitting alone and looking small, in dark, empty stands deep behind home plate.

"What a game."

"A good one, son. We'll have plenty to talk about at dinner."

"Uh, can't."

"Pardon me," my father said, deeply, severely.

I had never broken an appointment with him before. "That play at first with Sain. A big picture is going up at the Biltmore. They say it shows Sain is clearly safe. I have to cover everybody's reaction."

My father lit a Pall Mall cigarette, strong, unfiltered, king-sized. "Haven't they worked you hard enough today?"

"I've written about 2,500 words. Not Shakespeare, but okay. I can turn out another 2,500 if they need me to do that."

"I had looked forward to this chance to get together. We don't see each other that much anymore."

"After the Series, Dad." I was being polite, but after the Series I would need my father more than I knew.

A crowd in the Biltmore ballroom gawked at the AP photograph. Gil Hodges's right foot seemed to be in contact with the base. So much for Mize's wheelbarrow. But Sain's left foot was denting the bag, while the ball, highlighted with an arrow, was still four feet away from Hodges's glove.

"Look at that," Red Patterson said, over and over, shepherding reporters, troops of reporters, past the picture. "Did you ever see a worse call in your life?"

Stengel continued to maintain silence, a major effort. If he spoke out against the umpiring, Commissioner Ford Frick could punish him with a fine. Besides, Stengel knew that the photo spoke for itself.

Dressen unintentionally turned comic. "I see somethin' white under that arrow, and it sure ain't in Hodges's glove. But how do we know that thing is the ball?" (Mostly, I thought, but did not say, because that thing was round and had stitches.)

Fresco Thompson made a sensible summation of the Dodger position. "It doesn't matter what the photo shows or seems to. Baseball is an on-the-spot game. You can't make decisions the next day.

"If you want to rely on pictures, go to Belmont Park. They have photo-finishes every afternoon."

Arguments filled the evening. If Sain had been safe, could the Yankees have done anything more? Erskine had a world of stuff. But the right call might have put him under greater pressure. Gil McDougald could have bunted Sain—or a pinch-runner—to second base. The next hitters would have been Rizzuto, tough in a clutch, Mantle, and Mize and, if anybody else reached base, Yogi Berra.

The eleven-inning game had taken three hours to complete. Replays ran until the press bar closed.

Discussion of the game and the call persisted past the Series, and the umpire, Art Passarella, announced at length that he was "resigning" from the American League staff.

"It turns out," Dick Young said through a nasty smile, "that Erskine didn't really retire nineteen straight Yankees. He retired eighteen Yankees and one umpire."

It was only October, the Presidential election was four weeks away, but in Washington, D.C., work started on the grandstand for the inauguration of the next President, January 20. Way out in Seattle, Dwight Eisenhower challenged Harry Truman's stinging charge that he intended to return the American west to the prairie dogs. "But we don't need a Federal monopoly running the power plants out here," the general said.

We were back in Brooklyn for the sixth game. The politicians roaming the country were funny, ominous, loquacious, but a diversion. The real story would unfold further at Ebbets Field, where Casey Stengel was rediscovering the treasure of his tongue.

Reporters ringed Stengel in a dugout and tried to draw him into comments on the umpiring. No chance. Except when posed by star journalists, questions never interested Stengel. He would listen, then say what he wanted, questions be damned. "If you was watching," Stengel said, "you musta noticed they won the game for Brooklyn."

"Pardon, Casey," Red Smith said. "Who is 'they'?"

"Them outfielders is what I mean, Red. You can't get away from that. They make those border-line catches and they beat you and you can't kick on that. He [Charlie Dressen] had to have that outfield to win, but maybe if it's another day, they don't win that way."

Arthur Daley of the *New York Times* asked Stengel to be "a little more specific." Some of us laughed, but Stengel took his *Times* coverage very seriously.

"On some other days," he said, "the people out there in right aren't so quiet. An outfielder from the other side goes up to make a catch, they grab his shirt, they go for his arm. They grab the glove. They twist his fingers. They get the ball."

"You mean the fans?" Daley said.

"It was our ballpark, wasn't it, Arthur? Those people were supposed to be our fans. Raschi today. He will pitch good. My men are ready." So also was the magical Stengel brain.

Billy Loes flung six commanding innings at Stengel's men and when Snider drove a fastball over the screen, the Dodgers took a 1–0 lead. Then, nine outs away from the World Series victory, *the* World Series victory, Loes came unraveled.

Berra led off the seventh with a home run, much like Snider's drive. Gene Woodling singled up the middle.

"Time for Joe Black right now," I said to Smith. "Billy the Kid is losing it."

"And if the Dodgers lose the ball game, Skipper, who pitches tomorrow?"

"Preacher Roe and the rest of the staff. They can rest all winter."

It is simple to manage from behind a typewriter. All power and no responsibility. Dressen, with so much at stake, elected to stay with a twenty-two-year-old rookie. Or maybe, Dressen simply froze.

Loes threw a ball and a strike to Irv Noren. Then, as he stretched to deliver his third pitch, the baseball fell out of his right hand. The ball bounced behind the mound. The umpires called a balk. Woodling advanced to second base.

Loes steadied and struck out Noren. Billy Martin popped out. Stengel, with several pinch hitters available, let Raschi bat for himself. The big pitcher smacked a bounder to Loes's right. Afternoon sun slanted through the arches that supported the upper deck on the left side of Ebbets Field. Loes looked for the ball but the sun got in his eyes. The baseball bounced off his left knee, and caromed past Hodges. A pool-table single to right. The Yankees got the lead run in scoring position when the pitcher dropped the ball. They scored him when the pitcher lost a grounder in the sun.

Still Dressen stayed with Loes. Mantle opened the eighth inning with a 400-foot home run to left center. The Yankees led by two runs. Snider hit another homer in the bottom of the eighth and with two out Shotgun Shuba doubled. Stengel walked mournfully to the mound, where he muttered something to Raschi. Then both men turned toward the bullpen, where Allie Reynolds was throwing hard. Stengel pointed. Reynolds marched in. Raschi waited to wish him well. Reynolds nodded, but said nothing. He was going to work. The hitter was Roy Campanella.

Reynolds threw a fastball at Campanella's head. Then he threw two hard strikes. He threw an outside breaking ball. Campanella swung and missed. As the ball socked into Berra's mitt, Campanella's bat went spinning out across the infield. Reynolds literally had taken the bat out of Brooklyn hands.

My lead, spread across three columns on the front page, expressed a degree of wonderment.

> By using his two best pitchers, Casey Stengel got his Yankees even again yesterday and beat the Dodgers, 3 to 2, at Ebbets Field. Vic Raschi, the 33-year-old righthander, started and Allie Reynolds, the 37-year-old righthander, finished and the Yankees forced the World Series into a seventh game. . . .
>
> If the Yankees are to win their fourteenth World Championship, they will have to beat Joe Black, Brooklyn's best pitcher. Casey Stengel has no idea who will start today because Reynolds, his original choice, worked yesterday.
>
> So the Yankee manager will select Mr. X after a full night's thought and considerably less sleep.

The temperature dropped almost twenty degrees, back into the fifties, on October 7, the final day. Summer was past. It was time to bring the World Series to a close.

As everybody expected, Dressen went with big Joe Black. This was a third start in seven days, but Black was strong. Frank Graham,

Jr., the Dodgers' scholarly publicist, pointed out that Christy Mathewson made three starts in six days during the World Series of 1905, and pitched three shutouts. But Mathewson was the nonpareil—in twenty-seven innings he walked only one batter—and besides the ball was dead. He didn't have to throw the modern rabbit to the likes of Mantle and Berra in a small ballpark. Dizzy Dean started three World Series games in seven days in 1934. He lost the middle one, but finished with a six-hit shutout. "I don't feel tired," Black said before the game.

Stengel chose Ed Lopat, the lefthanded loser of Game Three. Except for Snider and Shotgun Shuba, all the Dodger starters batted right and Snider, on a record pace, seemed to be hitting everything, anyway. Stengel declined to discuss his reasoning. "Why doncha just watch the game?" he grumbled. "They give ya free tickets. Watch the game." We were left to conclude that Stengel preferred Lopat's experience and pitching wiles, to the younger, stronger, rested right arms of Tom Gorman or Tom "Ploughboy" Morgan.

Lopat nibbled at corners, changed speeds and spin and kept the Dodgers scoreless for three innings. Black looked strong and held the Yankees hitless until the fourth. Then Rizzuto doubled to left and advanced as Mantle bounced out to first. The hitter was Mize. Black would stay away from his power, the inside part of the plate. He threw a low outside breaking ball. Mize changed his swing and tapped a gentle single to left field. The Yankees led by one run.

The Dodgers countered quickly. Snider singled to right. Robinson bunted deftly toward third. Even though the Yankees were anticipating a sacrifice, nobody could make a play. Campanella bunted toward the same spot and beat Ed Lopat's throw to first base. Stengel hurried to the mound and lifted Lopat for Reynolds, who would now pitch in his fourth game this World Series.

Gil Hodges, who had come to bat eighteen times without hitting safely, lined out to left and Snider scored. When the outfield throw went bad, Robinson ran to third base. The game looked as though it might explode. But Reynolds reached back and struck out Shuba. Then Furillo bounced out. Going into the fifth, the game was tied.

Gene Woodling drove a home run over the screen in right.

Later, Cox doubled and Reese singled. The game was tied again going into the sixth.

Reynolds and Black were wearing down. Strong, brave, heroic, but wearing down. Rizzuto opened the sixth with a liner that Reese was able to snare. Mantle caught up with a fastball and hit a very long home run, over the scoreboard in right, over the sidewalk beyond, over Bedford Avenue beyond *that* and into a parking lot. A swarm of civilians scrambled for the ball. Dressen replaced Black with Preacher Roe.

Reynolds retired the Dodgers in the sixth. McDougald singled in the seventh. Rizzuto sacrificed. Mantle shot a long single to left. The Yankees led by two. Stengel replaced Reynolds with Vic Raschi. He was using the heart of his starting rotation, his three finest pitchers, in a single game.

One day after his enervating struggle against Billy Loes, Raschi was wild. He walked Furillo, got an out, fell behind to Billy Cox, who singled, and walked Reese. The bases were loaded with one out and here came the hottest batter in the cosmos, Duke Snider.

The crowd made raucous noises. Thirty-three thousand, a full house in Brooklyn, was less than half a Yankee Stadium crowd, but twice as passionate. So far, in a triumphant Series, Snider had hit four singles, two doubles and four home runs. Red Smith was calling him "The Archduke Snider." A single now would tie the score. A long double would put the Dodgers ahead. Another Duke Snider home run? . . . The thought turned Brooklyn fans giddy.

A decidedly ungiddy Casey Stengel was not surprised to find Snider coming to bat with the ballgame and the Series on the line. As in classic drama, the major figures would play the principal scenes. Stengel was, in fact, prepared. One Yankee spearcarrier, 6-foot 2-inch Bob Kuzava, out of Wyandotte, Michigan, threw hard, lefthanded stuff. Kuzava was a career .500 pitcher, win one, lose one, never a star, just someone you needed to pitch the innings. In 1948 Kuzava lost sixteen games with the Baltimore Orioles of the International League. But one batter Bob Kuzava mastered that season was the star center fielder of the Montreal Royals, Duke Snider. Stengel was not a man to disregard history. He replaced Raschi with Kuzava. The issue was joined.

Snider worked the count full. If he could win this game, the Duke would be anointed King, Pope, Grand Rabbi, and Czar of all the realms of Flatbush.

Snider bore down. So did Kuzava. He threw a tailing outside fastball. Trying to drive the pitch to left, Snider lifted a mighty pop fly over third. Gil McDougald tapped his glove. Two out.

The hitter was Jackie Robinson. Two strong right arms were active in the Yankee bullpen. Stengel made no move. Kuzava threw hard stuff to Robinson who fouled back four consecutive pitches. Now came the play that decided the Series.

Trying to drive a single to right, Robinson lifted a pop fly toward first base. Kuzava called the play, shouting, "Joe, Joe." But Joe Collins, who had replaced Mize, was looking into the same light pattern that brought down Billy Loes the day before—blinding sunlight slanting through the arches behind the third base stands. Collins, a fine fielder, never saw the ball.

Billy Martin suddenly realized what was happening. He raced in from his spot at second base. The wind was blowing the pop fly away from him. Running with two out, Furillo and Cox crossed home plate. If Robinson's pop-up landed safely, the score was tied. Martin lunged and caught the baseball, ankle high.

The Dodgers never threatened again and when Reese, who had played so well, made the final out, the Yankees' 4–2 victory became living history. Brooklynites wept in the grandstands. Gladys Goodding serenaded the ballpark with a song from *South Pacific*.

She played "This Nearly Was Mine."

From my earliest years, I'd heard Brooklyn fans cry out in defeat, "Wait till next year." My lead for the front page of the *Herald Tribune* leapt through the peanut shells residing in my portable typewriter:

"Every year is next year for the Yankees."

Red Smith peeked at my typewriter. "Good lead, sire," he said.

When Casey Stengel relaxed into a monologue, he was preacher, comic, sage, and spellbinder. "Yessir, gentlemen, we, uh, captured this important victory because we always win on the road. We like it rough.

We couldn't win them games at home because the ground was too smooth. But we win on the road, the rough ground, and we win when the going is rough and how about them players I got. Ain't they tree-mendous?"

"How do you feel about winning four World Series in a row?" Rud Rennie asked.

"It's a short record. Won't stand up." Wink. "You got to win eight, maybe nine, before it gets attention." Two winks.

"Uh, now, let me say this. The other fellas [Dodgers] tried every-thing and they almost got away with it. Don't let anybody say the other fella [Dressen] ain't a good manager. He made those guys play ball.

"He had them bunting, didn't he? And we couldn't do anything about it. That heavy catcher [Campanella] even he bunted and beat it out.

"Listen, they were rough and I mean it."

Stengel went off to pose for pictures. When he returned to his temporary office in the visitor's clubhouse, he explained his pitching strategy. "That boy [Kuzava] got Snider out in the minor leagues. I knew that and now you know it, just like I did. That's why I brought him in. But why did I leave him to face the righthand fella who makes speeches [Jackie Robinson] with bases full? Don't I know percentages and etcetera?

"The reason I left him in is the other man [Robinson] has not seen hard-throwing lefthand pitchers much and could have trouble with the break of a lefthander's hard curve, which is what happened.

"My first pitcher [Lopat] did all I asked him to. Those bunts loused him up. My second pitcher [Reynolds], his back was hurting him today, but he took us out of a big hole. And my third pitcher [Raschi] took me out of another hole. He just had too much stuff. The ball was moving so much he couldn't get it over the plate enough, but if he did, with all that stuff, they weren't going to hit him. All my guys played great.

"And I hope you gentlemen enjoyed these two excellent teams. They played splendid."

At the age of twenty, Mickey Mantle had arrived, batting .345 with two important home runs. "Nice Series, young man," Rud Rennie said. "What are you up to now?"

"Headin' back to Oklahoma. I got me a job working down in the mines."

"Work in the mines? The winning share is more than $6,200. You don't have to do that now."

"Yes I do," Mantle said. "You know my dad died and I got seven dependents who're counting on me." Mantle named three brothers, a sister, his mother, and his wife.

"That's six," Rennie said.

"A baby is due in March," Mantle said. "I don't know whether I'll be in the electrical crew or the pump crew or whatever." The Yankees' slugging hero of the Series smiled pleasantly. "I'm just lucky the mining company offered me a job."

That evening at the Biltmore Red Smith said the Series was "the best entertainment" since 1934, when the Dean brothers, Dizzy and Daffy, carried the Cardinals to a seven-game victory over Detroit.

"Entertainment?" said Rud Rennie. "Does that include Grand Opera?"

"And light opera as well," Smith said.

Tommy Holmes of the *Brooklyn Eagle* said that this was better than the 1934 Series, which ended with an 11–0 Cardinal victory. "First, almost every game was close and exciting," Holmes said. "Second, the Dodgers looked better than any losing team has ever looked in a World Series."

"You may be right," Smith said. "The '34 Series was the first Cardinal Series I covered when I was a newspaperman in St. Louis. Maybe I make it better than it was."

"And this guy," Tom Meany of *Collier's* said, pointing at me. "Before this year he's never written a line of big-league baseball in his life. Look at what falls into his lap. Just the greatest World Series ever played."

Like Mantle, still focused on a job in the Oklahoma mines, that didn't mean much anymore, I had a lot to catch up on all at once. I had written four front-page stories in seven days. Bob Cooke said "the brass" was happy with my work. I had seen Olympian baseball. Char-

acters like Casey Stengel and Allie Reynolds were my willing guides. I
had won praise from Red Smith. Where, then, was a sense of triumph?
Young and suddenly successful, I felt confused.

I found a telephone and called Brooklyn. "Dad?"

"They lost."

"I know."

"But they have nothing to be ashamed of."

"I know that, too. I'm calling to see if we can set up dinner."

# CHAPTER SIX

# The Natural

## or
## True Tales of
## The Big Leaguers

*The whole history of baseball has the quality of mythology.*

—BERNARD MALAMUD

W
E ALL WANTED TO WRITE THE GREAT American novel. Some thought it ought to be a baseball book. "Except," said Frank Graham, Jr., the Dodgers' intellectual publicist, "look at England. They've been writing books longer than we, and has any Englishman ever written the great cricket novel? I don't believe so and neither did Virginia Woolf." That was the healthy, skeptical wit of youth. Like the rest of us, Graham nurtured his own ideas about a big, fictional baseball book whose pages would open up a world.

By 1952 baseball had entered American writing like no other sport or pastime, providing huge harvests of juvenile fiction, ghosted memoirs, instructional works, team histories, and biographies. Christy Mathewson, once a member of the literary society at Bucknell, tried his hand at a novel with *First Base Faulkner*. As you may suspect, *First Base Faulkner* did not bump *Moby Dick* off library shelves. Earlier, helped by a professional journalist, Mathewson composed the memoir, *Pitching in a Pinch*. "He has been a student and something of a writer, having done newspaper work during the big series," John Wheeler wrote of Mathewson in 1912. "He has kept a sort of baseball diary of his career and, frequently, I have heard him relate unwritten chapters of baseball history filled with the thrilling incidents of his personal experience.

"'Why don't you write a real book of the Big Leaguers?' I asked him one day.

"And he has done it. It's as good as his pitching. This is a true tale of Big Leaguers, their habits, and their methods of playing the game, written by one of them."

A true tale of the Big Leaguers. What a seductive idea. Mathewson did a creditable job with the memoir; such colleagues as salty John McGraw spring to life. Early baseball days, the times themselves, are palpable. The reader learns of "scientific baseball" and of "failures of the inside game." A pleasant wit pervades. "There are few vacancies in the Big Leagues," Mathewson writes, "for the man who is liable to steal second with the bases full."

This was a ground-breaking effort. It can be read today as a visit with Christy Mathewson, the most successful and most scholarly of the early twentieth century pitchers. As such it is quite wonderful. But even as long ago as 1912 some sensed there was more to be done, grander designs to plot, if we were to realize or even approach John Wheeler's "true tale of the Big Leaguers."

Four years after *Pitching in a Pinch* appeared, Scribner's published a book consisting of six short stories, with continuing characters and loosely connected plots, under the title *You Know Me Al.* Ring Lardner chose to tell his story in the form of letters composed by Jack Keefe, a fictional rookie pitcher for the Chicago White Sox, just up from the Central League. Keefe writes steadily to his best friend, Al, back home in Bedford, Illinois.

Keefe's spelling, grammar, and character are unique. He is vain, stingy, insensitive, gluttonous, self-pitying, a boob and a fourflusher, and as soon as *You Know Me Al* appeared, Jack Keefe captivated the country. For Lardner's lout is also curiously sympathetic. In his definitive and neglected biography, *Ring Lardner*, Donald Elder writes that Jack Keefe "is not very much worse than anyone else; he is real. He is not quite like yourself, but he bears a fatal resemblance to your friends."

"My father's 'busher' letters," John Lardner pointed out, "were not written with artistic prestige in mind. [Jack Keefe, of course, was the epistolary busher.] They were written because there was an urgent need around the home for the $200 that each of the [short stories] brought when they first appeared in the *Saturday Evening Post*. . . . Almost as soon as the *Post* began to publish them, the letters made their author as famous as the President of the United States. . . . This turn of events startled my father, but it totally failed to cause him to think that what he had written was literature." (Ring earned more than John knew. The Post paid him $250 for the first story, then increased his rate by $250 for each succeeding piece until he reached $1,250, the magazine's top price and a bonanza eighty years ago.)

When Keefe lost to Detroit, 16–2, in his first major league start, he blamed a sore arm, poor fielding, a rough infield, and bad pitch selection by his catcher. On another occasion he lost because, "My fast one was jumping so. Honest Al it was so fast that Evans the umpire couldn't see it half the time and called a lot of balls that was right over the heart." Keefe's bravado remains beyond assault. "As soon as my name is announced to pitch the Cleveland Club is licked or any other club when I am right and they don't kick away the game behind me."

After Keefe is sold to San Francisco, he falls in love with Hazel, "a great big stropping girl that must weigh one hundred and sixty lbs." The White Sox reacquire him and Hazel writes to Keefe, asking for $100 so she can come to Chicago and marry him. Keefe sends her $30 and Hazel never makes the trip. Soon after that Keefe informs Al:

I am the happyest man in the world . . . Al she is married. Maybe you don't know why that makes me happy but I will tell you. She is married to Kid Levy the middle weight. I guess my thirty dollars is gone because in her letter she calls me a cheap skate and she inclosed one one-cent stamp and two twos and said she was paying for the glass of beer I once bought her. I bought her more than that Al but I wont make no holler. She all so said not for me never to come near her or her husband would bust my jaw. I ain't afraid of him or no one else

Al but they ain't no danger of me ever bothering her. She was no good.

Virginia Woolf, who never saw a game of baseball, read *You Know Me Al* in the early 1920s. Jack Keefe, she wrote, was a character, through whom "we gaze into the depths of a society. . . . Mr. Lardner provides something unique, something indigenous to the soil, which the traveller may carry off as a trophy to prove to the incredulous that he has actually been to America and found it [not an appendage to England but] a foreign land."

Virginia Woolf's implication is clear. Ring Lardner was a genius.

Baseball was the final mythology of my youth. Like other young people in my set—or rather in the set in which my parents lived their radiant lives—I read Bullfinch's Mythology, learned passages from Homer, heard, in my mother's ardent telling, the stories of Icarus and Daedalus; Theseus and the Minotaur, and, back to Homer again, sulking Achilles, who slew the noble Hector; and wily Odysseus, who survived the Trojan War and after that the Lotus-Eaters and the Sirens *and* the Cyclops, and made the grandest of all long journeys home.

At first these magnificent stories held me entirely. The Greek heroes became my heroes. The Greek gods presided over the pantheon of my home. But as I grew older, a passion for baseball came to intrude on—and sometimes to replace—my inherited Brooklyn Hellenism. I took to idolizing Flatbush ballplayers over the ancient Olympians, whom my mother worshiped as both a classicist and a true believer.

Not all at once and not entirely, either. At least not for very long. But as my father's well-told baseball tales spun out their magic, Mathewson, Ruth, and Zack Wheat grew mythic in my imagination. It followed naturally that I found new mythic figures in the ballplayers I actually saw myself—Mungo and Fitzsimmons and Dolph Camilli and Pee Wee Reese. Somehow Cookie Lavagetto superseded Hermes and Leo Durocher became more powerful than Zeus. This surely hurt my mother. I was not only embracing baseball—"a mere game"—but at the same time I was rejecting her deities.

In her late years, she mentioned that her dream for me was that I become the world's preeminent translator of the Greek tragic dramatists. I was doing well enough at the newspaper, but did I realize that Sophocles defeated Aeschylus in the Athenian playwrights' contest when he was only twenty-seven years old?


Distance is first, if mythic heroes are to flourish. To flash forward briefly, distance disappears daily in our electronic world. Today's ballplayers exist no farther from us than a bedroom television screen between our toes. We see them play close-up. Replay brings them even closer. Soon, like nose hairs, their mortality begins to show, more vividly than one would wish. We hear ballplayers speak and watch them perspire during broadcast interviews. We learn of their misdeeds in the tabloid press. Mainstream reporters scrutinize the smallest details of ballplayers' contract negotiations. Few things are less conducive to mythology than a newspaper account of a salary arbitration hearing.

But in my youth, when writers worked on typewriters and automobiles came with running boards, the ballplayers remained remote as Gods. I saw them only from the distance of the grandstand. They wore baseball caps, of course. You couldn't tell which ballplayers were red-headed or blond or bald. You never heard them speak, except in the distant wondrous chorus of infield chatter. Newspaper stories bathed the players with praise and generally provided only one-dimensional accounts of games. To go further, to find the True Tales of the Big Leaguers, my generation of children turned to books: *The Kid from Tompkinsville; The Redheaded Outfield; Fence-Busters; Baseball Joe Hits a Home Run.*

These are real titles. The fictions presented an always sunny land, where all the ballplayers were clean-cut, except for the villain, necessary for the plot. He was a cardboard cutout who occasionally uttered "vile oaths." Perhaps, at times, the villain took a drink. Before the end of the book, however, he would have stopped cursing, forsworn beer and begun a journey toward redemption. This linked baseball with the revivalist spirit, the born-again current that still persists in American life.

The good ballplayers had no need to reform. After all, their favorite drink was lemonade. They didn't smoke. But they were rugged, too, and unafraid of spikes. They may have known fear, as all children who played hard ball came to know it, but in the end they triumphed over fear and became brave and unconquerable, even before they reached the major leagues.

In one tale by the prolific Harold M. Sherman, Jeff Dugan, star slugger at Baldwin High, gets beaned. After he recovers, Jeff's batting touch is gone. He pulls away from pitches and strikes out. You can't hit a baseball hard when lunging away from it. But the kindly coach stays with Jeff even into the championship game. As the climax gathers, Baldwin High needs a double to tie and a home run to win the game in the ninth inning. Jeff looks bad at the plate. He misses with two cringing, flailing swings. Larry Wilkins, his best friend, rushes up and punches Jeff in the face. Jeff punches back. The two schoolboys roll in the dirt. "You aren't afraid of a punch," Larry cries. "Then why are you afraid of a baseball?"

Jeff gets up and hits the homer that wins the game.

At the age of ten I loved reading such stories. By the time I was fifteen I had played enough ball to realize that they were mostly nonsense. I switched my reading away from juvenile baseball fiction to Sinclair Lewis, Jack London, and Thomas Wolfe and to the poetry of Keats and Shelley.

But as I loved to play ball, I still hungered to read about baseball. I had just about memorized *Pitching in a Pinch*. The subtleties of Lardner's Jack Keefe, Virginia Woolf's American friend, played out beyond my adolescent ken. Somehow, I thought, there must be more to baseball literature than what I knew.

Or anyway, there ought to be.

But there was not. The harvest of good baseball books lay years into the future.

My father was prompt for dinner at Gage and Tollner's, a restaurant of great charm on Fulton Street in downtown Brooklyn, five blocks from the Dodger offices at 215 Montague Street. The room was lit by gaslight. Smoked mirrors covered the long walls. Gage and Tollner's made me think of women with ostrich-feather hats.

The waiters were all black men, wearing blue uniforms with a vaguely nautical essence. Each waiter was given a hashmark to sew on his sleeve for each five years of service. After ten years, he added a gold star. After twenty-five years he was awarded a golden eagle. With one glance at the sleeve, you could tell whether you were about to be served by a rookie or by an old pro, who had served up three thousand dinners.

The veterans were haughty. Not unpleasant, but haughty. It pleased me that the captain and our golden-eagle waiter both knew who I was. My father had made the reservation in his own name, but my recent flurry of front-page bylines made me a semicelebrity in downtown Brooklyn.

"Tough series to lose, Mr. Kahn," the captain said to me. My father weathered that salvo and insisted that dinner was his treat. I had, after all, gotten him a Series ticket.

"But you paid me for the ticket, Dad," I said.

"Bosh. This is my treat."

We settled into serious baseball talk. I would eat the standard ball-club dining-car fare: shrimp cocktail, steak, baked potato, lettuce and tomato salad, apple pie. My father, more adventurous, chose corn chowder, followed by a delicious house specialty called clam bellies, then shoestring potatoes, and, as a family gene asserted itself, another helping of apple pie.

I said I felt distressed that the Dodgers had lost the Series on a set of flukes: Erskine falling off a stepladder, Loes committing that odd balk, then losing a grounder in the sun. My father said there was nothing fluke-ish about Allie Reynolds's arm or the fact that in Game Seven, with bases full and the Series on the line, Brooklyn's two best hitters, Duke Snider and Jackie Robinson, popped out.

We turned to managing. Stengel had broken in with Brooklyn in 1912 and stayed there for six seasons, a solid centerfielder who hit with power, and a popular character among young Brooklyn ballplayers like my father. Now, forty years later, Stengel had given everyone, including Charlie Dressen, a lesson in the manager's art. My father delineated Stengel's triumphs. He used Reynolds, his ace, in four games. Reynolds won two and saved one. He used Raschi, his bellwether, in three games. Raschi won two. "Stengel showed me an uncanny knack," my father said, "of getting the most out of his best, and having his best in the right place at the right time. As that Civil War general, Nathan Bedford Forrest, almost said, 'He gets the mostest out of the bestest.'"

Stengel is often remembered today as the comical manager of dreadful New York Met teams, which finished in tenth place for four consecutive seasons, and lost 120 out of 160 games in 1962. "The youth of America," Stengel called that club, in resignation. By then he was seventy-two and he had difficulty working with the players he was given, most of whom had only minor-league skills. But managing a roster of top athletes, Stengel was matchless. While I moped for the vanquished Dodgers, my father fastened on to the essential Stengel gifts. "You could argue," he said, "that Stengel won the 1952 Series, which would be the first time a World Series was won by a sixty-two-year-old."

He grinned. "Cheer up. Your stories weren't bad. Not bad at all. Now all you have to do is keep it up."

Deep down, I didn't want to keep it up. Deep down, I had begun to dream, like newspapermen everywhere, of holing up in a cabin with a typewriter and perhaps a pretty girl and emerging months later with a bearded chin and a finished epic. SPORTSWRITER'S FIRST NOVEL HAILED. AN AMERICAN CLASSIC. It was somewhat easier to conceive the headline than to compose the book.

But I didn't want to talk about deep dreams. I knew my father, whose analysis of the Series was better than mine. I knew enough not to say or even hint that finally having found success at the ripe age of twenty-four, I felt restless, discontented, even unhappy.

My father also knew me. "We're not talking about forever," he said. "But stick to your last at the *Trib* for the next few years. There's no telling what good things life will send your way."

A problem with writing a baseball novel, Ed Fitzgerald, the editor of the popular *SPORT* magazine, pointed out, went like this. If you wrote a book and included a lot of game detail, slides into second base, sharp curve balls, and such, the novel would resonate like a juvenile. It would sound like *Baseball Joe*. After all, how many ways *are* there to describe someone sliding into second? But if you left out the detail, you were losing an important part of the story. Sliding into second is a significant part of a ballplayer's life. Catch One.

Paul Lapolla, a gifted editor at Doubleday, said he could offer modest financing for a baseball novel, if I wanted to try my hand at one, but was that what I ought to write?

"Baseball is a profound game," I said. "Look what happens to the people in it. Rookies at the age of twenty-five. Veterans at the age of thirty. Washed-up old men at thirty-four. How do you cope with time rushing past you like that. I think that's a theme for a novel."

"What about golf?" Lapolla said. "Think of a touring pro from a small town in Texas, Wichita Falls, who gets to be a champion. The setting becomes one gorgeous country club after another. Lush greens. Elegant bars. The golfer moves among rich men. He seduces their wives. Wouldn't you like to write a novel about that?"

"Not my world, Paul."

"Then imagine it," Lapolla said. But I had no inclination to hazard a work of pure imagination. Besides, I didn't know a nine-iron from a driver and felt disinclined to learn.

Hiram Haydn, a ranging man who worked at Random House and edited *The American Scholar*, thought a baseball novel was "something to put in your sights." He took me to lunch primarily to urge me to write a baseball article for *The Scholar*, but the talk soon moved to fiction. "My concept," Haydn said, "centers on someone who can play well enough to approach the major leagues, but not well enough to stay there. *The Gates of Heaven*, if I may. Care to give that one a crack?"

We talked at length. Heywood Broun, marvel though he was, failed with a baseball novel called *The Sun Field*. Lardner, with his Jack Keefe, was a thing apart. The editors and the writers and the newspapermen talked and wondered and postulated and raised glasses of whisky. After that they talked some more.

Then an obscure English teacher from Brooklyn, a small, balding, unknown mustached man who was thirty-eight years old, published his first novel, a baseball book. It later became the basis for an entertaining film, complete with the dazzling looks of Robert Redford, a home run that loosed a shower of stars, and a deliciously happy ending.

That wasn't the story that seized so many—baseball people, literati, newspapermen, and just plain readers—in the work that Bernard Malamud called *The Natural.* Seized and repelled. That was the movie plot. To this day, *The Natural*—the novel—remains a controversial, and to me wonderful, story in many ways—haunted and terribly sad.

"Roy Hobbs pawed at the glass before thinking to prick a match with his thumbnail." I read those lines after the baseball season of 1952. Roy Hobbs, *The Natural,* is riding a train through the night on his way to a tryout with the Chicago Cubs. In his mind's eye, Roy sees "a bone-white farmhouse . . . alone in untold miles of moonlight, and before it this white-faced, long-boned boy who whipped . . . a glowing ball to someone hidden under a dark oak." That is himself, or was himself, in childhood. Roy is traveling with a bassoon case, in which he carries the bat he has carved, an almost magic bat, that he calls Wonderboy. As I read this opening long ago, I thought of the phrases "bone-white" . . . "white-faced" . . . "long-boned" playing against each other in the darkness beyond the train. I knew I had come upon a writer.

For decades critics and scholars have had their way with *The Natural.* It often is described as a work of Arthurian legend. The ballplayers on the fictional team, the Knights, are said to symbolize the knights of King Arthur's court. The bat, Wonderboy, is akin to Arthur's sword, Excalibur. The pennant is the Holy Grail. Spells of drought and rain symbolize impotence and fertility. One can go on in this manner for some time.

As far as I know, Malamud's novel is the first book to suggest that tragic elements truly exist in baseball. The story includes two significant deaths, one attempted murder, and patterns of violent and troubled sexual behavior. Bringing these elements into a baseball book changed the nature of serious baseball books for all time. Whether or not one likes the novel, it cannot be ignored.

The Robert Redford film, which so many millions have seen, distorts the original story. I am not suggesting that the Redford movie is less than first-class entertainment. But it is not Bernard Malamud's *The Natural.* In the book, Hobbs sells out for money, strikes out, weeps. The movie is Redford's *The Natural.* He changed Roy Hobbs's terrible

and dishonorable defeat into Roy Hobbs's ninth-inning victory, bringing back the old, juvenile plot line. *Baseball Roy Hits a Home Run.*

When I read *The Natural* after the great World Series of 1952, I
noted that Roy's intense sexuality was an accurate rendering of many a
ballplayer. Except when he was being excessively fanciful, Malamud's
accounts of baseball action rang true. Describing a wall as embracing
an outfielder's body showed how a fine writer could set down details
of a game in an innovative way.

Unlike Ring Lardner, Malamud *had* set out to write literature. To a
great extent, he succeeded. We have been blessed with many fine baseball books in subsequent years and each has worked the game more
deeply into the American consciousness. To me that is more significant
than whether Roy Hobbs was supposed to be Percival or Parsifal or
the Perfect Fool and when I finished *The Natural*—it is not easy reading—I felt cheered not simply for Malamud but for myself.

If you were good enough, you *could* write a baseball book and make
it literature.

# CHAPTER SEVEN

# Two Naturals
## Leo and Willie

U NINVITED, DEATH TOOK MY FATHER on the evening of October 16, 1953, and I thought, "But we weren't finished talking.

"We wanted to play another game of catch."

My mind was speaking clearly and I listened very hard to hear what my father said in explanation. I listened over and over. But the answer was only the terrible silence of one just dead.

Then it was spring and older now and barren in mood, I journeyed to a desert, feeling banished to a barren land. I missed my father every day, but there, in Arizona dust and grit, the vulgar, vital exuberance of Leo Durocher renewed me, and after that I was refreshed by the only magic ballplayer of my lifetime—he was *better* than Roy Hobbs— young Willie Howard Mays.

But first let me tell you about Leo Durocher, the skipper, or as Leo himself would have put it, the fucking skipper. He was cheap and obscene and devious and suspicious and wholly magnificent.

. . .

By the time I got to Phoenix, where the Giants took spring training in 1954, and still do to this day, I had behind me two solid years of baseball writing, across two seasons in which the team I covered won the pennant. I had created solid relationships with Jackie Robinson and Pee Wee Reese and Walter O'Malley. I had written such strong stuff on baseball's rampant and persistent bigotry that Robinson hired me to help him start a black magazine named *Our Sports*. I had displayed independence and some toughness. The editors of the *Herald Tribune* said they regarded me as the sportswriter most likely to succeed Red Smith. I had been a nervous, novice baseball writer at twenty-four. Now at twenty six humility was not one of my problems.

Leo Durocher liked to take the measure of everyone around him. In checking me out, he came to know these things, or most of them, and I suppose alarm bells jingled. I could be a problem in the docile fiefdom Durocher ruled.

Unlike the man from the *Daily News* who drank before breakfast, or the man from the *World-Telegram* who drank all day and missed ballgames, or the man from the *New York Post* who drank and couldn't pay his bills, or the man from the *Times* who gambled and longed to be a stand-up comic or at the very least to meet celebrities—unlike these tame and malleable newspapermen, I displayed no immediately apparent vulnerability. To Leo's hard and baleful eye, that made me dangerous. Hell, I might actually write about what I saw, rather than what Durocher wanted me to see.

Like Joseph Goebbels, Leo believed that the press first of all had to be controlled. Control, to be sure, required serious scheming. Typically, Durocher lent $500 to the deadbeat reporter from the *New York Post* and said, "If you ever knock me in the paper, I'm gonna tell your editors you owe me money." So much for the crusading *New York Post*. As long as his debtor covered the team, Durocher never made a mistake on the *Post* sports pages.

But what about the new man from the *Tribune?* What are we gonna do about him? The word is that he likes to shake things up. Durocher elected to welcome me to his domain with courtship and a threat.

"Well, kid," he began in the lobby of the Hotel Adams. "I know we're gonna get along just great." He was wearing a dark, well-tailored suit, French cuffs with diamond links, slacks pressed to a razor's edge and pointed black shoes that sparkled in the lobby light. Durocher was bald, big-jawed, of medium height and build. Though hardly handsome, he was quite distinctive looking, somehow attractive. Energy charged through his being; he became animated when he spoke. His voice could roar in anger, or sink to the most confidential whisper. His hands were always moving. They were large hands, strong hands. In younger days he had been a wonderful shortstop.

"We don't do things here the way they do in Brooklyn," Durocher said. "They're still kinda *bush* over there."

"I never found Jackie Robinson bush."

"Hey, he's a player. He's my kinda player. He don't just come to beat you, he comes to kill you." Durocher's voice rose in enthusiasm. "That Robinson. He hits a ton. He hits one fucking ton. But that wasn't what I was talking about. I mean some of the writers there in Brooklyn. They knock the club.

"Hey, kid, if you weren't covering baseball, where do you think you'd be? Covering woman's golf, maybe. Yeah, you get some good fannies to look at when they putt. But not much of a sport for a real writer.

"The way we do it here, we don't knock the club. We're all working together. The players and the coaches and the writers. That's how we beat the Dodgers in 1951. It wasn't Thomson's home run. We all worked together. Fucking together. Yessir. And we're gonna do that this year, too.

"I tell the writers here, we don't need anybody scooping anybody else. Why should the writers beat each others' brains out? You get a story, you tell the other writers. They get a story, they tell it to you. That way nobody makes anybody else look bad.

"Now you want to talk to one of my players, that's okay. They're grown men. They're allowed to talk to the writers. But if you really want to look good back at your paper, then after you talk to a player come and run it by me. Tell me what he said and I'll tell you if what he said makes sense. I'm the one who knows what's going on.

"Stick with me." Durocher paused and looked around. Nobody was loitering nearby. "Look," he said, quietly. "When I told you the writers share, I didn't mean *everything*. Stick with me and I'll tell ya stuff nobody else knows. And when you write that, you're gonna look like the best reporter in New York.

"But if I tell you something for background, if I tell you something and then I say use it but don't quote me, and then you go ahead and use my name, I'm gonna tell the other writers and I'm gonna tell your boss, Bob Cooke, whom I happen to be good friends with, and you know what I'm gonna tell him?

"That you're a no-good, lying, cocksucking, motherfucking son of a bitch."

Durocher smiled. His eyes were hard. "Whaddya say, kid? We got a deal?"

We did not have a deal.

Baseball language was routinely gamey, often in ways that I found humorous. "What time is it, Carl?" I asked Furillo one day when my windup watch stopped.

Furillo checked his wrist. Then he said, "Two-oh-fucking clock."

That was the casual, innocent vulgarity of the game. But Durocher was neither casual nor innocent. His mix of obscenities, while inventive, sounded nasty and intimidating, which is exactly the way Durocher intended his words to sound. There was nothing humorous about Durocher's vulgarity, nothing humorous at all. In the late winter of 1954, with my gentle father so much on my mind, I found Durocher's language, and indeed his character, shocking and objectionable. But fascinating also, dammit, fascinating. Beyond that, he possessed a hard and brassy charm, which worked strongly on major league ballplayers and beautiful women. He was an earth force, rumbling with danger.

A blonde European movie star clattered across the lobby and said, "Hello, Leo."

"Hi," he said. He called her name. "I'll be up in ten minutes."

I gaped after the actress. "Like that foreign stuff?" Durocher said.

"Umm."

"I'm fucking her, you know. That's why you don't see me around the lobby in the nighttime. I'm up in the room with her."

I could not believe what I was hearing. "You," I said, very slowly. "You and *her?*"

"Sure, kid," Durocher said, "but I got to stop banging her on Wednesday."

"Why is that?"

"Because my wife is flying in."

Bald, loud Leo Durocher had to stop sleeping with one beautiful movie actress because his wife, the beautiful movie actress Laraine Day, was coming to town. My face showed amazement and green envy.

"Like I said, kid," Durocher said, "stick with me. Write good positive stuff and I'll teach you how to get movie stars to go to bed with you."

Mephistopheles Durocher was posing another bargain. Write what he wanted me to write and he would deliver glamour girls in heat. Ah, Lana. Ah, Ava. Ah, Rita. Whoosh.

I was tempted, all right, but I had read Faust. *No, thanks.*

After a while, he decided to offer me a specific lesson in seduction without demanding anything in return.

"Pick 'em up at seven o'clock," Durocher said. "Sit down next to her on the couch."

"Oh, I've done that," I said.

"Now five minutes into your date, at 7:05, put your hand on her crotch."

"Beg pardon."

"On her crotch. Her snatch. If she leaves your hand there, you know all you gotta know. You're gonna get laid. If she knocks it off, well it's early yet, just after seven o'clock. You got plenty of time to call up someone else. But you'd be surprised, kid. A whole lot of famous and beautiful broads don't knock your hand off their snatch."

From time to time, I tried to understand what made Leo run. Durocher didn't care for questions that probed. He stuck to a set-piece explanation for the sources of his drive. "I was born on the third floor of a three-deck wooden house in West Springfield, Massachusetts, born right on the kitchen table there. Two days later my mother was back at work. She was a maid in a downtown hotel. She worked hard. I work hard. It's as fucking simple as that."

Of course, it was not simple, seeking the sources of Durocher's ruthless ambition. The poor boyhood, a continuous rebellion against the Roman Catholic Church—his roots were French Canadian—tell us something. But Durocher is one of those impetuous men of action, probably better described than analyzed. You might as well try to ana-lyze an oncoming spear.

"Let me tell you about Leo," Dick Young offered, before I boarded the twilight train that carried me west. "Figure, you and Durocher are shipwrecked and you both end up on this little raft with sharks swim-ming all around. Leo slips into the water. A shark closes in.

"You dive in and pull him out.

"But while you're rescuing him, the shark comes up and takes your right leg. You bleed like hell, but somehow you survive.

"The next day you and Durocher start off even."

Durocher was concerned only and endlessly with himself. Others interested him only for what they could bring him—riches, flattering newspaper stories, fame, sexual pleasure, victory. "If I'm playing third and my own mother's coming home with the winning run," he told me in a rather odd boast, "I trip her up. Afterwards, I say, 'Mom, I'm sorry.' And I am. I truly am. But even my own mother don't get to score the run that beats me."

Durocher took pleasure in humiliating weak people. Before that spring ended, I saw him set fire to a page in the typewriter of one mildly inebriated sportswriter. When the writer grunted at the flame and tried to beat it out—his whole day's work was burning up, for heaven's sake—Durocher's laughter rose loud and merciless. He seemed surprised when I offered to help the writer prepare another story.

In his prime he was a great manager and a perfect villain. A very great manager (when he concentrated) and an exceedingly villainous villain. But that was old stuff to hard-eyed writers, like Dick Young. New in the spring of 1954 was the counterpoint to Durocher—the returning centerfielder from Olympus, Willie Mays.

Mays first joined the Giants on May 25, 1951, two weeks after his twentieth birthday. He was a very young twenty, out of an Alabama hamlet called Westfield, where the streets had not yet been paved.

(The family moved to nearby Fairfield a few years later.) Mays vitalized the 1951 Giants and became Rookie of the Year, but he batted an
earthbound .274 and hit only 20 home runs. He was good, a sunburst
of promise, but still decidedly mortal. Bobby Thomson, not Mays, was
the Giant deity that year. The following spring, after playing thirty-
four games, Mays was drafted.

He was hitting only .236, but Mays always was more than numbers,
a fielder beyond compare, a superb arm, speed and wonder and excitement. When the Army took him, the Giants were in first place by two-
and-a-half games. Without Willie the team sagged. The Giants finished second in 1952 and in 1953, with Mays stationed at Fort Eustis,
the team collapsed to fifth. Durocher lost interest in his job. He came
to work at the Polo Grounds as late as possible, often only half an
hour before game time, and left early, particularly when the Giants lost,
which they did 84 times.

The Giant club I found in the Phoenix desert in 1954 certainly was
competent, with such steady performers as Whitey Lockman, Monte
Irvin, and Alvin Dark. But there was no sense of fire, no rage to win
heating the air, except when Durocher decided to sound off. By contrast to the Dodgers of Robinson, Snider, and the rest, these Giants
seemed staid, even dull.

Then on March 1, the Army discharged Mays. He flew all night
from Virginia, and as soon as Willie walked into the dusty Phoenix
ballpark, wearing a yellow polo shirt and slacks rumpled by the long
plane ride, the New York Giants became a contending team.

I had struck up a friendship with Charles "Chub" Feeney, nephew
to Horace Stoneham who owned the Giants, and de facto general manager. Feeney knew Willie's discharge date well in advance and after a
drink or two, Feeney took to singing, to the tune of "Old Black Joe,"
"In seven more days/We're gonna have Willie Mays." The crooning
followed serious baseball talk. Why had Sal Maglie won only eight the
previous year? Sore back, or emotional problems? That trade, Bobby
Thomson to Milwaukee for Johnny Antonelli, a twenty-three-year-old
lefthander, did that make sense? Antonelli didn't seem like much more
than a .500 pitcher. Feeney said Maglie's back was going to be a helluva
lot better as soon as Mays showed up. "Sal says with the kid in center,

all he has to do is keep the baseball in the park. Willie catches everything. And when Antonelli realizes he has Willie behind him, he just
might go out there and win twenty games."

"That's not entirely rational," I said.

"Neither is baseball," Feeney said. He was a droll, contained fellow, a graduate of Dartmouth and Fordham Law School.

"Duke Snider," I began.

Feeney lifted his martini, gazed at the olive, then at me, and began
to warble again to the tune of "Old Black Joe," "In six more days/
We're gonna have Willie Mays." He briefly quit the song for conversation. "And among center fielders, Duke Snider will be history. And
Mickey Mantle, too."

"You're addled, Chub."

"In six more days/We're gonna have Willie Mays. Finish your
drink."

The *Herald Tribune* insisted that in addition to composing seven
daily stories, I supply a Sunday feature each week. Feeney's fanaticism
prompted me to file an unusual dispatch for the paper of Sunday,
February 27.

Willie Mays is due to arrive in the Giant camp on Tuesday,
not a day too soon. By Wednesday half the Giant party will
have left the desert sun, flown to Cooperstown, and started
remodeling the Hall of Fame to include ten busts and five por-
traits of Willie.

It's only human to wonder whether this is man or superman coming to join the Giants. In my case the wonder takes
the form of questions, and after I asked every authority around
the swimming pool where I hang out, a good picture of Willie
Mays emerged.

Willie is ten feet nine inches tall. He can jump fifteen feet
straight up. Nobody can hit a ball over his head.

Willie's arms extend roughly from 157th Street to 159th
Street [the location of the old Polo Grounds in Manhattan].
This gives him ample reach to cover right and left as well as
center field.

Willie can throw sidearm from the Polo Grounds to Pittsburgh. . . .

Willie's speed is deceptive. The best evidence indicates he
is a step faster than electricity.

Willie does more for a team's morale than Marilyn Mon-
roe, Zsa Zsa Gabor and Rita Hayworth, plus cash. . . .

That's about all there is to Mays, except that every authority added, "And if you think that's something, wait till you see
him."

In 1954, you couldn't get a New York paper in Phoenix. I had no idea
what was happening to my stuff after I turned it over to a Western
Union telegrapher, who transmitted it to the *Tribune* in Morse Code,
laboriously clicking out dots and dashes on his "bug." (Fax? Modem?
Not in 1954.)

My request for airmailed copies of the paper was rejected, either as
too much trouble or as too much for the sports budget. I was writing
not only in the desert but in a vacuum. Only much later did I learn
that the story on 10-foot 9-inch Willie Mays so excited *Tribune* editors
that they illustrated it with a cleverly distorted photo, making Mays
appear gigantic. They featured the picture and my story on the front
page of the Sunday sports section.

Feeney had his song and I had my laugh. Then in the middle of
the morning of March 1, Willie arrived. It is forty-two years distant as
I write this, but I can see that morning as though it were today.

A wide pellucid sky. The baked hills wanting grass. Desert winds
blowing whirls of sand. Durocher had scheduled an intrasquad game,
but when Willie walked into the clubhouse the players still were warm-
ing up, mostly playing catch. On the field, in whispers at first, Giants
began telling other Giants, "Willie's here."

I walked into the clubhouse. Buck naked, Sal Maglie burst out of a
shower and shook Mays's hand.

"Where ya been?" Mays asked.

"In the shower," Maglie said.

"That's what I thought," Mays said and giggled.

Monte Irvin, Mays's old roommate, came into the locker room.
"How's your game, Roomie?" he said.

"What game?" Mays asked.

Irvin smiled and shook his head.

"You mean pool?" Willie said.

"Your game, Roomie," Irvin said. "I mean baseball."

Press photographers converged on Mays. They took pictures while he was buttoning his Giant shirt, tying his baseball shoes, shaking hands with everyone in sight. "I wanna get out and hit," Mays complained.

"You're too late," said Coach Fred Fitzsimmons. "Batting practice is over."

Willie looked as though he were about to weep. He started down a runway to the field. Durocher loomed up, threw both arms around Mays and wrestled him back into the clubhouse. They were hugging with real affection. Durocher had no bigotry, no bigotry at all. Sometimes he said that Willie was the son he always wished he had.

Finally Willie walked into the Giants' dugout where the docile Giants press was waiting.

"Durocher says he's really depending on you," a reporter said.

"I don't know nothing about that," Willie said. "If I worry I don't play good. So I don't read the papers and that way I don't worry."

"Have you signed a contract yet?"

"No, but I'm easy to sign. I love to play."

"There's a story out of Fort Eustis," I said, "that says you want twenty-thousand dollars."

Willie blinked. "That man Stoneham would take a gun and shoot me if I asked for that much money. Whew. Twenty-thousand dollars. Whew. You know those reporters. Sometimes they write on their own."

"I guess," I said, "you'd play for nothing."

Our eyes met. Willie offered a teasing grin. "Now *you're* going on your own."

Durocher held him out of the intrasquad game. Willie squirmed and paced. Durocher sent him in to the pinch hit in the fifth inning. Willie hit a 400-foot home run.

He had no chances in center field until the seventh. Then, with Bill Gardner on first, Harvey Gentry slammed a long drive to right center.

Willie raced to the right centerfield fence, speared the ball one-handed, whirled and threw a strike to first base. He doubled Gardner, a good base runner. Then, when a big country boy called Joe Cephus "Cash" Taylor blasted a tremendous wallop to dead center, Willie galloped fifty feet straight back and caught the ball over his shoulder, a simply phenomenal catch.

"May I point out," Chub Feeney said, "that Willie doesn't like airplanes that much. He's playing this well on zero hours sleep."

"Point out anything you want," I said. "Please just don't sing."

But of course I was awed. So was everybody else, Durocher and Maglie and Lockman and Feeney and the handful of fans and the umpires.

I began my account for the Western Union telegrapher: "This is not going to be a plausible story, but then no one ever accused Willie Mays of being a plausible ballplayer. This is simply the implausible truth. . . ."

I had been right all along. Willie the Kid really was 10-feet 9-inches tall.


Durocher was 20-karat Hollywood. When Dean Martin and Jerry Lewis asked to work out with the Giants, Leo stopped regular drills and turned the ballfield over to the actors. He was, he told me, a very close friend of Danny Kaye. He liked to joke with Jackie Gleason. His very closest Hollywood buddy, except for Mrs. Durocher, was Frank Sinatra. "You know," Durocher said, "when they make the movie of my life, Frank Sinatra is going to play me."

Another fine ballclub trained in Arizona that spring. Quiet, courtly Al Lopez managed the Cleveland Indians, who were based in Tucson. Hank Greenberg, the great home run hitter from the Bronx, owned a part of the Indians and worked as general manager. The Indians did not have Willie Mays, of course, but three of their starting pitchers, Bob Feller, Early Wynn, and Bob Lemon, would be elected to the Hall of Fame. Third baseman Al Rosen was as great a competitor as existed. Solid performers, Bobby Avila, Larry Doby, Vic Wertz, filled the lineup.

Having clowned about with the Giants, Martin and Lewis asked to do the same with the Indians. "Absolutely not," Hank Greenberg said. "Do I send my ballplayers on to your damn movie sets?"

The two teams played more than a score of exhibition games against one another that spring; the variousness of ball clubs could hardly have been more stark. Every day Durocher kept the spotlight shining on himself and Mays. He played pepper games with Willie and Monte Irvin. The men stood quite close and Leo drilled hard smashes at Willie's toes, knees, whatever. Mays's reflexes were such that he could field a hard line drive at ten or fifteen feet. And he loved doing it. Once in a while Willie bobbled a ball. Then, if that was judged an error, he owed Durocher a Coke. Durocher made great shows of cheating Willie. One morning he hit a hard smash on one hop, well to Willie's right, and Willie knocked the ball down with a prodigious lunge. But the ball trickled past him.

"Coke," Leo roared. "That's six you owe."

"Ain' no Coke for that," Willie said. His voice piped high and plaintive. "That's a base hit."

"Six Cokes you owe," Durocher insisted.

"Monte," Willie pleaded at Irvin. "What you say, Roomie?"

"Six Cokes," Irvin said, solemnly. Willie's boyish face slumped into a pout. "You're giving me the short end," the expression said, "but I'll get you guys anyway."

Sometimes Irvin hit and then there was added byplay. Not only did Durocher and Mays stab smashes—at the age of forty-eight, Durocher still had fast hands—they worked to rattle each other. Durocher seized a line drive, wound up to throw to Irvin, and with a blur of elbows and hands tossed the ball to Mays at his left. Durocher was a consummate juggler. Willie caught the toss, faked to Irvin and there was the ball somehow floating down toward Leo. Durocher reached and Mays slapped a glove into his belly.

"Oof," Leo grunted. Willie spun off staggering through his own laughter. This went on every day and it wasn't long before people started coming to the ballpark early, just to watch these marvelous games of pepper.

Leo talked about Willie constantly. Mays had come to him for a twenty-dollar loan to go to a movie, Durocher said.

"Twenty? A movie ticket is a dollar."

"But I gotta eat."

"Sure you do. That's another five."

"But Mistuh Leo. I got a *friend!*"

I heard Mays call the manager "Leo" and "Skip," never "Mistuh Leo"—except in Durocher's stories. There Willie always called him "Mistuh Leo." If you want accuracy, I suppose, walk away from Durocher and head for an Encyclopaedia Britannica.

By today's standards, Durocher may not have been politically correct, but he did play up to Willie every day, flatter him, praise him, and make him feel that he was the most important player on the team and just about the best ballplayer in the world. Since Willie had a profound hunger for praise, this was artful managing.

The Cleveland ballclub was vastly more staid. Not humorless. One morning when I was shagging flies in right, hours before a Giant-Indian exhibition, a tall, booted State Trooper marched up and ordered me off the field. "Why?" I asked. "I do this all the time."

The Trooper spoke very carefully. "You are making a travesty of our National Pastime."

The jack-booted trooper glowered and I did as I was told. Crossing the foul line I noticed that a long way off near home plate, Al Rosen was doubled up with laughter. Rosen had given the cop five dollars to make his odd, intimidating speech and run me.

Lopez regarded his players as adults and treated them with respect. Some of the Indians liked martinis before dinner and stingers afterward. Lopez demanded only that his ballplayers show up at the ballpark on time and in shape to play. Drink, deal, or chase, but be ready at game time.

Under Lopez, the Indians won more than 90 games in each of the three seasons, from 1951 through 1953. Each year they finished second to the Yankees. Lopez appeared to take those results philosophically, or, as one writer put it, with a patient melancholy. Hope continued to stir in the secret places of his heart.

Lopez asked me one day, with genuine concern, if I was enjoying this interesting spring and, if, by the way, in the intense Giant camp, I had been able to do any serious reading.

"Not much, Al. The ballclub has grabbed my concentration."

"Save some," Lopez said. "Refresh your mind. I've been reading a fine book, *From Here to Eternity*, by James Jones."

"I actually studied that," I said, "at a Writers Conference in a place called Bread Loaf. I think it's the best novel to come out of the war."

"The language is strong," Lopez said, "but I believe it has to be. Soldiers use strong language, same as ballplayers. So I think strong language is appropriate. Don't you agree?"

My father had told me about Al Lopez, nicknamed El Señor, who caught for the Dodgers across seven seasons and whose hands were so sure, he still could play piano.

"I know why your dad told you that," Lopez said. "One season the New York photographers had me sit down at a Steinway. The picture of my hands on the keys was in all the papers. It's true I never broke a finger catching, but don't take the piano picture seriously. Can't play a note. Never could."

The Giants and the Indians flew to Tulsa for an exhibition game. We then repaired to Pullman cars, three for each team, plus two diners, and embarked on eighteen days of barnstorming back toward the east. We stowed our belongings into upper berths and lived in the lowers. For almost three weeks, home was a lower berth. (Heaven, of course, was a shower.) The players, the managers, the writers, all rode the rails. Tulsa. Oklahoma City. Wichita Falls. Houston. Fort Worth. Dallas. Beaumont. A game a day on scruffy bush-league diamonds.

Wynn threw awesome knockdown pitches. Rosen was a murderous batter with runners in scoring position. Maglie seemed strong again. Antonelli, the kid lefthander, threw a nasty change-up that faded away from righthanded hitters. Durocher began an endless game of gin rummy with Cleveland's huge first baseman, Luscious Luke Easter. They played day after day in a Pullman car and Easter never seemed to care that one of the Giants' coaches was posted behind him and saw his hand. Easter lost sullenly, but kept playing. Later Durocher told me that he took $3,000 from Easter on the trip. Leo fleeced innocents and raved about Willie Mays. Those were his overwhelming skills.

A couple of Giants resented the fuss Durocher made over Willie. Not the smart Giants, not Whitey Lockman. "I'm glad to have him for two reasons," said Lockman, an enlightened son of the segregated South. "First, he's gonna win us a lot of ballgames and make us all some money when he does. Second, if he wasn't with us, I believe I'd pay my own money, not that there's that much, just to watch that young man play baseball."

"The fucking kid is overrated," said Ralph "Red" Kress, a sour-mash Cleveland coach.

"He won't hit .300," said Franklin "Whitey" Lewis, a normally solid Cleveland sports columnist.

"Let me get this straight," I said. "Willie Mays is overrated and he will not hit .300. I have forty dollars, that's twenty dollars for each of you. My money says that Willie hits .300."

"What are you, stupid?" Kress said. "Don't you know I'm a coach? People in baseball aren't allowed to bet."

"Some of that National League pitching is pretty soft," Lewis said.

"Twenty dollars, Whitey."

"You're on."

Tris Speaker came to the exhibition game in Beaumont. Tristram E. Speaker. *Spoke, The Grey Eagle.* The greatest center fielder who ever was. Or so my father told me. I heard my late father's bass-baritone again, strong in my mind. "Spoke played so close behind second base he caught a lot of singles. He went back so beautifully it was just about impossible to hit a ball over his head. He was a wonder. There's never been another like Tris Speaker."

"Sir?" I introduced myself feeling unusual humility. My father's heroes were ever greater than my own. Speaker was a poised, commanding, soft-spoken man with a wide brow. He didn't shout. He didn't have to shout. He knew who he was. Tris Speaker. He agreed to sit with me and critique Willie's performance. The ballgame was mostly routine. You can't make great catches unless you get hard chances. But Speaker quickly noted Willie's speed and ball sense.

Once Willie threw over a cut-off man's head. "Low," Speaker. "You keep your throws low. You don't want to throw over the cut-off man's head. But you knew that, of course. Mays probably knows that, too. He just made a mistake."

Compact tape recorders did not yet exist and I no longer have my notes. But I remember old Tris Speaker watching young Willie Mays play ball one afternoon in Beaumont, Texas, and how, when the game was over and I thanked him for his comments, Spoke Speaker gave me a little smile and said, "He'll do."

In his memorable memoir, *Nice Guys Finish Last*, written with Ed Linn, Durocher describes young Mays as "barely able to read and write"— lovable but an American primitive. That is Hollywood Leo, rewriting the truth. As the baseball train made its way east, a journey that lasted eighteen nights, there was plenty of time to get to know other people. I sought out Willie and we had numbers of serious conversations. I have been sensible here and preserved detailed notes.

At twenty-two, Mays had developed a strong, personal view of the major leagues. "I'd say there is really three things," he told me, as the baseball train moved on from Beaumont to Shreveport. "First you got to love the game. If you don't love the game, how you gonna learn about it? Second, you got to watch your drinking. I seen guys, good players, they liked to drink more than they liked to play ball. I don't think you can drink a lot and be a great player. Then you got to get your sleep. You don't have to go to bed by eleven, but twelve, twelve-thirty, something like that. You ought to be in bed by then because you have to get eight hours of sleep. You shouldn't get more. A fellow gets to sleeping too much he gets lazy. You shouldn't sleep too much and you shouldn't sleep too little. Eight hours."

I remarked that a few cars away some of the Indians were drinking hard. Willie shrugged. "Well maybe that Early Wynn can take a drink and them other fellers, but I know it wouldn't work for me. You think I could play like I been playing if I was drinking? No way. You got some writers here are drinking all the time. Tell me what kinda job they do?"

"Skip it."

"Tell me."

"They do a rotten job, Will."

He smiled. "I knew that already. I wanted to hear you say it."

I asked about his boyhood and Willie remembered happy times in the all-black Alabama villages of Westfield and Fairfield, where as far back as he could remember, he was good enough to be playing with the older kids.

"There was this man, Clee Holmes, who was the financier of baseball in my town. I mean he had money and he got uniforms, real good ones, and balls and spikes and all the stuff you need. He got them for the older kids. But if you were good enough, even though you were a little kid, you could play with the older kids. From the time I was really little, I played with older kids so I never had to worry about a uniform or spikes or anything like that. This Mr. Clee Holmes, he took care of that.

"I could always throw pretty good. Just could. You know in the outfield, you got to throw like a pitcher. Watch the way I look after I get off a real good throw. Sort of like I was a pitcher who's just thrown. And I had good breakaway. I could always breakaway for flies pretty quick."

"I never saw anyone break as quickly as you. You must see the ball the instant it leaves the bat."

"And I hear it. Sure I see it, but the sound helps me too, to know which way I gotta break."

I had to think that over. "I shag some flies."

"I seen that cop put you off the field."

"Not like you, but I'm trying to understand this. You're saying the sound tells you whether to break right or left, in or out?"

"Not just the sound, but the sound helps."

"Can you explain that?"

"No more than I just did. You gotta figure it out for yourself."

A 350-foot line drive coming off a bat makes a more assertive sound than a pop fly. I knew that. But here Willie was saying that a line drive to right center made a slightly different sound than a line drive to left center. Few mortals have ever heard this difference. Willie said he had. I have never been inclined to argue with him about anything, least of all the mysteries of center field.

"After I was playing all the time with older kids, I begun to have an idol. He was Joe DiMaggio. I didn't get to see him, but I heard talk from lots of ballplayers who had that seen him, and they said he could really catch them and throw and he could really hit, and that was what I wanted to be able to do. I played a lot of center field and I became much improved and the Giants signed me and sent me to play in Trenton, New Jersey. You ever been there?"

Willie crashed Organized Baseball, White Man's Baseball, in the Interstate League when he was eighteen. He batted .353 for Trenton that season, 1950. Here is the report Giant scout Frank "Chick" Genovese filed in September:

> Major League prospect. Possesses strong arms and wrists. Has some power. Hits to all fields. Runs good. Has good baseball instincts. Wants to learn. Gets good jump on fly balls. Has one of the strongest and most accurate arms in baseball. Hits with men. Winning type player. Personality excellent.

"In Trenton," Willie said, "I was nowhere near as good as I am now, but I have my own way to learn things and I did. People can tell you: 'Willie do it like this.' But that ain't the way to learn. You got to do it for yourself. Sure you're going to make mistakes, but it is very seldom that you'll see me make the same mistake more than one time, or maybe twice. You got to keep thinking: 'What am I doing wrong?' And you got to look around and watch the other outfielders and think: 'What are they doing wrong?' Then you got to be sure you don't do anything wrong more than once."

A year later Willie moved up to Minneapolis in the American Association. After a few weeks another scout, Hank De Berry, filed an exultation.

> Sensational . . . Outstanding player on the Minneapolis Club and probably in all the minor leagues . . . The Louisville pitchers knocked him down plenty, but it seemed to have no effect at all. This player the best prospect in America; it was a banner day for the Giants when this boy was signed.

"I was getting better in Minneapolis but I wanted to keep getting better all the time. Nobody never come to me and say like you see in a book: 'This is the way to play center field.' I used to wish someone would tell me just how you do everything. But it don't bother me now because I have learned that nobody can teach you nothing like you can learn yourself.

"You know what I mean. Leo is a friend of mine and he say this and that, but nobody can teach you nothing. Not me or nobody and nobody can write a book that will teach you.

"You got to learn for yourself and you go to do it your way and you got to become much improved.

"If you love the game, you can do it."

Hardly the words of an ignorant man.

Quite beautiful, it seemed to me.

*Willie's Song.*

Back in New York, Red Smith said he had no intention of asking me any questions about Mays. My stories had already answered them. "But what about the Indians. Are they ready to take the Yankees?"

"Absolutely not, Red. They're a solid club with wonderful pitching, but they drink and drink and drink. No team that drinks that much is going to win a pennant."

I was speaking in April. When I looked up it was September and the Indians stood above the Yankees, poised to administer the coup de grace.

Willie was leading the National League in slugging percentage and triples and impossible catches and he was going to hit more than 40 home runs.

Batting average?

Oh, yes. There was that twenty-dollar spring training bet with Whitey Lewis, the Cleveland columnist, who said that Willie wouldn't hit .300.

Lewis mailed me my check on an afternoon when Willie was leading the major leagues at .358. This season had a few weeks to go, but Lewis conceded gracefully. His concession note was brief.

"See you and Willie at the Series."

# CHAPTER EIGHT

# Clap Hands, Here Comes Henry

## or

## Present at the Creation

*E*XCEPT FOR ONE OBVIOUS REASON—the chance to make money—it's never been clear what drew Henry Robinson Luce to sports. Henry Luce, America's last titanic press lord, was a severe, humorless Presbyterian, passionately opposed to "atheistic communism" and dedicated to what he called The American Century. Inactivity made him uncomfortable. He never spent a leisurely day in the bleachers in his entire, vigorous life.

Luce was a calculating, brilliant, fervid character, who, since his death in 1967, has been the subject of half a dozen biographies. Only in books authorized by his family or by his huge company, Time Inc., does Luce appear likable. But Henry Robinson Luce was not about being likable. Luce was about being America's last titanic press lord.

Characters based on the publisher rumble and scheme their way through a dozen novels, some serious, some mere spoofs. The titles range from *The Death of Kings* by Charles Wertenbaker to *The Fun House* by William Brinkley. Wertenbaker was alarmed by Luce's congeniality with fascism. Brinkley was more concerned with copulation at a big picture magazine.

Luce hired, debated, and dismissed some of the finest journalists in the annals, including John Hersey and Theodore White. But hired or fired, those close to him never seemed to get over the experience of Henry Robinson Luce, an intimidating, contradictory, formal man who liked to be called Harry.

"The Lord gave you a fine mind," one of his mistresses wrote Luce, "and he gave you the ability to get money and power . . . [but] I think you ought to be all fear and trembling. I could imagine the Lord speaking. 'How about it? You got money and power. How could you help it when I gave you all that ability. But what *use* did you make 'em after you got 'em, Harry. That's the question.'"

Although he was a hard-drinker, a heavy smoker and a devout pursuer of women, Luce regarded himself as a moralist. He was a missionary's son. Worship Jesus, toil tirelessly, hands to work, hearts to God, Luce professed to believe, and thou shalt know salvation. But he was one abrasive Christian.

Luce preached rugged individualism and developed, in *Time* magazine, journalism's first collective farm. He spoke for truth in reporting, and published some of the most viciously slanted stories in American history. He was a slow talker, often pausing in the middle of a sentence until a subordinate leaped in to supply a seemingly elusive word. Luce then sneered, articulated his own word and went on lecturing. That was his way. He didn't like subordinates flirting with independence.

With a Yale classmate, Briton Hadden, Luce founded *Time* when he was twenty-four years old. The first issue, dated March 3, 1923, sold nine thousand copies. Covering a big week—American quarrels over prohibition, a famine in Russia, French troops occupying the Ruhr—*Time's* account could be read in half an hour. From the beginning, the news, according to Luce, had to be compressed and interpreted.

Timestyle, that clever, cloying combination of adjectival writing, backward-running sentences, and innovative words, showed up at the creation. So did group journalism. For decades, no one writing for *Time* was allowed a byline. The stories that appeared in *Time* were repeatedly rewritten to fit preconceived ideas. Without bylines, pride of authorship withered. No one could cry, "You're distorting my work." There was no "my work" at *Time*. There was only "our work." Someone said, "*Time* isn't written at all. *Time* magazine is edited."

Luce presided over his various innovations and his hirelings with utmost seriousness. "Careful, Harry," Briton Hadden taunted him. "You'll drop the world."

When Hadden died at thirty-one in 1929, Luce took over sole command of his growing and wildly successful "newsmagazine." Seven years later, proclaiming a "new era of photojournalism," he founded his picture magazine. Offering vivid photos of a woman in childbirth, *Life* sold out its entire initial press run, 466,000 copies. *Time* and *Life* became the twin towers of Luce's expanding empire, which also included *Architectural Forum* and *Fortune*. Time Inc., as he called his company, prospered implausibly, and Luce began paying significantly better salaries to editorial workers than did such other publishers as William Randolph Hearst and Adolph Ochs. In addition, Luce provided his staff with free medical care, a generous pension plan and profit sharing though special private mutual funds. By the time World War II ended in 1945, word spread through journalism that to join Time Inc. was to attain lifetime financial security. And if perhaps you were required to write things that you did not believe to be so . . . well . . . surely you could settle that score in later years by writing a novel about Henry Robinson Luce, the bastard who had made your early retirement possible.

The reigning sports magazine during the early 1950s was a monthly called *SPORT*, edited with style and brio by Edward E. Fitzgerald, who soon left the playing fields and became president of the Book-of-the-Month Club. A core of Fitzgerald's readership consisted of youngsters, the same group that once devoured baseball novels. *SPORT* offered them cheerful, competently written profiles of ballplayers. But Fitzgerald also courted fine magazine writers, men like John Lardner and W.C. Heinz, and published their work when they could make time for him. These articles were witty and sophisticated, or strong examples of journalism verité. Fitzgerald could get Lardner and Heinz because he didn't change their stuff. There was no collective journalism under Fitzgerald. You could be as good as you knew how to be. Some of the baseball stories Fitzgerald published in *SPORT* were better than anything appearing in wealthier and more pretentious magazines, the *Saturday Evening Post* and *The New Yorker*.

He gave me an assignment in 1954, asking if I knew Don New-combe of the Brooklyn Dodgers.

"A little bit."

"We hear," Fitzgerald said, "that he's a sensitive fellow."

"And big," I said.

"That's the point," Fitzgerald said. "Here is this huge man coming out of the Army and getting back into the major leagues where every-body is expecting him to become an instant 30-game winner. But he may have a lot of adjusting to do." Thus prompted, I looked for com-plexities in Newcombe's return. The piece I wrote preached caution. Newcombe won only nine games that season. Later Fitzgerald encour-aged me to write thirty pages on Jackie Robinson and racism, a story that made other editors nervous. "Fitz" was not afraid to think on his own. He encouraged his contributors to do the same.

For all Fitzgerald's efforts, SPORT was limited. The lead time, the period needed for a story to go from the editor's desk to the news-stands, was three months. Keeping the magazine up with the news was not possible. Also, Fitzgerald's budget was restricted; the most that he could pay for an article was $500. *The New Yorker* was offering $1,200 for baseball profiles. The *Saturday Evening Post* paid $1,500. John Lardner wrote for all three publications, but said he liked writing for SPORT when he could afford it "because the other joints have people who believe they are being paid to change my copy."

From his office forty floors above Rockefeller Center, stern, bushy-browed Henry Luce glowered down on SPORT and baseball and asked himself a penetrating question. Couldn't a weekly magazine, with a well-paid full-time staff, steal SPORT's thunder and double or triple its profits? Numbers of deputies said no. They argued that sports was too narrow. The new Time Inc. Magazine should be called *Leisure*, with a section on sports, sure, but also material on music, theater, books, resorts, and movies.

Luce listened in his hard, cold way and shook his by now balding head. He wanted a sports magazine. Discussions ended. Harry Luce would have a sports magazine and he would make it work more prof-itably than any sports magazine had before.

Luce hired scores of people and put them to work preparing a dummy magazine called *MNORX*. Luce intended to buy the title, *SPORT*. By calling his nascent publication *MNORX*, he gave the design people a chance to play around with a five-letter title and try graphic games with the central letter "O." Sample covers of an embryo magazine began to appear, under the logo *MNORX*. In all versions, the central "O" looked rectangular and aggressive.

As the baseball season of 1954 unfolded, an interesting season, a grand one, I felt my strongest pangs of weariness with life as a newspaper baseball writer. I started with the Giants, who played fine, exciting baseball. Then I moved on to the Yankees, where I was immersed in the wonder that was Casey Stengel. The baseball part of the job was ever more vivid and fascinating. But the travel, the relentless Willy Loman travel—Chicago, Milwaukee, St. Louis, Detroit, Chicago, ground at my nerves. I didn't sleep well on Pullman cars. I could leave a team briefly and fly on my own, but in those days few planes could climb above bad weather. My adventures inside thunderheads, flashes of lightning, hail beating on propellers, side slips, dizzying drops, and unscheduled landings took the glamour out of air travel soon enough.

"Say, you know Luce is starting up a sports magazine," Arch Murray told me. Arch was a stumpy, genial Princeton man who worked for the *New York Post* and worshiped Durocher.

"They've hired an articles editor who likes martinis. Have lunch with him. After he starts drinking, you can sell him anything."

"*Anything*, Archie?"

"I sold him two pieces the *Saturday Evening Post* rejected. He paid me two thousand dollars."

In press boxes, the new magazine *MNORX* was known first as an easy mark. Everywhere baseball writers began blowing dust off old articles and peddling them. Occasionally a *MNORX* reporter appeared. I was covering a game at Ebbets Field when Duke Snider poled a home run high over the scoreboard in right center. A tweedy man introduced himself as a reporter for "the new sports magazine," and asked me how far Snider's home run had traveled "from bat to landing place."

"I can't say precisely. It left the ballpark where you see that sign that says 344 feet. It was maybe 60 feet up. You'd be safe in writing that it traveled about 400 feet."

"My editors don't want 'about,'" the tweedy man said. "We're doing a new kind of journalism. My editors want precision."

He turned to Dick Young. "Could you tell me precisely how far that home run traveled?"

"I can tell you precisely that you should have paid precise attention to what Mr. Kahn told you. Or you can go hire a surveyor. I'm busy, fella. I gotta write a fucking story."

After the tweedy man—his name turned out to be Coles Phinizy—retreated, Young resumed cursing. "Fucking guy like that. Knows nothing. Probably makes twenty-five thousand dollars. More than either of us. Knows nothing at all. Fucking magazines. They steal from the newspapers, that's all they know how to do, and they sell the stuff they steal and make a fucking fortune. How much do you think that guy's sport jacket cost?"

Young's loathing for the new sports magazine was extreme. He practiced immoderation in all things. Generally sportswriters regarded *MNORX* as silly and irrelevant—rather than larcenous—except, of course, if you sold them an old retread of a baseball story for a cool thousand. Then *MNORX* became as relevant as your wallet.

Luce never could buy the title *SPORT*. The relatively small company that owned the name refused to sell. Luce liked one-word titles for his magazine: *Time, Life, Fortune.* Now he had to settle for the laborious handle *Sports Illustrated.* He was going to publish wonderful sports photography; illustration etched with the finest cameras and fastest film was important to his concept. But to this day no one with an ear for language has suggested that the five-syllable name *Sports Illustrated* falls trippingly from the tongue.

Unlike Arch Murray of Princeton and the *New York Post*, I never could get the alcoholic articles editor to meet me over lunch. I did, however, receive a telephone call from a man named John Knox Tibby suggesting that I might, just might, mind you, have a golden future at the magazine.

Tibby identified himself as "news editor of *Sports Illustrated.*" I had been wondering who the top editors at the new magazine would turn out to be. Stanley Woodward, with all his ideas and integrity, culture, knowledge, feel for sports, would be a perfect editor-in-chief, I thought. Ed Fitzgerald, with his practical gifts, his steady, attentive ways, his great good sense, his love for good writers, his tolerance for their idiosyncrasies, would make a splendid managing editor.

Henry Luce approached neither man. Each was, in fact, pretty much what he did *not* want. As perceived in Luce's ordered mind, sports was merely a department of journalism, like foreign affairs or national news. Editing and writing sports required intelligence, but no unique background, no special expertise. As first-class Timestyle journalists moved easily from foreign to nation and back, and shifted from *Time* to *Life*, so Timestyle journalists could move from *Time* and *Life* to the new command posts at *Sports Illustrated*. Luce wanted top editors who were schooled in *Time's* collective thinking, so that they could impose it on ingenuous recruits at *Sports Illustrated*.

I came to understand this. But now, I wondered, who the hell was John Knox Tibby, anyway?

"The martinis at the English Grill [beside the Rockefeller Center skating rink] are served at a temperature six degrees cooler than those at Holland House," Jack Tibby informed me. "So we'll go there."

"Fahrenheit or centigrade?"

"Fahrenheit, of course," Tibby said, as though I had raised a serious question. He was a trim, buttoned-down fellow, with some white in his brushed-back hair, and a pleasant triangular face. Tibby wore plastic-rimmed spectacles and spoke deliberately, using the Luce trick of seeming to grope for a word. About like this: "As the baseball season wanes and we come to that most beautiful of seasons . . . mmm . . . mmm . . . er . . . "

"Autumn."

"As we come to that most beautiful of seasons . . . *fall* . . . "

Tibby said he had been following my work and that *Sports Illustrated* was prepared to offer me $9,500 to leave the *Herald Tribune* and join the staff as principal baseball writer. My articles would be bylined. Mr. Luce was a generous man and if everything went as

Tibby expected it would, in a few years I could pretty much write my own ticket at Time Inc.

Tibby then began to talk about himself; he came out of Pittsburgh, had worked as a pollster for Gallup, got hired by *Time*. He had a beautiful wife who played viola in the Port Washington Community Orchestra. He lived in a great old waterfront home in Sands Point on Long Island Sound and at night from his back porch he could see the green light, the very green light, that was so symbolic to Jay Gatsby. If everything worked out, as Tibby expected it would, a similar lifestyle would soon be open to me.

While Tibby was in college and the Depression raged, he had heard about a man who turned an instant fortune. This fellow walked into the headquarters of the Coca-Cola Company in Atlanta, which then made a syrup that had to be mixed with seltzer. He said just two words—"Bottle it!"—and became a millionaire. Tibby traveled to Cincinnati, home of Procter and Gamble, the manufacturers of Ivory Soap. "I said my two words. 'Powder it!' They threw me out and I had to get a job."

Until recently Tibby had been senior editor at *Time*, in charge of the back of the book—culture, education, sports. This new magazine, he maintained, was the most exciting thing he had ever encountered. "You see," Tibby said, "what we're going to do is equate sports, specifically baseball, in terms of Americana. Nobody has done that before. We're going to add depth, dimension, color, and vitality to one of the most remarkable areas of American life. We call it 'The Wonderful World of Sport.'" Tibby paused longer than usual, signifying something pretentious was coming. "More than that," he said. "We're going to raise group journalism to an art form."

I sipped my martini and wondered when we'd get around to sitting. The mutton chops at the English Grill were reputed to be outstanding.

"An advantage to coming here now is that your slice of the pie will be fair, which certainly isn't so at newspapers. I understand you like poetry. I can see you spending rewarding years as *Sports Illustrated*'s preeminent baseball writer, then moving on to *Time* and writing essays on the state of poetry—Eliot, Pound, and their successors. How does that sound?"

I never got near the mutton chops. After three martinis, Tibby led me to a drugstore lunch counter, where we each consumed a chocolate malted. Martinis and malts were the original *Sports Illustrated* power lunch. Most serious work went on either in the morning, or late at night.

"I have no doubt that you'll work out very well," Tibby said, across his malted, "but before we officially offer you this position, premiere baseball writer, $9,500 a year, Harry Luce wants you to submit a sample article."

"I publish articles every day in the *Herald Tribune*."

"Something specific for our magazine," Tibby said. "We will, to be sure, compensate you."

I felt miffed, but I wanted the job. "Allie Reynolds is really struggling." I said. "He's a great pitcher, a tremendous competitor, but now he's thirty-nine, and he's having trouble winning games."

"He's with the Yankees isn't he?" Tibby said.

"Right. He is the heart of the Yankee pitching staff. He started strong and now he's struggling. But Reynolds is one tough Indian."

"An Indian?" Tibby showed a flicker of interest. "And he's having a very difficult time." Tibby paused. The malted milk glasses were empty. "I . . . um . . . can see a story here . . . An Indian and struggling. Here's your title," Tibby said. "Allie Reynolds' Trail of Tears."

At Yankee Stadium Reynolds asked if this new magazine hired me, would I earn more money? When I told him my salary would jump by 60 percent, he said simply, "Well, let's go to work." He stood naked but dignified in the Yankee locker room. Naked with a towel wrapped around his head, a sort of turban. For more than an hour, Reynolds talked pitching to me. How first you had to have a strong arm, and then you needed confidence in your arm and that you had to train yourself to despise hitters. Maybe I knew that, he said, or maybe not. Reynolds said he was a pretty easygoing feller; oil royalties had long since made him financially independent. "But I'm not easygoing when I pitch. As soon as my foot hits the mound, it's war. The hitter is trying to beat me and I've got a lot of pride. I'll knock him down, as you've seen. That's to put some fear into him. But batters duck away from pitches at their head. They can't get away from a fastball at the ribs. If

I want to hurt a hitter, I drill his ribs. If you get my fastball in the ribs, you cough for a week."

These things were said in gentle tones, as Reynolds moved about to a lounge and then to the trainer's room. I never had to ask about the towel turban for finally he stepped into a whirlpool tub. His back was killing him, he said, but please don't write that. He didn't want hitters to know how bad it was. "Just say I got more aches than I used to. More aches, but also more pride."

"Are you going to pitch next year?"

"The Yankees want me to," Reynolds said, "but I'll only come back if I can really do the job. I'm going to be forty in February. I've been here for eight years. Two no-hitters. Seven wins in the World Series. Seven wins in the World Series and four saves. You could say—you, not me—that over the years I've been the best World Series pitcher ever."

"I'll say that for you, Allie, sure."

Then hard-muscled Allie Reynolds, the toughest pitcher of his time, stepped out of the whirlpool, drew the towel from his head and began to dry himself. "I'm not trying to tell you what to write, but if you think I've been that good, if you believe it in your heart and you do write it, I'll remember that you did."

Casey Stengel was querulous. "I don't like none of them magazines," he said. "They ain't like the newspapers. The magazines take what you say and hold it for a month and when it comes out in print, its all twisted, the way they want it, not the way you said it, but you been one of my writers, so I guess I gotta help you, kid." We were standing at the end of the bar in the press room underneath Yankee Stadium, and Stengel was drinking. Whisky didn't anger the old man as it angered his volatile successor, Billy Martin.

"All right," Stengel said, and spoke a paragraph that I have never forgotten. "Reynolds is the greatest two ways, which is starting and relieving, the greatest ever, and I seen the great ones, Mathewson and I seen Cy Young and I wondered who that fat old guy was, which tells you what a dumb young punk I was. You could look it up."

"You actually hit against Christy Mathewson?" I said.

"A splendid pitcher and a splendid gentleman, which had been to a fine college in Pennsylvania, but you was asking me about Reynolds and I have informed you with my thoughts."

Tibby paid me one thousand dollars for the Reynolds story and as September began I joined *Sports Illustrated* at $9,500 a year. "We'll see if we can get you a substantial raise for Christmas."

"When does my Reynolds article run?"

"It, um, doesn't. The er . . . ah . . . fellow in charge of articles doesn't like to publish stuff that comes in through the news department. That's us. He's a bit of a problem that way."

"Damn."

"If we had decided to publish 'Allie Reynolds' Trail of Tears,'" Tibby said, "I think you should know I would have had to make one deletion. That section where the Yankee manager . . . um . . . Stengel . . . is talking about those old-time pitchers . . . um . . . Mathewson . . . er . . . Cy Young."

"Cut *that*?"

"Yes," Tibby said. "The way you have Stengel speaking isn't . . . um . . . believable."

"That's how he really speaks."

"Um," Tibby said. "I'm sure. But that's another issue. Another issue . . . um . . . altogether."

As news editor, Tibby ranked number three, or perhaps two and a half, in the hierarchy. Sidney L. James, a short, glad-handing, former *Life* executive, presided. "You're going to write better than ever here," James informed me. "I know about the press boxes. I used to be a newspaperman in St. Louis. The newspapermen think if you X out a line, and then rewrite it to make a story read better, you're a sissy. We believe in X'd out lines at *Sports Illustrated*."

Tall, sardonic Dick Johnston, the man who refused to run the Reynolds piece, stood second in command. He was a mustached libertine from the Pacific Northwest, once a radical, but now a functionary, a hedonist, with no surviving beliefs, let alone ideals. Johnston had covered the Chinese civil war and filed dispatches to *Time* describing corruption and ineptitude in the camp of Chiang Kai-shek. Luce championed Chiang and permitted no criticism of him in the magazines.

Who was assigned to rewrite Dick Johnston's radical dispatches to conform with Luce's company line that only Chiang could save the far east from atheistic Communism? The answer is predictable: Jack Tibby. At *Sports Illustrated* neither man would discuss the episode.

Luce believed that placing adversarial people in competitive positions drew the best work from each. He put Dick Johnston in charge of *Sports Illustrated*'s long articles, features, and fiction. Tibby ran news coverage. Enemies and equals. Competing for space and power, the two regarded each other with distaste, and each man worked very hard.

"I should warn you about two things," Dick Johnston said on my first full day in the old Time-Life Building on 49th Street. "First"—he paused for effect—"researchers." The magazine was stacked with research assistants, almost all female, poised, serious, and attractive, who were charged with fact-checking every story, every word, that was published. "They look tempting, particularly after a drink," Johnston said, "but researchers are dangerous. They don't have much of a future here. The company doesn't encourage women to write. After a while, they tend to see a future in marriage. Marriage to a writer. That's where the danger lies. New York alimony laws are brutal."

I said I was troubled by a system where the reporter was not finally responsible for the accuracy of what he wrote. "You shouldn't be required to give that responsibility away to some person from say, Vassar, no matter how bright she happens to be."

"I agree with you, at least in theory," Johnston said. "Harry Luce does not. But there seems to be some confusion here. You are talking journalism. I was discussing fornication."

My father, still beside me in this curious new world, sometimes quoted Marlowe's lines from *The Jew of Malta*:

*Thou has committed . . .*

*Fornication? . . . But that was in another country; and besides, the wench is dead.*

I heard my father speaking in his rich bass voice. Dick Johnston's voice in counterpoint grew urgent. "Be very careful with your immediate superior, Mr. Tibby. He is a typical humorless Time Inc-er. He will lay a heavy hand on your stories, sometimes whether they need editing or not."

"This isn't *Time*," I said. "My stuff is going to be bylined."

"He will lay a heavy hand . . . Ask the fellow who's done the baseball writing up to now. He's our office virgin, Robert Creamer."

I blinked.

"Every office needs a virgin," Johnston said. "Creamer is a very good one. Blonde. Pale. Earnest. We were down in South Carolina on the plantation of Tom Yawkey [who owned the Boston Red Sox], trying to let baseball people know that we existed. There was a lot of drinking at this conference and all of a sudden a huge wind came up and blew us all into a whorehouse.

"All except Creamer. He wouldn't go. He explained that he was a Roman Catholic." Johnston wore a mustache as lecherous as the ones you see on old movie villains, a big, soft-faced fellow, and world-weary. "So Creamer is our virgin. You certainly won't find another, no matter how hard you look and I suspect you will, among our estimable staff of researchers."

I remember one research assistant, black-haired, 5-feet 9-inches, attractive rather than beautiful. She listened patiently in a cocktail lounge while I held forth on the wonders of baseball, the Yankees, the Indians, Willie Mays, Durocher. And wasn't that new Dodger manager, Walt Alston, a bit of a clod? She listened patiently, over a number of drinks, then looked at me and said, "Please. Could you stop talking baseball and tell me a joke with the word 'fuck' in it?"

Work, some like to remark, spinning off Thorsten Veblen's axiom, is the curse of the drinking class. There was work to be done, at *Sports Illustrated,* formerly *MNORX.* With two weeks remaining, the Cleveland Indians, my friends from spring training, held a five-game lead over the Yankees, even though Stengel's team was winning at a better clip than any Stengel Yankee team had ever done before. With Wynn, Lemon, and Mike Garcia, powerful righthanded starters, performing at their peaks, plus Bob Feller, now thirty-five, working spots, and two crack relievers, Don Mossi and Ray Narleski, the Indians were getting the best pitching on the planet. The earned run average for the entire staff was under 2.80. (By contrast the Giants' staff, with Johnny Antonelli bursting into stardom, was posting an ERA of 3.10. The Brooklyn Dodgers' collective ERA exceeded 4.30. The Philadelphia Athletics' ERA was 5.18. Of course, the A's would lose 103 games and finish last.)

Additionally, the Indian pitchers usually finished what they began.

At the end of the 154-game 1954 season, Cleveland starters had completed 77 games. Fully half of Cleveland's victories came with a single pitcher going nine innings, usually allowing fewer than three runs. Some believe that the 1954 Indians were graced with the best pitching staff ever assembled in the long, curve-balling history of the major leagues.

How could the Indians possibly fall out of first place in September? Well, perhaps, the sight of Yankee uniforms might turn Cleveland knees to jelly, and Cleveland hearts to water as cloudy as Lake Erie. Perhaps, some said, this fine team would "choke." The Indians had not been able to defeat Stengel's Yankees in the past.

The teams would meet in a double-header on Sunday, September 12, at Municipal Stadium in Cleveland. Jack Tibby said this would be an important double-header, was he right?

"The season, or anyway, the American League season, is going to come down to the two games next Sunday. Yes, it is important."

"Then we'll be sending you to Cleveland," Tibby said. "I think you'll enjoy traveling for the company. Did you know that for a time Harry Luce published *Time* in Cleveland?" We were meeting on a Thursday morning. Suddenly Tibby looked stern, a stern Sunday school teacher, and demanded: "Just who is going to win those important games in Cleveland *this* Sunday?"

"Beg pardon."

"Cleveland or . . . um . . . er . . . um . . ."

"New York?" I said.

"The Yankees," Tibby said. "Who's going to win?"

"As a matter of fact, I don't have any idea. This isn't theater. There isn't any script. Who's going to win? Who'll win? Dammit, Jack, that's what I go to the ballpark to find out."

"I think," Tibby said, "we'd better go to um . . . um . . . ahh . . ."

"Lunch," I said.

"Cocktails."

My training in the *Herald Tribune* sports department dictated strongly *against* anticipation. Say, you were going out to watch a mighty Yankee team play a double-header against a Philadelphia team so weak

# I
# The Setting

April in Brooklyn. Cherry blossoms proclaim the spring at the Botanic Garden.
*Corbis-Bettmann*

The Flatbush Avenue Trolley pauses beside a fashionable department store in downtown Brooklyn.

*Archive Photos*

A portrait of the author as a very young man. His mother, Olga, presides.

*Author's collection*

The author's father, Gordon Kahn, a retired City College third baseman.

*Author's collection*

Van Lingle Mungo, winding up, one foot against the sky.

*UPI/Bettmann Newsphotos*

Pee Wee in Louisville. A portrait of th shortstop as a very young man.

*Brooklyn Public Library Eagle Collection*

Pennant! Brooklyn fans lift Reese to their shoulders in 1941.

*Brooklyn Public Library Eagle Collection*

Parade! The 1941 Dodger victory parade starts at the Soldiers and Sailors Monument.

*UPI/Bettmann*

# II

# The Scribes

Christy Mathewson. The
greatest pitcher of his age
loved to write books.
*UPI/Corbis-Bettmann*

Ring Lardner. His fic-
tional ballplayer wowed
Virginia Woolf.
*UPI/Corbis-Bettmann*

Heywood Broun. Modern, sophisticated baseball writing starts here.
*UPI/Bettmann*

Red Smith in his prime at the *New York Herald Tribune*.
*Author's collection*

Stanley Woodward at the keys, as a football coach, "Jock" Sutherland, looks on.
*Associated Press*

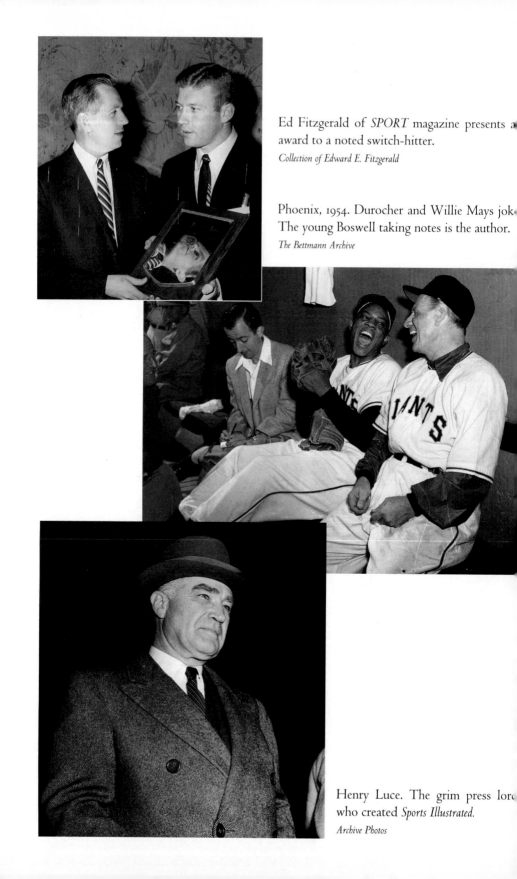

Ed Fitzgerald of *SPORT* magazine presents a award to a noted switch-hitter.

*Collection of Edward E. Fitzgerald*

Phoenix, 1954. Durocher and Willie Mays joke The young Boswell taking notes is the author.

*The Bettmann Archive*

Henry Luce. The grim press lord who created *Sports Illustrated*.

*Archive Photos*

John Tibby, the news editor at *SI*.
*Sports Illustrated*

Longtime *SI* writer, editor, and loyalist Robert Creamer.
*Sports Illustrated*

Bernard Malamud. He looked to baseball for literature and wrote *The Natural*.
*Archive Photos/David Lees*

THE WEATHER

Today: Fair and continued cool;
moderate northwesterly winds.

Tomorrow: Fair and continued
cool; moderate northwest to
westerly winds.

Temperatures Yesterday: Max., 44.1; Min., 11.4.
Today's Probable Range: Max., 44: Min., 46.
Humidity at 3 p. m. Yesterday: 71%
Expected Humidity This Afternoon: 43-55%.

Detailed Report and Map—Page 34

# NEW YORK
# Herald

European Edition Published Daily in Paris

112th Year VOL. CXII NO. 18,473

Copyright, 1952
New York Herald Tribune Inc.

WEDNESDAY, OCTOBER 8. 1952

# Yankees Win 4th Series in Row;
# Defeat Dodgers in 7th Game, 4-2

## Mantle, Woodling Wallop Home Runs

### Stengel Uses 4 Pitchers; Kuzava Foils Brooklyn Attempts for Late Rally

By Roger Kahn

Every year is next year for the Yankees.

Yesterday, at Ebbets Field, Casey Stengel's proud Bombers swept past the Dodgers, 4 to 2, and retained the championship of the baseball world. The Dodgers have never held the title. It is a birthright of the Yankees, who now can boast fifteen and the last four in a row.

The bitterly earned victory gave New York the forty-ninth World Series, four games to three, after the Dodgers had won three of the first five. Never before has a Yankee team managed by Stengel been forced to scramble so hard to win and in taking the three previous series six games were the most the Bombers needed. This time they were forced to the limits of their man power and their endurance. There was a ring of greatness in the way the Yankees responded, as individuals and as a team.

**Mantle Bats In Two Runs**

Mickey Mantle, the twenty-year-old golden boy, was a hero because he hit a home run in the sixth inning and put the Yankees ahead, 3 to 2. Then he hit a single in the seventh that scored Gil McDougald with the final run.

Bob Kuzava, the strong left-hander, was a hero because when Stengel summoned him he responded with perfection. Kuzava became the fourth Yankee pitcher when he replaced Vic Raschi after the Dodgers had loaded the bases with one out in the seventh. He was the last pitcher the Yankees needed since he stopped Duke Snider and Jackie Robinson, ending Brooklyn's last threat to Yankee domination. The eighth and ninth innings were easy for Kuzava.

There were lesser heroes, too. Johnny Mize, who batted in the first Yankee run with a fourth-inning single, slapped away from his power; Gene Woodling, whose homer scored the second New York run in the sixth, Allie Reynolds who fought fatigue, pitched two innings and was credited with the victory. All can be proud of their effort.

**33,195 Chilled Fans Sit**

For Brooklyn, Pee Wee Reese, the professional, who singled home Billy Cox and tied the game in the fifth and Joe Black, who started and lost, falling under the burden of a season's weariness, were game and gallant in their failing cause.

But it was the Yankees who were the great ones yesterday—the Yankees as a team.

A crowd of 33,195 fans sat in

Associated Press

THE WINNER IS ON THE LEFT—Yankee Manager Casey Stengel being congratulated by Dodger Manager Charlie Dressen after Stengel's team won the seventh and final game of the Series

## Beria Warns 'U. S. Imperialists' Of 'Invincible' Soviet Strength

### Party Congress Cheers as Secret Police Head Prophesies 'Disaster' for War Makers

By The United Press

MOSCOW, Oct. 7.—Lavrenti P. Beria, a Soviet Deputy Prime Minister, charged tonight that the United States is pushing the world's peoples "into the abyss of a world war." Mr. Beria told wildly cheering delegates to the Soviet Communist party congress here that such a war would speed up the Americans' "own collapse and their own disaster."

After Mr. Beria spoke, the congress approved a Central Committee report reviewing the last twelve years and promising that "capitalist nations" will be defeated "if they dare to attack the motherland."

World War II showed the world that Soviet strength is "invincible," Mr. Beria said.

"However," he added, "the lessons of history have not been learned by all. The American imperialists who have become opulent on two world wars are drunk with the mad idea of establishing world domination."

He said the Americans "are again , pushing peoples into the abyss of a world war, although there is no doubt in

## 3 Magistrates' Courts Set Up On Fire Hazard

### Murtagh Announces Policy; 'Bad Area' Inspections Planned Block by Block

Chief Magistrate John M. Murtagh announced yesterday that he and two other magistrates henceforth will devote themselves exclusively and "indefinitely" to fire hazard cases.

Announcement of the new policy was made by Mr. Murtagh after a conference in his office at 100 Centre St. with Frederick S.

## South Koreans Exceed G. I.s At Front by 50%

### Lovett Praises Them as 'Very Good Force,' Their Fatality Rate Is Higher

By C. B. Allen

WASHINGTON, Oct. 7.—Secretary of Defense Robert A. Lovett said today that South Korean troops on the Far Eastern firing line outnumber Americans by 50 per cent, are suffering proportionately higher fatalities in battle and have generally demonstrated that they are "a very good fighting force."

He added that "we are doing all we safely can" to put still greater numbers into the defense of their homeland consistent with adequate preparatory training.

Secretary Lovett told a pentagon press conference that the combat record of the South Koreans was "a great credit to the Army's training system" under which they have been schooled. He said it has been and will continue to be the Army's policy "to employ South Korean

# Allies Retal
# Two Outpos
# In Korea Hi

## ROKs Plug Brea
## In Bayonet Bat

### RedsFire93,000 Rou
### in 24-Hour Barr
### Their Heaviest of

By Mac R. Johnson
From the Herald Tribune Bure
Copyright, 1952, New York Herald Tribu

TOKYO, Wednesday, Oct
Troops of the Republic of
9th Infantry Division recap
an outpost position on White
Hill on the Korean central
early today. In a separate s
U. N. troops also recapture
outpost that had been lost
Reds on Finger Ridge.

Fighting was heavy too
half a dozen points along
battle line, with most of it
fined to the Chorwon area.
Horse Hill bore the brunt
Communist fall offensive
though the 8th Army doesn'
it an offensive.

**Heaviest Barrage of Wa**

In the twenty-four-hour
the Communists fired their
est barrages of the war, som
000 rounds. The Communists
been stockpiling ammunitio
the front despite Air Force
to cut railroads, blow up
bridges and burn rolling sto
trucks. It was a record out
Red guns. The 8th Army est
it was twice as heavy as any
ous Red barrage in the
eight-month-old war.

Fighting was still quite
on White Horse Hill, Arr
Ridge, east of Kumsong, so
Pyonggang.

[The Associated Press re
from Seoul that Gen. James
Fleet Wednesday said the
munists in North Korea ha
strength for "sizable limite
jective attacks throughout O
and November." The United
8th Army commander said
ever, the Reds could not a
a general attack for s
period.]

**Seesaw Battle**

In the action on White
Hill, the ROKs had beaten
Chinese company at 7:30
yesterday, but two hours la
the outpost to two Chinese
panies in hand-to-hand f
on the crest that lasted for
minutes.

U. N. artillery and mort
then hammered the Red-he
(Continued on page 4, colu

## Road Is Paved With
### By the Army in K

SEOUL, Oct. 7 (UP).—
"prospectors" chipped aw
roads in the area of Pyong
day after it was discover
highways were surfaced wi
ore.

"The gold rush is on,"
Army officer who explaine
engineers had coated the

**une**

## Late City
## Edition

West 41st Street. New York 36, N. Y.
Telephone PEnnsylvania 6-4000

**FIVE - CENTS**

# ...hower Sees Revolt
# ...mocratic Ranks on
# ...ght Control' Issue

## ...ys He Will Destroy ...cy'BeyondRepair'

### ...He Asserts Eisenhower Joins ...enace, Has No Solution

...s address at Detroit—Page 16.

Adlai
that
h the
Unit-
nd he
...it D.
...ly" in
...ounist
...as of-
...silence
5,000
here,
...s first
when
...bun-
great

...e said.
...unism
...ealing
..e, long

before Sen. Joseph R. McCarthy
R., Wis., "suddenly appeared on
the scene and began his wild and
reckless campaign against the integrity of our government itself."
Gov. Stevenson asked what Gen.
Eisenhower proposed to do;
whether he planned to dismiss J.
Edgar Hoover, the Federal Bureau
of Investigation director; Gen.
Walter Bedell Smith, head of the
Central Intelligence Agency, and
other "experienced men" whom the
Governor promised he would keep
on in his administration.

"I think we are entitled to ask:
'Is the Republican candidate seriously interested in trying to root
Communists out of the government, or is he only interested in
scaring the American people to get
votes?'" Gov. Stevenson said.

The Governor said that while
(Continued on page 16, column 3)

## Cites Loyalty Oath FightatConvention

### GeneralatPortland,Ore., Warns of 'Whole-Hog' U. S. Forestry Control

Text of Eisenhower address at Portland, Ore.—Page 14

**By Homer Bigart**

PORTLAND, Ore., Oct. 7—Gen.
Dwight D. Eisenhower today as-
sailed the Democrats as "the party
of thought control," and insisted
that the Republicans opposed reg-
imentation in political thinking.
He said his "crusade" welcomed
differences of opinion so long as
the diverse groups supported basic
American ideals.

He told a capacity crowd of
5,000 in Portland's Civic Auditori-
um that the Democrats tried to
impose "thought control" on various party elements at the Democratic convention. Independent
elements of the Democratic party
were now in revolt against dicta-
tion by Administration leaders, he
said.

The general returned to his attack on what he called "whole-
hog" Federal government and
warned that Federal agencies were
seeking monopolistic control over
the nation's forests.

Thousands cheered the general
along a two-mile drive through
downtown Portland.

#### Cites Agencies' Squabble

He said the national forests
"should not be turned into a vehicle for Federal control of the nation's entire forest economy," and
charged that two Federal agencies
in Washington, the Department of
the Interior and the Department
of Agriculture, were squabbling
over which should supervise forest
lands.

"In another bureau," he said,
"actual fraud and favoritism crept
in. Only last summer, in your own
State of Oregon, a Federal court
canceled the sale of Indian timber
as fraudulent and ordered its re-
sale to the highest bidder, not to
a favorite!"

He accused the Administration
of trying to "corrupt" the purpose
of the forest and land management agencies. "Their political
bosses," he said, "have departed
far from the purpose laid down by
that great Republican conserva-
tionist, Gifford Pinchot. They have
reached out to acquire more and
more private land with more and
more dominating control."

#### Speaks at Tacoma

Earlier, at Tacoma, Wash., he
told a crowd that corruption in
Washington had become an inter-

## ...tal Truman Says ...on Presidency Is ...249 Civilian's Job

### ...nt of Calls Professional Soldiers ...rnout Unfit for Post; Labels ...Mark Eisenhower 'Deceitful'

Text of Truman address at Colorado Springs—Page 10

voters
..'s two-
...ncrease
record
...n 1944,
...e two-
...presi-

...8 was

...fonday,
...d that
...ttering
...shown
...always
...e turn-
...that of

...e regis-
...he first
...h that

1948
317,382
174,332
201,900
138,976
16,335

**By James E. Warner**

DENVER, Oct. 7.—President
Truman, arriving here tonight on
his whistlestop campaign, got a
tumultuous welcome from a crowd
of 10,000, who heard him continue
his attacks on Gen. Dwight D.
Eisenhower.

Mr. Truman, who spoke from
the steps of Union Station,
declared: "Professional generals
should not be President. A man
who spends all his life in the
army can't possibly learn political
life . . ."

He said a civilian should always
head the government.

Mr. Truman quoted what he said
was a statement made in 1948 by
Gen. Eisenhower that a military
man is not qualified for the Presi-
dency, and got a big laugh from
the crowd.

Zachary Taylor and U. S. Grant,
both generals who became Presidents, were "babes in the woods"

A front page to remember.

# III
# The Artists

Dodger manager Charlie Dressen and Brooklyn fans. *UPI/Corbis–Bettmann*

World Series action at Ebbets Field. *AP/Wide World Photos*

swing to remember. Roy Campanella puts one in the seats. *AP/Wide World Photos*

ackie Robinson as a guest expert on "Information, Please." Others, from left: John Kieran,
Rufus Clement, Franklin P. Adams. *UPI/Corbis-Bettmann*

Joe Black firing the hummer.

*Author's collection*

In your face. Robinson arguing with umpire
Al Barlick.

*UPI/Bettmann*

He's in charge here. Casey Stengel, manager
of the Yankees.

*UPI/Bettmann Newsphotos*

Good form. Nice power. Mickey Mantle blows
a bubble.

*Author's collection*

It only happened once. The Brooklyn Dodgers win the World Series. Though injured, Jackie Robinson, number 42, still leads triumphal charge from dugout to mound.
*UPI/Bettmann*

The centerfielder from Olympus plucks one. Cleveland manager Al Lopez called this catch and the throw that followed "the best play ever made by anybody in baseball."

*Author's collection*

that not a single starter was able to win ten games. You anticipated the Yankees winning two. As you drove to the ballpark, you composed a lead. "The Philadelphia Athletics made a serious mistake at Yankee Stadium yesterday. They showed up." You liked the flippant tone of that lead. But the Athletics surprised you and many others when Arnold Portocarrero held the Yankees to six hits in the second game and Philadelphia won, 4 to 2. You now had to compose a lead not for what you anticipated, but for what actually happened—a split double-header. You had to discard the lead you wanted to write. That complicated the process of writing against a deadline. Worse yet, you might try to preserve your little joke and write something like this: "For a time at Yankee Stadium, it looked as though the Athletics had made a mistake by showing up. But . . ." Bad reporting when the story of the day is one Arnold Mario Portocarrero, a big kid from New York City. How had the Yankees let him get away?

I explained all this to John Knox Tibby over our first chill martini at the English Grill. He listened courteously; Jack Tibby was unfailingly a courteous man. But when he responded, he glossed over my point. "We are, um, professionals. I, mmmm, imagine you agree with that. As professionals we know more than the spectators. Actually, most of the time, we do have a pretty fair idea of who is going to win, wouldn't you say?"

"If I knew with any certainty, I'd bet."

That was bravado. But actually, in his polite, bulldog way, Tibby was on to something. Training says, make your mind blank. Never anticipate. If you're going to be a good baseball writer—or a good poet—you have to be willing to be surprised. But underneath, deeply within, you do think you really know who is going to win. Some days the feeling is strong; some days it's faint. But it's always there. On this Thursday at the English Grill in Rockefeller Center, unfortunately I had a powerful hunch. But I was damned if I'd tell Tibby.

He ordered two more martinis and continued to press me. Who was going to win? Near the end of the second drink, I cracked. "Time's up for the Yankees, Jack. It's the Twilight of the Gods."

"Let's get back to the office," Tibby said.

Upstairs, he came out from behind his desk armed with paper and pencil. "Here's the layout," he said, and sketched quickly. "This page, the opener, has one big picture, and you know what that picture says? That picture says 'Baseball.' Here, on the second page, we run a smaller picture. That one says, 'Crowd.'"

He was clearly excited. "Now"—Tibby indicated the top of the second page—"here is where we run your marvelous headline." He drew:

### The Twilight
### Of the Gods

"And here, just below that, we have your byline." He printed my name in letters as large as the headline, leaned close and said intimately: "What do you think?"

"It's not my wonderful headline. It's Wagner's. The German word is Götterdämmerung."

Tibby looked beyond me and said as if in shock, "Of course. You seem to have forgotten that my wife, Emily, is an orchestral musician. Obviously, what I mean is, your . . . um . . . utilization . . . of Wagner in this context is what's marvelous.

"We're going to fly you out to Cleveland, first class."

I did some serious rooting after that. Come on, Yankees. Come on Casey and Whitey and Yogi and Mick. You can beat these guys. I liked the Indians, but I was rooting against them because I knew that there was only one way to save my article from flying that pompous Wagnerian headline. The Yankees had to win. Damn, the English-Grill martinis. Why had I opened my mouth? I didn't need that racist bastard, Wagner, intruding himself into my stuff.

When Sunday came, I saw a double-header for the ages. I was not alone. Fully 86,563 people, then the largest crowd ever for a major league game, filled Cleveland's Municipal Stadium. The Stadium seating capacity was officially stated as 73,500—inexact because there were benches rather than seats in the center field bleachers and capacity varied with many factors, including the girth of the fans and the weather.

On a cold day, when people wore overcoats, fewer bottoms could wedge onto those distant benches.

This was a hungry crowd, assembling from Ohio and Western Pennsylvania and Western New York State. A Midwestern crowd, panting and lusting to see the arrogant Yankees—Snooty New York, Swaggering Snobs, Big Eastern Bucks—to see the arrogant Yankees put to death. Cleveland was 6 ½ games ahead, with thirteen left to play, a good lead, but not a safe lead in a pennant race against Stengel's Yankees. Many thought there was no such thing as a safe lead over Stengel's Yankees.

If the Yankees swept, won both ends of the double-header, they would come within 4 ½ games of the front-runners—and momentum would be powering the New York team. If the ballclubs split, the Indians would be back in the pregame situation: "safe lead, but is any lead safe?" But should the Indians win two and go 8 ½ games up with eleven remaining, this rousing American League race would be settled. Al Lopez's Cleveland Indians would win.

On the morning of September 12, buses, trains, aircraft, and cars poured excited ball fans into the city that lay on the shore of murky Lake Erie. The Yankees breakfasted downtown at the Hotel Cleveland. I sipped coffee with Jerry Coleman, the fighter pilot back from Korea, and now Stengel's favorite utility infielder. "You come to bury us?" Coleman said.

"Win and I get to praise you."

"Sure," said Charlie Silvera, backup catcher behind Yogi Berra. "I'll write your lead. The slowly dying Yankees. The slowly dying Yankees leaking blood. Very funny."

Stengel motioned for me to join his table. "So you've gone to work for some magazine," he said. "You gotta watch them magazine people. They'll make yer stuff look funny, if you let 'em, and I defy anyone to say this team ain't worth a quarter. I don't want to blow up another club, because the race is still going, you can be sure, but Cleveland has played tree-mendous and we been trying to catch 'em, so how can you say our team ain't worth a quarter?"

I rode the Yankee players' bus to Municipal Stadium. Less conversation now. The men were getting ready. Even Stengel fell silent.

Around the batting cage, the Indians seemed nonchalant. "This is not a rough day," said handsome, black-haired, high-cheekboned Bobby Avila, of Vera Cruz, Mexico. "All year we play. Now we play. Good team. We play okay."

"When you write your story, can you forget the choke-up stuff?" Al Rosen asked. "I don't know if you can. But, look, I'm playing out here every day. I know what's going on. Bobby here is gonna lead the league in batting [at .341]. I'm gonna knock in 100 RBIs again. We don't beat the Yankees because they choke and we don't lose to the Yankees because we choke. Don't overcomplicate it. The team that wins is simply the better team that day."

I found Al Lopez sitting in his office. He winked and said, "Doing any reading *now?*"

"Are you going out into the clubhouse to give a pep talk to your team?"

"Like Durocher?" Lopez said. "No. I'm not. Not a chance. This isn't Little League. I don't have to go into the clubhouse to talk to my players and hold their hands. They know what's going on. I don't have to go in there and talk to them like they were children. Lemon starts the first game. Wynn goes in the second."

Bob Lemon, thirty-four years old, and at his peak, had already won 21 games. He had been a 20-game winner in six of the last seven seasons. He threw a sinking fastball and a slider that he spotted with precision at the knees on the outside corner. He kept everything low and kept the batters beating the baseball into the ground.

Stengel started his marvelous twenty-five-year-old lefthander, Whitey Ford, who threw a wide variety of pitches, probably including an illegal "scuff ball." Opposing players claimed that in tight spots Ford scuffed the baseball, with his belt buckle, and that these scuff balls became unhittable sinkers. The umpires said hell no. Batters who made out, they insisted, always griped that they were being cheated.

Against these starters, neither team would do much hitting. Ford went six innings, then told Stengel his left shoulder felt tight. With the teams tied 1–1, Stengel sent Allie Reynolds to relieve in the seventh.

The Superchief had better stuff than he had luck. With one out, leftfielder Al Smith beat out a bunt. Reynolds walked Bobby Avila.

Larry Doby bounced to first—the ball was hit too slowly to start a double play—and both runners advanced. Al Rosen, just about the best clutch hitter in the league, stood in looking grim. Reynolds brushed Rosen with a high, tight fastball. Rosen glared. Reynolds glared back and threw a hard slider low and away. That is textbook pitching, intimidate the batter with an inside blazer, then throw a breaking pitch low and away. Rosen was not intimidated. He leaned in and cuffed the slider on a line toward the right center field gap. Mickey Mantle raced over, but muffed the ball. Two Indians scored. Rosen had just batted in his 99th and 100th runs. He had now batted in 100 runs or more for five consecutive seasons.

Al Smith was safe on an infield error in the eighth. Avila singled to right and Smith scored when the ball skipped through the legs of Enos Slaughter. In their most important game of the season, the Yankees had made successive errors. Bob Lemon and his sinker were taking away the Yankee bats. He struck out Mantle three times. No Yankee homered. Lemon handcuffed Stengel's powerful team. In effect beating both Ford and Reynolds, Cleveland won this exciting game, 4–1. The Indians' lead was a commanding 7 ½ games.

During the double-header intermission I made my way through the crowded grandstands to the Cleveland dressing room. It was a slow trip, among celebrants. By the time I got to the clubhouse, most of the Indians had returned to the field for Game Two. Lemon sat alone in front of his locker, drinking a beer and smiling at the ceiling.

"Can you tell me how it feels?" I said.

He met my eyes. "Grand," Bob Lemon said. "It feels like a wedding day."

Early Wynn was a great-chested competitor out of small-town Alabama, every bit as fearsome as Allie Reynolds. Wynn threw a fine fastball, a good overhand curve, a hard knuckler and a harder knockdown pitch. "Burly Early Wynn," the sportswriters called him, and Burly Early despised batters and losing with a great, crackling fire of hatred. "What's wrong with that?" he demanded. "When a damn salesman loses a sale, he doesn't laugh. When I lose a ballgame, keep the hell out of my way."

Knocked out one day, Wynn went into a rage in the clubhouse and threw furniture and clothing. He flung his sport jacket into the air and it popped a ceiling panel and stayed there, dangling in an odd way. Noting the jacket after the game ended, Al Rosen asked: "Wynn hang himself?"

Wynn seemed to enjoy knocking down hitters, watching them dive onto dirt. When an interviewer wondered if he would throw at his own mother, Wynn had a quick reply. "I'd have to," he said. "Mom was a pretty good curveball hitter." He had a nice, rough humor, but merriment vanished when he took the mound. Wynn was a warrior.

Still, as Stengel had reminded me, this beleaguered Yankee team was worth more than a quarter, and before Wynn settled into his rhythm, Yogi Berra cracked a knuckle ball into the upper deck in right for a two-run homer. The Yankees held that lead into the fifth inning. Then, with two out, Tommy Byrne, the Yankee starter, tried to fool Wynn with a change of pace. Wynn lined a single to center. Al Smith followed with another single. Stengel stayed with Byrne; his bullpen was weary. Avila singled, Wally Westlake doubled, and the Indians led, 3–2.

Now in the fading light, this fine Yankee team tried desperately to reach Wynn for the tying run. Or even reach him for a hit. But the big pitcher seemed to draw strength as he went along, draw strength from the very earth. Stout-chested, hard-throwing Early Wynn became untouchable. Stengel sent Enos "Country" Slaughter up to pinch hit in the ninth. Wynn struck him out with a hard, low knuckle ball.

Mantle hit next—twenty-two, the next DiMaggio, a world of promise. Wynn threw a high fastball by Mantle for strike three. It was Mantle's hundredth strikeout of the year.

Berra up. Home run in the first. Another would tie it. But Wynn had given up his homer for the day. He fanned Berra for his twelfth strikeout and the ballgame and the pennant. It was a long time ago, more than forty years, but I can still see Early Wynn, fierce master of the mound, exultant as he triumphed in the twilight.

I believe this was the best double-header I have ever seen. Two wonderful teams. Neither knew how to quit. Rosen and Berra and Bauer and Bobby Avila. Gladiators.

Of the four pitchers who started on that mild September day in the vast old Cleveland Stadium, three—Wynn, Ford, and Lemon— have been elected to the Baseball Hall of Fame. I mean it was hard to get a hit.

Gripped by excitement, I withdrew to my hotel room and wrote three thousand words in just four hours. I don't remember exactly what I wrote, but I ended with Bob Lemon talking. *Grand. It feels like a wedding day.*

Then I filed the story to *Sports Illustrated* by Western Union and the next morning I flew home and hurried to the office. I had done a hard job, I thought, and done it well.

"That was quite a lot of writing under pressure," Tibby said. "I don't believe anybody else at the magazine could have done that much work that quickly."

"Thanks." Perhaps Jack really wasn't such a stuffy guy. Different, sure, but not bad. Maybe today I'd buy *him* a martini.

"But if you have a minute, come into my office, won't you? I, uh, want to go over a thing or two."

He threw out my lead and typed a few lines on the size of the crowd, rewriting a wire service story. Then he composed an extraordinary paragraph, that would appear under my byline.

> The largest crowd that ever gathered to watch a baseball game went back to the fascinated contemplation of what had brought most of them to Municipal Stadium in the first place—the Cleveland Indians' effective demonstration that they are a better team than the five-time World Champion New York Yankees. As drama, it might very well have been entitled *The Twilight of the Gods*. While a band played brassily in left field, the Yankees followed Thor and Wotan into eclipse.

Tibby grinned as he wrote; he grinned and chuckled. "There it is," he said, when this dismaying paragraph was finished, "and it's just terrific, thanks to you."

"Jack," I said, slowly, "I don't write like that. Too many adjectives. You don't need the word fascinated before the word contemplation. You don't need the word effective before the word demonstration.

And now that I see it on paper, the Wagner stuff is a reach. Pretentious. And here. Look. You've written that the band played brassily. Bad adverb. It's a brass band, for God's sake. How is it going to play? Woodwindily?"

"Everybody here admires your sense of humor," Tibby said. Then he wrote, "The Yankees died hard and Cleveland watched with deepgrained satisfaction."

"Cleveland is a city, not a person," I said. "Cities don't see. Deepgrained doesn't seem right, either."

"This is coming along beautifully," Tibby said. "You really are giving us great stuff."

When Tibby reached the passage in which Al Rosen hit a slider for two bases, he wrote, "Rosen hit a slider pitch."

"You don't say curveball pitch, or fastball pitch," I said.

"But this is different," Tibby said. "Who would know what a slider is, if we don't explain?"

I thought the story that appeared under my byline was truly awful. I saw myself humiliated before old newspaper colleagues, Smith and Rosenthal, before Al Lopez and Al Rosen and Casey Stengel. I didn't write with all those fruity Timestyle adjectives. Why bother with a byline if you publish collective prose?

"Why, indeed?" Red Smith said. Luce had hired him to write a weekly column and then assigned Tibby to edit Smith. "I assumed Luce wanted me because he liked my stuff in the *Trib*. I was in error. They change everything at that magazine and there is this one fellow up there, Tibby, who spends his days putting words into my copy that I have spent my life not using."

"Such as?" I said.

"Such as *moreover*. I'm going to resign as soon as I can without creating a fuss."

When I reviewed the proofs of my Cleveland story, I discovered not only a plateful of extra adjectives. I saw that even my carefully crafted conclusion was missing. The story now ended with some sharp comments by Stengel, but Bob Lemon's wonderful wedding-day observation lay in a dust bin.

"I did that," Sidney L. James, the managing editor, told me with pride. "That wasn't Jack Tibby killing that quote. That was me."

"Lemon said those things. He said exactly what I quoted him as saying."

"I'm sure he did," James said, "but that doesn't matter.

"It just didn't seem to me to be the sort of thing a winning pitcher actually would say, even though he did say it, if you understand me. In this magazine, we want them saying appropriate things, things that they ought to say. The wedding day comment was not appropriate. It was even a little effeminate.

"Yes, I'm sure this Lemon fellow said it.

"But I run this magazine and I'm the man who took it out."

I did not look at the mutilated Cleveland story again until the magazine bearing it appeared on newsstands. Then I noticed a curious thing. In their enthusiastic and imperious editing, Sid James and Jack Tibby had knocked out the score of the second game. The fact-checker failed to notice that the score was missing. She was not trained to check a fact that wasn't there.

Is there a worse sin in baseball writing than neglecting to tell the reader the final score of a ballgame?

Group journalism as an art form had a way to go.

# Willie's World Series

WHILE HENRY LUCE'S LATEST MAGAZINE was inventing the wonderful world of sport, the Giants and the Indians, springtime playmates, bore down on one another without veering, hellbent for a collision in the fall. This World Series would be one of the most memorable—and surprising—ever.

Months before, most expected yet another Yankee-Dodger World Series, the third in a row. With four Hall of Famers among eight starting position players, the Dodgers appeared to be the strongest team in the National League. But after losing consecutive World Series to the Yankees, Brooklyn changed managers for 1954 and the switch from gabby, open Charlie Dressen, to dour, brooding Walter Alston didn't work. Alston antagonized several veterans, including Jackie Robinson and Don Newcombe, and seemed indecisive. He was used to managing in the minor leagues where a ballclub numbered seventeen men. The twenty-five-man major league roster confused him. Alston didn't throw in pinch hitters the way Durocher did. He had no touch with pitchers. His players lost confidence in him and the rookie Brooklyn manager ran his veteran team out of the race.

The Milwaukee Braves with the great sluggers Eddie Mathews and Henry Aaron and the splendid starters, Warren Spahn and Lew Burdette, clearly were a coming powerhouse. But not yet. The Braves were three years away from a pennant in this rugged and contentious league.

No, the summer of 1954 was Willie's time and Leo's, a grand season for saturnine Sal Maglie and, say, that trade the Giants made with Milwaukee—the legend, Bobby Thomson, for the black-haired young lefthander, Johnny Antonelli—really worked. Thomson broke a leg sliding and played in only 43 games. At twenty-four, Antonelli matured all at once, won 21 and led the league with an earned run average of 2.30.

Every day that summer Durocher told Mays that he was the greatest ballplayer in the world. Sublimely happy, Willie batted .345 with 41 home runs. He became what Durocher told him that he was, the greatest ballplayer in the world.

"Now the dago pitcher," Durocher said, referring to Maglie, "is a different kettle of fish. If I let him get happy, he don't pitch good. So I get him mad. I say, 'Whatsa matter, you stupid wop, you choking?' He gets so mad he wants to kill me, but he don't. He takes his dago temper out on the fucking hitters." Like Wynn and Reynolds, Maglie was a master of the knockdown pitch. He was nicknamed Sal the Barber, in part as a racial comment on Italian barbers, but also because Maglie's fastball "shaved" chins. He told me once that he didn't believe in throwing knockdowns with a two-strike, no-ball count. "Then the knockdown is routine. It's expected. A good time to knock somebody down is when the count is two and two. To do that you've got to get your curveball over with a full count. I can."

The crowd at *Sports Illustrated* was excited by the idea of a World Series. "Who's going to win?" Jack Tibby said.

I fled for a drink with Bob Creamer, Dick Johnston's virgin, and Gerald Astor, the photo editor, both of whom had a decent feel for baseball. Creamer previously worked for an encyclopedia; the thought of covering a World Series transported him toward ecstasy. He was a Giant fan and bubbled quite a bit.

"You're the happiest man in America, except for Willie Mays," I suggested.

"It was cold in the encyclopedia offices where he worked," Astor said, "and dark."

I complimented Astor on a photo that ran with the Cleveland double-header story. Taken from ground level with the then novel 35-millimeter, single-lens-reflex camera, it caught Early Wynn in a fierce silhouette against the darkening September sky. In a way, Jack Tibby had gotten his wish. This picture did say baseball. Artistically, it was leagues beyond what any newspaper sports section was printing at the time.

"Yeah," Creamer said, "but we're running so many photos there isn't any room in the magazine for text."

"Sid James is a photo man," Astor said. "I don't entirely agree." Astor—Tibby described him as looking like Phil Silvers with hair—grinned and said: "I keep telling Sid, 'A word is worth a thousand pictures.'"

"Who's gonna win the World Series?" Creamer asked me.

"How the hell should I know?"

"You covered the two teams in spring training," Creamer said. "They played against each other twenty-one times."

I thought of that Pullman ride from Tulsa to eternity.

"The Giants won thirteen of the twenty-one," Creamer said. "That says something."

"You're rooting," I said.

"Damn right," Creamer said.

"The bookies," Astor said, "are picking Cleveland at nine to five."

"Look," I said, "I have an idea, but I'm damned if I'll tell you guys. Creamer, you'll blab to Tibby. Jerry, you're always with James. You guys will talk and they'll get some kind of preconceived idea and ruin my story again."

Astor looked thoughtful. "They can ruin your story without us," he said.

After a while, I found myself holding forth. "The rule of thumb is that pitching wins the Series. It has since Mathewson pitched those three shutouts in 1905. Why do the Yankees murder Brooklyn? Because of pitchers like Vic Raschi and Reynolds.

"Look at the Indian staff. Wynn, Lemon, Mike Garcia, Bob Feller. The best staff in the world. Cleveland has won III games. You want to hear my pick?"

"If we must," Astor said.

"All right. In this World Series, between the Indians and the Giants, whichever team has Willie Mays playing centerfield is going to win."

The first World Series day, September 29, broke beautiful and festive. The Polo Grounds, that old green horseshoe sitting in the flats between the Harlem River and the rise called Coogan's Bluff, was decked in bunting. An old, eccentric, rundown sort of character suddenly sported finery.

However frequently I visited the Polo Grounds, the shape of the playing field always was startling. The field ran just over 250 feet down the right and left field foul lines. Little League distances really. In dead center, where a green blockhouse rose between twin stands of bleachers, the distance was ridiculous in a different way: 483 feet to the blockhouse. Almost a tenth of a mile. Want to propel a baseball out of center field at the old Polo Grounds? Buy a bazooka.

"The World Series came to the Polo Grounds," Bob Cooke wrote in the *Herald Tribune*, "with its special All-American appeal, and with it came a crowd as traditional to our country as broad stripes and white stars. . . . In the balcony, the bleachers and the boxes, people watched shoulder to shoulder as though the ballpark were a vast living room. This well-mannered and cosmopolitan crowd seemed almost to be guests of the New York Giants."

General and Mrs. Douglas MacArthur watched from a box near the visitor's dugout. Laraine Day, Durocher's wife, sat with Spencer Tracy. Senator Herbert H. Lehman shared his box with Mrs. Carmine G. DeSapio, wife of the leader of Tammany Hall. Elsewhere you could spot Mrs. Lou Gehrig, Jackie Gleason and Don Ameche and Danny Kaye and Mrs. John McGraw. Mrs. John Hay Whitney, the former Betsy Cushing, attended with John Sims (Shipwreck) Kelly, a one-time Kentucky football star who had burst into high society. William G. Rabe of Great Neck, a vice-president of the Manufacturers Trust Company, arrived with his brother Frederick and five guests. They traveled up from the foot of Wall Street in a sixty-foot cabin cruiser. "The Polo Grounds," Cooke noted, "was a place for people to see and to be seen and call friendly greetings. But as game time approached everyone grew hushed with expectation."

Perry Como sang the National Anthem. The Giants ran onto the field and Maglie walked to the mound. A control pitcher, he threw three balls to Al Smith, Cleveland's lead-off hitter. Then Maglie plunked Smith in the ribs with ball four. "If I'm going to walk you," The Barber was pointing out, "I might as well hurt you."

Bob Avila singled to right, where Don Mueller fumbled the ball. Smith went to third. Lefthander Don Liddle began throwing in the bullpen. Maglie retired Doby and Rosen on pop flies, but Vic Wertz, a lefthanded power hitter, poled a triple over Mueller's head. The Indians led, 2–0.

The Giants tied the score in the third on singles by Whitey Lockman and Alvin Dark, a walk to Mays and a base hit by Henry Thompson. Then the game settled into a tense pattern, as tie ballgames often do, when nobody will get any more runs until a starting pitcher tires.

Maglie wobbled in the eighth. He knocked down Larry Doby, and then walked him. He snapped a curve, but missed his spot, low and away, and Rosen grounded a single to deep short. Durocher sent his coach Fred Fitzsimmons to the mound to tell Maglie that he was coming out of the game. Durocher always left this mission to a coach. He didn't want pitchers arguing with him; their disputing a deputy would, of course, be pointless. Don Liddle, a lefthander, came in to face the lefthanded Wertz.

The dressing rooms in the Polo Grounds were lodged in the blockhouse behind center field. While Liddle took his eight warmup pitches, Sal Maglie made his way toward the clubhouse. His shoulders were bent. His face was coated with sweat. He limped a little. The New York crowd rose to applaud. Maglie made a little wave of thanks to the people in the bleachers who were cheering him.

Bob Creamer and I had left the press area behind home plate. I said vaguely that I wanted to get a feel for the crowd. Creamer followed. We were standing at the back of the lower deck, between third and home. Liddle threw a shoulder-high fastball and Wertz hit a tremendous high line drive to center. I had a nice view of the wallop. It was a monster. "Ballgame." I thought. When you see a game every day, as I had for three seasons, you judge the ball more quickly than the fans. *Ballgame, ballgame, ballgame.* This was three bases. Two runs for the Indians. Then surely somebody would score Vic Wertz and . . .

At the instant of impact, bat on ball, Willie Mays turned his back and fled. He had taken one, quick, professional look and now he ran, with his back to the plate, on a straight line toward the bleachers, just to the right of dead center field. The bleacher wall was 450 feet from home plate. Mays ran and ran. As his toe spikes touched the narrow cinder track at the base of the bleachers, and the wall—a hard, unyielding wall with no padding—loomed before his face, he took the ball almost directly over his head. It carried a shade to the left of the button on his Giant cap. Then Willie stole the baseball out of the air. He spun and threw on the fly clear back to the infield. All Cleveland got out of Vic Wertz's prodigious drive was a worthless base for Larry Doby who tagged up and advanced to third. Durocher replaced Liddle with hard-throwing Marv Grissom, who walked the next hitter but held the Indians scoreless.

In the tenth inning with one out Lemon walked Mays. He had seen Willie hit all spring; he was aware of Willie's power. On Lemon's first pitch to Hank Thompson, Mays broke for second. The throw from backup catcher Mickey Grasso bounced fifteen feet short of the base. Willie told me later that the steal was his own idea. When Lemon loosened up to pitch the tenth, Grasso had not thrown the last pitch through to second base, as custom dictates. "When I saw that," Willie said, "I figured this catcher had a sore arm. I can beat him. And I did."

Hank Thompson walked. Durocher sent a free-swinging, hard-drinking Alabama country boy named James Lamar Rhodes to pinch hit for Monte Irvin. They called Rhodes "Dusty." Some said that *all* big leaguers named "Rhodes" are nicknamed Dusty. (According to my record books, only one "Dusty" Rhodes—a pitcher—ever played in the big leagues before.)

Lemon threw a good outside breaking ball and "Dusty" Rhodes pulled it gently in the air to right. Second baseman Bobby Avila ran back, but the fly had just enough carry to reach the first row of seats, above a sign marked 257 feet. I had never before seen an infielder run back for what would be a home run.

Creamer loosed a quiet, intense, "Yea."

"Stop cheering, Bob, and figure out this game for me. Vic Wertz hits a 450-foot line drive and he's out. Rhodes hits a 258-foot popup and it's a homer."

"I can't figure out this game," Creamer said.

No matter. The Giants had won, 5–2.

A curious episode took place in the winning clubhouse. Harold Rosenthal of the *Herald Tribune* asked Durocher if Mays's catch was the greatest catch Willie had made.

Durocher turned ugly. "What the *fuck* are you talking about, Harold? Willie makes *fucking* catches like that every day. Do you keep your *fucking* eyes closed in the press box?" Durocher went on in this vein for several minutes. Twenty reporters were gathered around him. For some reason, perhaps simple nastiness, Durocher was humiliating Rosenthal before colleagues. Nor was there any way to stop him. Durocher's voice could shatter bulletproof glass. Besides, he was the big man in this crowd.

I steered Rosenthal to the Cleveland dressing room. "It was a fine baseball game," Al Lopez said. "The only thing I didn't like about it was the Rhodes homer. A game that good should end with something a little more, er, what's the word I mean."

"A drive longer from bow to stern?" Bob Cooke said.

"Something like that," Lopez said.

I told him about Durocher's comments and Lopez grew indignant. "I've been playing ball since I was a kid. I've been around the major leagues for thirty years. That was the greatest catch I've ever seen. Just the catch, mind you.

"Now put it all together. The catch. The throw. The pressure on the kid.

"I'd say that's the best play anybody ever made in baseball.

"I got no idea, no idea at all, what Durocher is taking about."

The Series was over. The 1954 World Series was settled when Willie made his catch. Some will disagree, but after the catch, the Indians had no chance. Deep down they knew the transcendent truth of that base-ball season. Nobody could defeat a team with Willie Mays. He did whatever it took to beat you.

This Cleveland team, this winner of 111 games, did not roll over. They were better and braver than that. Early Wynn went out next day and began to pitch a masterpiece. With Lemon defeated, Cleveland looked to Wynn, winner of 23 games. "If there was one ballgame that I had to have and I could pitch anybody in our league," Casey Stengel told me, "it would be the big, mean feller that pitches for Cleveland and which is named . . . wait . . . I got it . . . Wynn."

Johnny Antonelli opened Game Two for the Giants with a fastball and Al Smith cracked it over the roof of the nearby left field stands. Wynn led, 1–0. He then set down the Giants in order through four innings with flawless and commanding no-hit pitching.

But in the fifth, Wynn walked Mays. Having seen all that pound-ing power through those twenty-one spring exhibition games, the Cleveland staff wanted to make sure Mays got nothing he could hit out of the park. That sort of ultra-careful pitching leads to bases on balls. And in this case an end to Wynn's perfection.

Hank Thompson singled Mays to third. Durocher sent Dusty Rhodes to hit for Irvin. Wynn decked Rhodes, a fastball, spinning the batter face down into the dirt. Rhodes got up and hit a short fly to center, where Larry Doby was playing too deep. The ball bounced. Mays scored the tying run and Thompson went to third, beating Doby's weak throw. In the press box, Red Smith suggested, "We're witnessing a tale of two center fielders." When Cleveland failed to turn a double play on Johnny Antonelli's one-out grounder, Thompson scored and the Giants took a 2–1 lead.

Rhodes went out to play left field and came to bat again in the seventh inning. Wynn once more knocked him into the dirt of the bat-ter's box. Now when he got up, Rhodes slammed a line drive against the roof of the stands in right center. The Giants won Game Two, 3–1.

One postgame episode burns in my memory. After this tough defeat, Early Wynn sat in full uniform on a three-legged stool in front of his locker. He held a large paper cup of beer in his right hand. His left hand gripped the stub of a cigar. He was staring downward. Reporters fluttered around Al Lopez, talked to Al Rosen and Larry

Doby, but none dared approach Wynn. The pitcher looked something like Rodin's "The Thinker," but in a great rage.

"What about this ballpark, Early?" I said. By giving him a chance to knock the Polo Grounds, I thought I might start dialogue.

"Horseshit park."

"Um, ah, on the homer, what did Rhodes hit?"

"Horseshit pitch."

"Was it a slider or what?"

"Horseshit knuckler."

For the first time, Wynn looked at me. He drew his right hand back ever so slightly and a disturbing thought struck. If I asked another question, Wynn would throw his beer into my face. I moved on.

In later years, after we had become friends, Wynn said, "You had that just about right. But you wouldn't have gotten the beer in your face. All over your suit is more like it. That way you woulda got stuck for a cleaning bill, which you deserved. I didn't appreciate your talking to me just then."

The Giants flew to Cleveland on a chartered Capital Airlines plane. The Indians rode home on a New York Central special. Next day the Giants took a six-run lead against Mike Garcia and three relievers and won, 6–2. Finally, on Saturday, October 2, the New York Giants won cruising, 7–4, and clinched the fifth and final World Series victory in their long history.

Back in New York, Jack Tibby wanted to know what I intended to write.

"I'm never sure until I actually type my story."

Not good enough. Tibby hustled me to Martini City—the English Grill—and started his patterned, painstaking interrogation. I mentioned Durocher's strange attack on Harold Rosenthal. That wouldn't do, Tibby said. Our readers didn't care about the problems reporters faced and anyway the story was . . . a . . . little . . . *nasty.*

"That's the idea," I said. "Durocher is a nasty character."

Tibby thought for a while. "Do we really want to introduce that concept into the wonderful world of sport?"

I described Early Wynn in his anger.

"Even if you clean up the language there," Tibby said, "what's the point?"

"The point is that it is very, very tough to lose a game in the World Series. It's horrible to lose after you've pitched well."

"*Sports Illustrated* is about winning. We're not about losing."

"Mays," I said. "There's a winner. I want to write my whole story about Willie Mays."

"I've been following this World Series closely," Tibby said. "Aren't there other important players? This pitcher Antonelli? This pinch batsman Rhodes?"

"They're part of it. But I think I ought to concentrate on Willie, who is just the greatest player in the world. Maybe go up to his apartment right now and talk to him."

"That approach is too restrictive. We need something more general."

Was I imagining this, or was Jack Tibby resisting the idea that my World Series story—the story that would lead the magazine—should focus on a Negro?

Was the magazine racist? Or was it just elitist? Whatever, it was not a happy place.

The story I wrote on the 1954 World Series was adequate. As recently as 1994, someone paid me to reprint it in an anthology. But it is pallid compared to what I should have done and what I might have done with more encouragement and less neurotic editing.

Robert Creamer wrote the best story in *Sports Illustrated*'s first World Series issue. It began:

> Henry Thompson scudded over the foul line, almost awkward in his anxiety, and clutched the weak little pop foul. He jumped up and down in his excitement, waved the ball over his head, ran to Pitcher John Antonelli for a moment and then turned, still clutching the ball and made for the Giant dugout. It was the third out of the ninth inning of the fourth game. The World Series was over. Cleveland had lost.
>
> Under the grandstands a fat-faced hawker held the price on miniature celluloid baseball dolls at a dollar.

"The Series is over," a prospective buyer said. "I'll give you half a buck."

The hawker was impassive.

"You can't bargain with me," he said. "The price is a dollar."

"The Series is over," the buyer insisted. "When do you think you're going to sell them? Tomorrow?"

The hawker looked away, his face still impassive.

"The price is a dollar," he said, almost sullenly.

It was difficult for anyone from out of town to understand the hawker's attitude, but the city of Cleveland knew how he felt.

*Sports Illustrated* ran this piece anonymously in a section called "Soundtrack" which began with the following item:

**Say hey!**
*SI* went to its first World Series last week.

"We could both quit together," Red Smith told me, "except I've already resigned. I don't see how they can stay in business, anyway." The magazine was said to be losing between $60,000 and $70,000 a week. Staffers at *Time* and *Life* were furious. The losses were cutting into their profit-sharing plans. Henry Luce didn't much care. He was going to make *Sports Illustrated* a profitable magazine, even if it took him ten years.

When I told Tibby I would be leaving, he invited me to his home and gently said that I was making a mistake. He and I, he insisted, had already begun to revolutionize sports journalism. "I liken you to a modern Donner," Tibby added. "Except you've crossed the pass to safety without realizing it."

Next day I cleaned out my desk as quickly as I could.

# The Mick
## Hercules or Bacchus?

*I loved playing baseball. Nobody could have
loved playing ball as much as me.*
—MICKEY MANTLE

## I

He came out of northeastern Oklahoma, a wonder of power, a whirl-wind of speed. But there were problems even as he materialized godlike in the outfield at Yankee Stadium. That first season, he signed on with an agent, one Allen Savitt, who guaranteed him a fortune from endorsements, his life story and such. Commission? Oh, er, ah, the agent said, 50 percent of all your earnings, but wait until you see how much we make. We're talking millions.

Millions? That sounded great to a lead miner's son. But say, friend, fer how long will this dern contract run? Oh, er, we'll get along great, Savitt said. We'll be together making millions of dollars for the rest of your natural-born life.

The kid signed. He signed away 50 percent of his collateral income for all eternity. Part of the kid was bumpkin; the rest was yokel.

When Allen Savitt slid toward bankruptcy, he sold half the con-tract to a stripteaser named Holly. The kid didn't mind. He thought Holly was beautiful. Besides, he got to sleep with her.

Then, after a while, Holly needed money. She sold *her* story to
*Confidential* magazine, the *National Enquirer* of the era. *Confidential*'s headline, above Holly's story and picture, shattered the customary Yankee
calm:

I Own Twenty-Five Per Cent of Mickey Mantle!
And Sometimes . . . 100 Per Cent!!

The Yankees were the most corporate of the sixteen major league
teams; the men who owned the franchise liked to project an image of
grandeur. Control and grandeur. They loved those newspaper stories
that began: "The lordly New York Yankees." Now here came the
team's great prospect, the future of the Bronx, exposed in a sordid
business deal, and charged implicitly with sleeping with a woman of
surpassing congeniality. No high crimes or misdemeanors lurked here.
When these events broke, in the summer of '51, Mantle still was an
unmarried man. But he was supposed to conduct himself like a Yankee, moving, as DiMaggio and Gehrig before him, with a suggestion of
elegance.

"You know and I know that these things go on," the late Arthur
"Red" Patterson, the Yankees high-powered publicity director, remarked during a pleasant lunch in Anaheim a few years ago. (Patterson
left the Yankees during the season of 1955; he eventually became president
of the California Angels.) "There's nothing unusual in a ballplayer getting
taken by a sharpie, or climbing into bed with a girl. But that stuff was not
supposed to hit the papers. It never did with Ruth. It never did with
DiMaggio, at least not until DiMaggio got started with that famous
dame [Marilyn Monroe]. I mean, the press today, anything goes, but
we're talking about the 1950s when there were rules and limits on what we
let the press do.

"My job, and Casey's, too, was to sell this kid as the *next* DiMaggio. We had 70,000 seats in the Stadium to fill every day. DiMaggio
was 'dago' to his teammates, but we sort of made him into a Roman
emperor. This kid from Oklahoma, we wanted him packaged fresh and
clean, like a grown-up Tom Sawyer. The regular writers from the *Daily
News* and the *Times* pretty much went along with what we wanted. A
few drinks here, a nice Christmas present there, a free trip to spring

training for the wife, and you had them. When I was running the show, the regular writers never gave the Yankees any trouble.

"But *Confidential.* How the hell could you control something like that? You couldn't, and you couldn't ignore the thing, either. It was selling a million copies every issue. People were reading it and talking about it all the time.

"Groucho Marx was supposed to have a weakness for younger women. *Confidential* ran a couple of messy exposés. Groucho sat down and wrote them a letter. He said, if you put me on the cover one more time, I'm going to cancel my subscription.

"Well, that hands you a laugh, but it doesn't solve anything. The Yankees I worked for weren't big on humor. When the *Confidential* story broke, we had a bunch of high-level meetings and my boss, George Weiss, said that good as this kid was, maybe we ought to get rid of him right now. He sounded like a peck of trouble. Weiss kept saying over and over: 'No one ballplayer is as big as the New York Yankees.'

"After a while I told Weiss he was right, but if he did dump the kid or trade him, he would need a new manager right away because Stengel was gonna jump off the Triborough Bridge. Mantle was the ballplayer Casey always dreamed of managing."

The immediate solution put no one, least of all Stengel, in a life-threatening situation. Mantle had signed with Al Savitt, the 50-percent agent, when he was nineteen. Since Mantle was a minor, under the age of twenty-one, the contract was not binding. Weiss called Frank Scott, once a Yankee traveling secretary, later an energetic sports agent, and Scott went on to represent Mantle skillfully, for a 10 percent commission, from the 1950s clear into the 1990s. "A really good fella," Frank Scott says, "and generous. People don't know that. But Mickey was very generous to his friends."

One of Scott's first ideas called for a Mantle book. Clean. Wholesome. Lots of baseball. No strippers. He engaged a personable baseball writer from Arkansas, Ben Epstein, as Mantle's collaborator and in the spring of 1953, Henry Holt published *The Mickey Mantle Story.* The text ran 108 pages.

A month later, Mantle approached Epstein near his home away

from home, the batting cage at Yankee Stadium. "I read that book," he said. "Every word. I liked it."

Epstein said thanks. His job at the *Daily Mirror* paid $120 a week; he needed all the outside work he could find.

"And you know something, Benny," Mantle said, open-faced and earnest. "That's the first book I ever read in my whole life."

By this time he was twenty-one. He had read only one book, and that was his ghosted autobiography. The young Mick was such an up-front yokel, the circumstance did not embarrass him. I don't believe that he had yet learned how to blush. Blushing never was Mantle's strong suit, anyway.

The older Mick became suspicious. Some of the writers were kind of nasty bastards, he decided. You had to watch out for them and their wise-guy questions. To cope with both, the writers he didn't like and the questions he didn't want to answer, he taught himself a cold, intimidating glare.

Some of those kids outside the Stadium who wanted an autograph gave him leaky fountain pens. "How do you like that? They want a free autograph and then their pen leaks over my shirt and I get a laundry bill." He had his sullen moments. I mean it wasn't any one thing, he said, but a lot of things, and you had to be damn careful. So many people want me, they oughta pay.

With time, in the crush of commerce, that early innocent book, *The Mickey Mantle Story*, was forgotten, like the early innocent bumpkin. During the last decade of his life, Mantle put his name on no fewer than four autobiographical baseball books. He didn't write any of them, of course, but he promoted each with great energy, and he deposited the royalty checks.

By then, he had reached a state where he would autograph anything, even the nail on your great toe, if you gave him fifty dollars. Mantle had evolved from yokel to hustler; not a bad fellow, as Frank Scott said, but still a hustler.

Some say something similar about baseball.

*To this day it's a fine game, but damn, it's gotten too commercial.*

People discuss the flawless baseball instincts, the stunning foot speed and, of course, the home runs that almost beat *Sputnik* into orbit. These made him famous and in time wealthy. But crosscurrents cut harshly through his life—a desperate rage to live, a wild, primitive, and ultimately terrifying hunger.

I didn't care for him much in the beginning. In New York then it didn't seem that there was much to care for. Mantle was always being compared with his great rivals, Willie Mays and Duke Snider, and his idolized predecessor, Joe DiMaggio. Donald Honig, the fine baseball historian, describes the early Mantle in terms of missing attributes. "He lacked the bubbly innocence of Willie Mays," Honig writes. "He did not have the cool dignity and mysterious persona of Joe DiMaggio. Unlike Duke Snider, he did not flare out and berate the naysayers . . . Though secure in his talent, Mantle projected no definable image in an image-conscious city. Where DiMaggio had been [perceived as] noble in his quiet modesty, Mantle seemed dull."

Youth and responsibility. Triumph and sadness. The glory and the lead mines. Power and lust. Later a double Jack Daniel's on the rocks. Mantle lived on many levels and swung through many moods, but I think you begin with a poor boy, a lead miner's son, who ran with the hounds of poverty at his mercurial heels.

That and the shadow of cancer. His own ghastly, self-fulfilling prophecy that cancer, which killed his father and his favorite uncle, was lurking close and soon would drag him to eternity. Yet, and for all that, Mantle was often a happy guy.

Robert Frost once told me that the three threads of his life were poetry, teaching, and farming. "When I was young," he said, "my family thought that I was going to waste my life and become a pitcher. Later on they thought I'd waste my life and be a poet—and they were right."

The threads of Mickey Mantle's days also were three: baseball, whiskey, and pretty women. He said he loved playing ball, hitting the grand home runs, hearing the cheers. Baseball jerked him up from poverty and now, instead of a beer or two, or three, the way it had been for his father, Elvin "Mutt" Mantle, and for his Uncle, Tunney Mantle, and for his father's good buddy, Trucky Compton, it was vintage Scotch—Chivas Regal—and fine bourbon. And then the women. Begin with Holly. Then Molly, then Lolly, then Polly, and flight attendants and waitresses and even a movie queen. "Her back," Mantle remarked of a tall blonde actress, "is as strong as mine.". . . In the end when his vitality ebbed, he took pleasure in lifting the skirts of pretty girls he had just met and simply staring at their loins. Hello. (Trumpet no righteous nonsense here. Breathes there a man with soul so dead that he doesn't *sometimes* wish that he had Mantle's nerve?)

You cannot possibly approve of Mickey Mantle. All by himself he embodied most things now termed politically incorrect. But as so many of his teammates say in one way or another, "No, you couldn't *approve* of Mickey Mantle. What you could do was love him."

He was born in a town of a few hundred called Spavinaw, in Mayes County, Oklahoma, near the chain of lakes that feed the Tulsa water district. Despite the lakes, it is dry country, not much for farming. His family lived a hardscrabble life. Lived and had lived. He said the Mantles and his mother's family, the Richardsons, went back three generations in northeastern Oklahoma, back to when the land was Indian territory. His roots were English mixed with bits of Dutch and German. He said his mother, Lovell Richardson Mantle, had been a beauty, tall and slender with light gray eyes and reddish blonde hair.

Lovell gave birth to her first child on October 20, 1931, in a two-room, unpainted house, set on a hill above the northern edge of Spavinaw. The Depression was breaking across the country and the Mantle family was not so very different from the Joads, the famous Okies of John Steinbeck's *The Grapes of Wrath*. But where the Joads pulled up stakes and rolled down Route 66 toward California, with all their goods strapped to a tin lizzie, the Mantle family chose to stay and fight. So they struggled in the rough, dry country of northeastern Oklahoma, where the water troughs smelled of sulphur and where the topsoil turned to dust.

The father, Elvin Clark Mantle, comes down to us in photos, wearing boots and a work shirt, looking severe and weathered by the rigors of his life. He worked in road gangs, tried tenant farming and, when his first child was less than a year old, moved the family from Spavinaw to Commerce, a town of about 2,200 souls, thirty-five miles away, close by the borders of Kansas and Missouri. The Eagle-Picher

Zinc and Lead company operated mines near Commerce. Mutt Mantle found work there—underground—as a shoveler.

Mutt was a semipro ballplayer, a St. Louis Cardinal fan, like most in the area. But Mutt's special favorite was Mickey Cochrane, a stand-out American League catcher and a fine hitter until "Bump" Hadley of the Yankees beaned him in 1937. The pitch fractured Cochrane's skull. After that, ballplayers said, Cochrane was "a little funny in the head."

But in 1931, when he was twenty-eight, Cochrane batted .349 with 17 homers for the Philadelphia Athletics. The A's won their third straight pennant that year, finishing 13 ½ games ahead of the Yankees. Three weeks later Mutt named his newborn son Mickey Charles Mantle, after Cochrane, and swore to Lovell that he would make the boy a major league star.

Mickey's description of his father as a ballplayer shines through the best of the Mantle books, his 1985 effort, *The Mick,* written with Herb Gluck.

> [My father] ran, pitched, fielded most any position, batted both ways, hit for distance, had a shotgun arm and threw strikes . . . he was the best damn ball player in the territory. Only the professional scouts never saw him play. They never got a glimpse of him. There's no doubt he would have made a fine major leaguer if given the chance.

Actually there is plenty of doubt. Scouts traveled the country, even during the Depression, watching, talking to semipros, listening. A superstar, the Mutt Mantle of Mickey's memory, might have been overlooked for a season or two, but hardly for the length of an entire ballplaying career. What Mickey provides is not a professional scouting report, but a son's adoring testament to his father. That surely touches all of us from Commerce, Oklahoma, to Brooklyn, New York, who came to love the game and learned to play the game under the severe, demanding, caring gaze of the overworked, irreplaceable person we called Dad.

Departing the lunatic cocoon that was *Sports Illustrated* preserved my liver and a portion of my sanity, but once out of there, I felt disoriented. Where were the promises of a future amid poets? Where were the paychecks? *The Herald Tribune* offered the then extraordinary newspaper salary of $10,000 a year, if I would come back and resume writing baseball. I tried, but that time was over. The road was still the road, and I'd had enough of the Schenley in Pittsburgh, the Warwick in Philadelphia, and the Knickerbocker in Chicago, described by one sportswriter as "the only hotel in America with all inside rooms." By summer I had left to freelance, mostly for *SPORT* magazine, flourishing in a bright age of baseball writing, nurtured by Ed Fitzgerald. Working with a small budget, but with keen intelligence and concern, Fitzgerald assembled a stable of splendid writers. These included Arnold Hano, who wrote the small classic, *A Day in the Bleachers*; Ed Linn (*Veeck as in Wreck*) and John Lardner, son of the immortal Ring, and in his own right a matchless baseball stylist. Here is John Lardner in *SPORT* on Babe Herman and the Brooklyn Dodgers:

> Floyd Caves Herman, known as Babe, didn't always catch fly balls on the top of his head, but he could do it in a pinch. He never tripled into a triple play, but he once doubled into a double play, which is the next best thing. For seven long years, from 1926 through 1932, he was the spirit of Brooklyn baseball. He spent the best part of his life upholding the mighty tradition that anything can happen at Ebbets Field, the mother temple of daffiness in the national game.

About as funny a magazine piece as I've read followed. It included no spurious "news peg." There was no windy rumination on Americana; no pomposity, no pomposity at all, just fun. Rereading it, I am reminded of something quite important. Baseball is a game and games are *supposed* to be fun.

When Ed Fitzgerald heard I was leaving the *Herald Tribune*, he asked me to lunch at a modest Third Avenue bar called Meenan's. "What were you making at the *Trib*?" he asked, without appearing to pry.

"Ten thousand. More than anybody but the sports editor and Red Smith."

"I have a proposition," Fitzgerald said. "Do a story for each of my magazines [*SPORT* and a sort of mini-*Esquire* called *Saga*] every month. That's two stories a month, but you're fast. Do that and I'll pay you $11,000 or $12,000 a year. You should feel that you are moving up, which you are. I'm offering you more money than the *Tribune* because I want you to be aware that you *are* moving up."

"Deal."

"To start," Fitzgerald said, "I'd like your first story, at $500, absolutely my company's top rate, to be called 'The Ten Years of Jackie Robinson.' That's how long he's been in organized ball now, isn't it? Ten years? I know you fellers get along."

"Including the racial stuff?"

"Especially the racial stuff."

Hard as this may be to believe, Fitzgerald's proposal was revolutionary for a major publication. Bob Cooke at the *Herald Tribune* resisted all my efforts to describe the tension around Robinson and to report on organized baseball's uneasiness with integration. This was 1955, the year the Yankees finally deigned to sign a Negro player, the dignified and reserved Elston Howard. Three ballclubs, the Red Sox, the Tigers, and the Phillies, employed no blacks at all. For whatever reasons, not the *Trib* nor the *New York Times* nor *Sports Illustrated* had anything to say about the slothlike tempo of integration.

I told Fitzgerald that the abuse Robinson had suffered and still was suffering was surely worse than even he realized. "I'd like to call this story 'The Ordeal of Jackie Robinson.'"

"I don't think so," Fitzgerald said. "But his ordeal will jump off the pages that you write. We don't need to telegraph our punches in the title." He paused and puffed his cigarette. "Robinson doesn't get along with many writers. How come he gets along with you?"

"I think he's a great man, Ed. I guess it shows."

We had, in fact, become friends and when I mentioned Ed Fitzgerald's proposal, Robinson said that it didn't sound like the worst idea he had ever heard, and how could he help?

Robinson gave me a ranging, candid, touching interview and my notes remain. "Whenever I get in a real bad [baseball] argument," he said, "I don't care about [Walter] O'Malley or anything like that. I'm kinda worried about coming home. What's Rae [his wife, Rachel] gonna say? Have I acted like a jackass? My real judge of anything is my family relations. That's the most important. The house [he had just built a large stone house on four acres in a previously all-white section of Stamford, Connecticut], you know the house wasn't so important to me. Rae, it's something she always wanted for the kids. It's no real mansion. I mean there's only four bedrooms."

We were talking on a team bus, jouncing down Olive Street along the way to the old ballpark in St. Louis. "Do *you* think you get involved in too many incidents, Jack?" I said.

"If I stayed in a shell, the way some of the writers want, personally I could be maybe 50 percent better off in the minds of the little people. You know, the people who feel I should mind my place. But people that I know who aren't little, you know, people who are big in their minds, I've lost nothing by being aggressive. I mean that's the way I am, and am I supposed to try to act differently because I'm Negro? Here in St. Louis, around the different cities in the league, you know how much progress has been made, not just in baseball but in human relations between Negroes and whites. Sure you know. That's why I'm talking to you. My aggressiveness hasn't hurt."

I interviewed a representative mix of baseball people. Durocher said, "He's my kinda player." Chuck Dressen said Robinson was "the greatest player I ever managed and there was never nothing I asked, bunt, hit and run, anything, that he didn't do." Duke Snider said, "I'll tell you this. When Jack believes in something, he'll fight for it harder than anybody I ever saw."

Walter O'Malley dismissed Robinson as "a shameless self-promoter" and publicity seeker. Larry Goetz, a top umpire, said Robinson was too loud. "He's gotta second-guess every call and keep his big mouth going all the time." Red Smith agreed to let me quote him, but anonymously. He said, "I just don't like the guy. I'm fed up with Robinson fights and Robinson incidents and Robinson explanations. He's gotten boring. I'm going to heave a sigh of relief when he gets out of baseball. Then I won't have to bother with him any more."

I began the story like this:

When the Brooklyn Dodgers are at home, Jackie Robinson
may visit the United Nations on a Monday and discuss sociol-

ogy with a delegate. "There is still a little prejudice in baseball," he will remark, "but we have reached the point where
any Negro with major-league ability can play in the major
leagues." That same Monday night, Robinson may travel to
Ebbets Field and discuss beanballs with an opposing pitcher.
"Listen, you gutless *obscenity*," he is apt to suggest. "Throw that
*obscenity* baseball at my head again and I'm gonna cut your
*obscenity* legs in half." If Jackie Robinson is an enigma, the reason may be here. He can converse with Eleanor Roosevelt and
curse at Sal Maglie with equal intensity and skill.

Fitzgerald ran the story, ten thousand words long. Robinson's candor—and the candor of those who didn't like him—provided the basis
for what I came to think of as my first grown-up magazine piece.
(Robinson was thirty-six years old in 1955; I was twenty-eight.) Fitzgerald wrote me a warm letter. "You've given me an ornament to the magazine." Tom Meany, the sports editor of *Collier's*, greeted me at Toots
Shor's after a few drinks and said, "If you learn to write about white
guys the way you write about niggers, you can sell a piece or two to me
for our magazine. We pay three times as much as *SPORT*."

I continued to work mostly for Fitzgerald, writing long pieces usually about interesting ballplayers, at least one a month, every month —
the ferocious Early Wynn; the great home run hitter, Eddie Mathews;
Marty Marion, a superb Cardinal shortstop, who was managing the
Chicago White Sox. By observing and listening, I learned more and
more about the game and the people who played it and what they were
like and where their roots lay. Wynn came from Hartford, Alabama,
and pitched for the town team when he was thirteen. He recalled riding mule wagons to nearby towns to pitch. In hard Depression times,
he said, the two teams sometimes had only a single baseball between
them. "So if someone hit the ball into the bushes," Wynn said, "it
meant the game was over, unless we found it. We always found it. You
had the whole population of two towns looking for that one baseball."

Mathews hit 47 homers for the Milwaukee Braves in 1953, when he
was twenty-one, but got a mixed press. "I cursed out some writers. I
ducked their questions. I didn't see why they were intruding on me. It
would go like this:

"'What kind of pitch did you hit, Eddie?'

"'Where's your white cane? Weren't you watching the game, or are you blind?'

"I guess I was afraid of what these guys would write. But I took some time to think, and I figured I would try—just for a while—to get along, to help the writers. Damn, some of them turned out to be all right. Some of them turned out to be nice guys."

The press, though seldom hostile unless provoked, was less benign than people tend to remember. After the White Sox lost a close game at Yankee Stadium, I watched Marty Marion respond to reporters, who came in distinct troops. He had taken out his fine starter, Billy Pierce, and a relief pitcher named Millard Howell threw a critical home-run ball to Mickey Mantle.

Marion told the first group, morning newspaper writers, "Sure, if I had it do over again, I'd have left Pierce in. But the game doesn't work that way. Anyways, you gentlemen can be sure of one thing. That feller that beat us with his homer today is gonna hit a few more homers 'fore he retires."

Marion was annoyed, but civil. He was equally amiable to the second contingent, afternoon newspaper writers, who also pressed him on his unfortunate pitching change. He had to answer the same set of questions twice.

Finally a third group, the strays of journalism, appeared. Marion asked mildly if they had been waylaid in the press-room bar.

"Nah," someone said. "We had to talk to Stengel first. And Mantle. Boy, getting two words outta that Mantle is a day's work. Anyway, why the hell did you take out Billy Pierce?"

For a third time, Marion offered the earnest self-effacing response. He refused to be drawn into a discussion on Mantle's moody silence. "I got my hands full managing my own players. I think I'll just let Casey go right on managing the Yankees. I b'lieve he's up to the task."

When the last newspaperman had left, I commended Marion and said, "The same questions three times. Deep down, when they second-guessed your pitching change, didn't you want to say, 'Go to hell'?"

"Not deep down," Marion said. "Right up top. Right on the surface. But that gets you nowhere. When you grow up in this game, like I did, you get to recognize that the press always has the last word. Even Mantle will find that out someday . . . Uh, don't use that last if you don't have to, at least not right away." Marion then began to break down the job of managing, as he defined it—press relations, pitching rotation, preparing a team to play six or seven days every week.

"How about teaching, Marty? How much actual teaching do you do?"

"None," Marion said. "By the time they get to this level, they know how to play and what they're supposed to do. Throw to the cut-off man, and all the rest. But sometimes they forget. There was some of that today. Then they have to be reminded. So, to answer you, as a major league manager, I do no teaching, none whatsoever, but boy, do I do a hell of a lot of reminding."

That October, the Dodgers won the World Series for the only time in the sixty-eight-year history of the Brooklyn National League franchise. The team had lost seven earlier Series, four in the relatively brief stretch since the end of World War II. Some said that before the Dodgers ever won a World Series, a new Messiah would have to appear in Brooklyn. Looking backward, perhaps that is what happened, but this Messiah, the Lord of Flatbush, arrived at various times, in multiple forms and bore a variety of names: Robinson and Snider, Campanella and Erskine, Labine, Podres, Gilliam, and Reese. A collective Messiah, a Supermessiah, if you will. It took the mightiest of forces to defeat the Yankees.

Damn, I thought, if my father had lived just another two years, we could have shared this. Dad and I could have shared Johnny Podres's seventh-game shutout and Sandy Amoros's fine catch in the sixth inning and Pee Wee Reese's finer relay throw to first base that choked a dangerous Yankee rally. The newspapers rightly praised the catch; it was a good play, rather than a great one. Reese's relay from left field, a blazing strike to first base that doubled Gil McDougald, was what excited me. Here was Pee Wee, the immortal shortstop, in the middle, at the vital center, as he so often was, while the tallest headlines went to someone else, as they so often did.

The game ended when Reese threw out Elston Howard by a step.

Following an uneventful Dodger victory party at the Hotel Lexington—Walter O'Malley was a part owner of the place—Reese and I made our way toward a stylish saloon on Fifty-seventh Street called Whyte's. He was known there and respected. A few people said things like "good going," but mostly we were left alone to talk. "You know," he said, "I've played in every inning of every Dodger World Series game from 1941 on. I don't mean to sound boastful but I'm the only man who has." Reese puffed his cigarette a few times. We all smoked so much in those days it's amazing any of us is still alive. "One thing about all those losses is that they cut a little deeper than the ballgames. You say to yourself, why *can't* my team win a World Series? And then you start to wonder, about your own character, your own courage."

"Well it's a great night, captain. I only wish my dad were here to share it."

"My own father," Reese said, "might have enjoyed it a little himself. He was a detective for the Louisville and Nashville Railway and when I signed to play in Brooklyn he was very concerned about his boy in a big city. You know what his going-away gift was? A pearl-handled revolver. I kept it locked in my glove compartment for some time."

We lifted glasses to our late fathers and after a while I said, "Two out in the ninth. You almost have your first World Series. Elston Howard's the hitter. Do you remember what you were thinking."

"Oh, sure," Reese said. "I was thinking, I hope he doesn't hit the ball to me." That summoned waves of memory, of tight ballgames alongside Lake Mohegan, tense games where I had thought the same thing. Hit the goddamn ball to somebody else. Let somebody else blow the goddamn game, not me.

That was not something I had ever admitted. Now here was Pee Wee Reese telling me he'd had the same thought.

"I know what you mean," I said.

"I'll bet you do," Reese said.

We had the same thought but we did not really play the same game. As played by Reese and Robinson and Early Wynn and Eddie Mathews, baseball presumed such exquisite disciplines and skills that it was not only (and obviously) better than sandlot ball, it was something else entirely.

Sandlot ball is a helluva game. The baseball these fellows played was an art form.

Toward Thanksgiving Frank Gibney of *Newsweek* telephoned and asked if I'd like "to sign on as our sports editor." Could I join him and John Lardner for lunch? "John thinks you're our man," Gibney said, "and we have a lot of respect for John around this campus." Gibney sounded bright, enthusiastic, and very Yale.

I had never met John Lardner but, of course, knew who he was and, more important, knew how *good* he was. One lead sentence he created for his weekly *Newsweek* column was a special favorite. Bill Veeck, the noted baseball hustler, had bought the St. Louis Browns, a franchise seriously in trouble. As the Browns sank, Lardner wrote a gorgeous summary of the situation: "Bill Veeck bought the St. Louis Browns, under the impression that the Browns were owned."

Tall, bespectacled, and shy, Lardner sat quietly at a table at the Algonquin. Gibney did much of the talking. He didn't know sports, he said, except for skiing, sailing, and tennis, but he did recognize that sports were important. Next to Gibney sat a wonderfully pretty young journalist named Elizabeth Knox, who came from the prosperous community of Sewickley, Pennsylvania. "We've just stolen Liz away from *Glamour* magazine," Gibney said. "We think she'll make a fine researcher for you."

"Do you know much about sports?" I asked.

Liz Knox looked at me with startling intimacy. "Well," she said, in a throaty voice, "I like to swim."

Gibney said my salary would be $11,000 a year. I said I was earning more than that as a freelance. Gibney said I could continue to earn more than that as a freelance. "The truth is," he said, "and John will confirm what I'm telling you: Being sports editor of *Newsweek* is only a three-day-a-week job."

"Unless you have trouble with a lead," Lardner said.

After Gibney and Liz Knox left, I told Lardner a bit about my adventures with *Sports Illustrated.* "It should be different here," he said. "You don't want to be the editor of *Newsweek*, do you?"

"Hardly."

"Then you should be able to stay out in left field, away from the office politics, and get your work done.

"They've been very strong covering the dog show at Madison Square Garden, but not much with baseball.

"I expect you'll be able to change that."

It took some time. Gibney's thought about Liz Knox—the preppie beauty as sports reporter—certainly was interesting. Sending a radiant girl to report on the all-male domain of sports had possibilities. But the time was wrong. A hockey star broke a lunch date. A basketball player failed to return four phone calls. Liz Knox began to feel rejected and overwhelmed. She was being asked to pioneer, but after a proper Presbyterian upbringing, she lacked the requisite brazen toughness.

The star jockey Eddie Arcaro told me that his colt, Nashua, the best racehorse in the country, "is one mean bastard. He'd bite me, if I let him. I win big purses with him, but I hate the fucker."

I thought this might form the core of a story and mentioned the idea to Liz, in cleaned-up, abbreviated form.

She offered me another of her intimate looks. "What's a Nashua?" she said.

I was wondering how to replace Knox without shattering her when she came to me one morning and cried a bit and said she recognized that she couldn't do the job. After that, I hired my own research people: Bruce Lee, in time an outstanding book editor, and Dick Schaap, later a ubiquitous television character. (Knox got herself transferred to *Newsweek*'s radio and television department. In that milieu, she achieved success.)

As I settled into *Newsweek* in 1956, at the age of twenty-eight, Mickey Mantle was embarking on the summer of his life, at the age of twenty-four. It had been a long time coming. I can't think of any great star, except perhaps Sandy Koufax, who had a more trying time establishing himself. (Mishandled by Walter Alston, Koufax did not win twenty games until his *ninth* major league season.)

Even after Mantle broke free from the avaricious agent, his career proceeded unevenly. When he became subject to the military draft in

1950, the Selective Service Board of Ottawa County in Oklahoma classified him as 4-F. He suffered from osteomyelitis, a chronic bone infection, near his right ankle. By the time Mantle joined the Yankees, war was raging in Korea and a nasty anti-communist fanaticism swept the country. Jerry Coleman and Ted Williams both took time out from baseball and risked their lives flying fighters over North Korea. Comparisons were inevitable and Americans found it hard to understand how a tremendously powerful young man could play outfield in the major leagues, hit 500-foot homers, and yet come up unfit to fight for his country. Under public and political pressure, Army doctors re-examined Mantle three more times. He remained 4-F. Dr. Austin Schlecher, an old schoolmate of mine then serving in the Medical Corps, saw x-rays of Mantle's legs in 1952. "With that osteo," Schlecher said, "and the cartilage damage in his right knee, there is no question of him coming into the Army. He couldn't make it through basic training. My question is, how can he play ball? He must have a very high tolerance for pain."

Unpleasant rumors lingered—Yankee influence had bought Mantle his deferment. As the Korean War dragged on in its bloody, indecisive way, some called Mantle a coward, actually shouting that from the bleachers. Others yelled "Commie." Someone said, "So what if his legs are shaky? All he's got to do is shoot the damn Reds. He doesn't have to kick 'em to death."

The taunts turned Mantle further inward. He didn't *want* to fight in Korea. Except, perhaps, for "Dugout Doug" MacArthur, nobody did. But it wasn't as if he had *asked* to come up 4-F. It wasn't as if he were a conscientious objector. Hey, wait a minute. Wait one fucking minute! Who said he owed explanations to anyone? The hell with that. He wasn't gonna say another word. While Mantle chose silence, the vague sense that he was a slacker—or at any rate less than a patriot—persisted.

By the end of the 1955 season, Mantle had hit the ball more than 500 feet on nine different occasions. But he was not the consistent home-run hitter his strength—and Yankee publicity—suggested that he should be. For his first four Yankee seasons, Mantle averaged only 21 homers a year. Duke Snider hit the ball almost as far and drove out

40 homers a year. Willie Mays hit 41 homers in 1954; the season after that Mays hit 51.

Fans at Yankee Stadium took to booing Mantle. In addition to everything else, the draft, the frequent strikeouts, the hard comparisons with Mays and Snider, Mantle was walking in the spike marks of a colossus. Joe DiMaggio himself never hit 50 homers and, with the exception of 1948, his post–World War II performance, while brilliant, was erratic. Twice DiMaggio's batting average fell below .300. But during his thirteen seasons as a Yankee, DiMaggio sustained a carefully fashioned image: humble perfection. He told stories well. He drank with the power columnists, Jimmy Cannon, Bob Considine, and Red Smith. He even picked up his share of tabs. When Smith told him he had not only outrun a 420-foot drive, but had made the catch look easy, DiMaggio offered a nice response. "People say that and I'm grateful, Red. But let me tell you the truth. It isn't easy. It isn't easy at all. It's hard as hell to do the things I do out there." The columnists loved this big-shouldered character from San Francisco, who played ball with a special, stately grace. DiMaggio's New York press was a long love letter.

DiMaggio seldom struck out. He didn't walk much. He'd swing at a bad pitch if he thought he could drive in a run. But for a big, powerful swinger, DiMaggio's ratio of turns-at-bat to strikeouts was phenomenal. In 1941, the year of his famous 56-game hitting streak, DiMaggio came to the plate more than 620 times. His strikeout total: 13. That works out to one strikeout every two weeks.

Mantle, the new DiMaggio, came to bat more than 620 times in 1952. His strikeout total: 111. No Yankee before, not even free-swinging Babe Ruth, had ever struck out that frequently. In 1954 Mantle led the league in a negative way again, this time with 107 strikeouts. The failures infuriated him and he took to kicking the big metal water cooler in the Yankee dugout. Trying to calm him one day Casey Stengel said, "That water cooler ain't striking you out, son."

There was never serious doubt about Mantle's strength and power. But after those first four seasons, some wondered about his intelligence. Sure the kid could slug, but could he *hit?* Bob Feller, Cleveland's mighty righthander, summed up the general thinking. "His physical development is all there," Feller said. "Now it's a question of his mental development coming along. If he can get this thing up here tuned up"—Feller pointed to his brow—"then he'll set a lot of records."

When such comments appeared in sports pages, Mantle began to shun the sportswriters who covered him every day. Leaving the Stadium on afternoons, he stalked past children, asking for an autograph, literally knocking some aside. The lead miner's son had made the major leagues. His dream, his father's dream for him, had come true. Why, then, was life so disappointing? He didn't understand.

In the 1955 World Series, leg injuries kept Mantle out of the starting line-up for five of the seven games. Across ten turns at bat, he hit only .200. Was this moody, sullen kid with the bad legs, this almost-but-not-quite-new DiMaggio slipping into an early downhill slide? The power was there. Would Mantle ever know the glory?

The Yankees and the St. Louis Cardinals both trained in St. Petersburg, playing exhibition games on alternate days at Al Lang Field. During Cardinal workouts, I liked to stand at the batting cage, for the sheer pleasure of watching Stan Musial hit. Musial coiled his supple body, picked up the ball out of the pitcher's hand and uncoiled with a swing of ferocity and control. He had already won the National League batting championship six times, led the league in doubles eight times and consistently hit 30 or so homers. He struck out only 35 times a year and even the strikeouts were frightening as that droll character, Preacher Roe, earlier reminded us.

In a quiet dugout conversation in the spring of 1956, Musial said I ought to keep an eye on Mantle this season.

"He's always had that power," Musial said. "You know that. But the other day [March 20] he hit a homer off Larry Jackson that cleared my head [in right field] by more than any homer I remember. The ball traveled more than 500 feet."

"How many times did he strike out?"

"That's the real point. He's looking better. People think that a hard swinger strikes out, just because he swings hard, but that's only part of it. It's not only the swing, it's the pitches that you decide to swing at. Mickey used to get impatient, make up his mind early and swing at some curve balls in the dirt. And he'd chase the high fastball. Well, you don't want to do that in the major leagues, or else you'll see a lot of high fastballs out of the strike zone.

"This spring the kid is letting bad pitches go. If he keeps it up, and he bats .350 I can't say I'll be surprised."

On March 11 Mantle was batting lefthanded against a young Cardinal pitcher named Bob Mabe. A street ran beyond the left field fence at Al Lang Field. Beyond the pavement lay a sprawl of lawn. Past both street and lawn, the waters of Tampa Bay stirred in the sunlight. With two men on base, Mantle crashed one of Mabe's fastballs over the fence, over the lawn and into the water. According to eyewitnesses, this monstrous opposite-field shot scattered an armada of pelicans, which had been fishing for lunch. Nine days later he hit the huge drive Musial remembered. Counting wallops of normal home-run length, he hit four home runs in ten games. He added another 500-footer against the Dodgers on March 24 at Miami Stadium. Then he bruised his right leg sliding and couldn't play for a week. "Is Mantle Superman?" Dick Young wondered. "Hardly. He's as strong as Superman maybe, but Superman isn't breakable. Mantle obviously is. At best, he's Superman in glass."

He was back in a week and this year his legs did not betray him. Batting lefthanded against Camilo Pascual on opening day at Griffith Stadium in Washington, Mantle hit two very long ones. One cleared a high wall 420 feet distant from home plate, carried across a street and landed in a clump of trees. "They tell me the other feller which hit that tree was Ruth," Stengel said. "When his ball landed, it shook some kids outa that tree. The tree's got bigger in twenty-five years, and so's the kids the Babe shook outta it." The other homer, slightly to the right of center, landed on the roof of a house at 2014 Fifth Street.

Four days later at Yankee Stadium Mantle hit what Ted Williams called "the hardest ball I've ever seen hit off a Red Sox pitcher." Righthander George Susce threw the pitch, a fastball, and Mantle hit it on a rising line to right. It struck a seat high up in the third deck still carrying hard 415 feet from home plate. Although dispute persists, apparently no one had, or has, hit a fair ball out of Yankee Stadium. "If the seat hadn't stopped that one," Tom Brewer, another Red Sox pitcher said, "the ball woulda gone out of the Stadium and maybe outta the Bronx."

Mantle hit four home runs in April and 16 in May. By June 1 he was batting .421 and his home run pace—20 in the first six weeks of the season—was the briskest power start in the annals. When Babe Ruth hit 60 homers in 1927, he had sixteen through May. When Hank Greenberg hit 58 in 1938, his six-week total was twelve. The newspaper headlines repeated and repeated: MANTLE AHEAD OF RECORD RUTH PACE.

My own efforts to introduce baseball writing into *Newsweek* were meeting with questionable success. My immediate superior, a sad-faced fellow out of Bridgeport named Jack O'Brien, insisted that newspapers covered baseball so intensely that there was nothing left for the magazines. We went to a nearby bar to argue and as I scored some points, O'Brien suddenly took a small volume of Cicero's speeches from a coat pocket and began reading them—in translation—by the dim light of the saloon. After a while I said, "You must have some real peace of mind to be reading Cicero in a bar."

"Wrong," O'Brien snapped. "If I had peace of mind I wouldn't *have* to read Cicero—or listen to you!"

"I read the stuff myself back in school, Jack. But, of course, we read it there in Latin."

O'Brien's boss, Frank Gibney, had no interest in baseball and so it went up the line to John Denson, the strange and rather unusual editor-in-chief. Denson was a reformed alcoholic who kept a case of Jack Daniel's under his desk to demonstrate that he could be close to booze and not have to drink it. He could be funny. When he was issued a Diners Club card, Denson told me, "I'm going to see if this thing is any good. I'm going to use it to buy *Newsweek*." But his attitude toward baseball was colored by an appalling prejudice against blacks.

At John Lardner's urging I went over the heads of O'Brien and Gibney and proposed directly to Denson a revised, condensed, updated version of "The Ten Years of Jackie Robinson." Denson's dental plates fit poorly; when he grew excited his teeth clicked and rattled. I began to hear strange noises. Then Denson made a hiss out of the word "no."

"Why not?" We had been having a pleasant lunch at a German restaurant called The Blue Ribbon.

"I don't want nigras in the magazine," Denson said. "I don't want that oily dago Frank Sinatra in the magazine and I don't want any *nigras*."

"I can't run a sports section and exclude Negro athletes."

"Don't be so damn self-righteous."

"Well, I can't, and you can't tell me who or whom I have to exclude, John. It's my sports section."

The teeth rattled. "Yes, but it's my magazine." At length we struck a compromise. I *could* write about Mr. Denson's *nigras*, but I would not insist that he run photographs of them.

He sensed that the conversation was getting out of hand. "They tell me you like to read books," Denson said. "What in your opinion is the greatest novel of this century?"

I nominated *A Portrait of the Artist as a Young Man* and spoke a bit about the poetic accomplishments of James Joyce. Denson listened politely. When I was finished he said, "But have you reread *Gone with the Wind* lately?"

In early June 1956, Denson summoned me to his office and asked if I thought I could write a cover story "about a clean-cut, nice-looking white kid."

"I don't see why not. I'm something of a clean-cut, nice-looking white kid myself."

"Don't get smart with me. Do you want to write a *Newsweek* cover on Mantle or not?"

"You bet your ass I do, sir." As I left the boss's office, his teeth rattled dangerously behind me.

I would come to know Mantle best in the course of writing three different magazine stories about him for three very different editors. Now I was embarked on number one.

"I've gone and done it," I told John Lardner. "I've agreed to write a cover story on the worst interview in baseball. Mantle has nothing to say and when he does talk, every third word is 'fuck.'"

"His bat talks clean English," Lardner said. "Everybody else in baseball will have something to say about that."

*Newsweek's* cover photo, devised by Denson and Ed Wergeles, would emphasize Mantle's switch-hitting power. Out of a single base—that is Mantle's body from the waist down—Mantle would appear on the front of *Newsweek* in the issue dated June 25, 1956, batting both lefthanded *and* righthanded. This required Wergeles to work with double-exposures for half an hour while Mantle took alternate batting stances in front of a black background.

"How did the photo session go?" Robert O. Fishel, the Yankee publicist who had replaced Red Patterson, wanted to know.

"Okay in a sense," I said. "Mantle showed up in the little studio the photographer set up next to the dressing room and he posed for a while, pretending he didn't know who I was. About fifteen minutes later, he finally spoke to me. He said, 'How the fuck much longer is this fucking thing gonna take?'"

Fishel looked pained. A gentler soul, and a more passionate baseball fan, never lived. "This cover story is important to me and to the entire Yankee organization," he said. "We feel it gets us beyond the sports page and that's something we really want. But I can tell you this: Mantle wouldn't have showed up for *any* photos if we hadn't ordered him to show up. I spoke to him. Casey spoke to him. But orders only get you so far." We were sitting in the Stadium press box. Fishel looked across the playing surface, tan and white and green and huge. "Good luck with the interview," he said, "but we had to order him do that, too. Mickey said, 'Hey, I'm getting a thousand to go on Perry Como. Why do I have to speak to this magazine for free?'"

Mantle met with me three times in the clubhouse and mostly offered stares and grunts. "Could we talk about your boyhood?" I said.

"What do you need to know that shit for?" Mantle said. "There wasn't no lullabies for me back home. Instead Dad'd play the ballgame on the radio from some station up in St. Louis." At length Mantle added that his father was a good guy who died of a form of cancer called Hodgkin's disease.

"I hear you're concerned about contracting that yourself."

"Who told you?"

"Somebody on the team [Yogi Berra] said there was a clubhouse meeting about the players' pension plan. You told the guys that pensions didn't concern you because you weren't going to live long enough to collect a pension. You were going to die of Hodgkin's disease before you were forty."

Mantle glared. "I did a little research for you, Mick," I said. "Hodgkin's disease is not hereditary."

"Fuck your research," Mantle said. "My uncle died of it, too."

At our next session, I tried to draw him out on hitting. He said he was always looking for a fastball. He could adjust to a slower pitch, like a slider or a curve. But if he started out looking for, say, a slider, the fastball could buzz past him before he had time to readjust. "You gotta know that already. How could you be covering this game and not know that?"

"I want to ask you about the strikeouts."

Another glare. Then, grudgingly, "What about 'em?"

"Why so many?"

"Look, if you're gonna hit the ball as far as I do, you gotta *start* your swing, start it, pretty much when the ball is still in the pitcher's hand. So you're more liable to get fooled by a pitch than if you wait longer, see the ball longer, and just try to hit a single. But nobody, me included, wants me to just hit singles, and why the hell are you asking me about my strikeouts instead of my home runs?"

"About the homers," I began. But Mantle was walking away.

The cover story in a major national magazine—surely a triumph for a man of twenty-five years—was turning into something of a war. "I'm supposed to ask," I said at our final session, "whether you'd rather bat .400 or hit 60 homers."

"Stupid question," Mantle said. "The way I swing, if I do hit .400, with maybe 220 hits, I get the 60 homers easy. Couldn't you figure that out for yourself? Anything else? I wanna go take batting practice."

"Yeah," I said. "I saw you on Perry Como the other night. The way you act, Mantle, you better not lose your bat."

He began to grin. "What do *you* know?" he said. "After that show the phone was ringing all night when I got home. Two o'clock. Three o'clock. Why don't that damn [Hollywood producer David O.] Selznick leave me alone?"

That started me grinning and it was then that I asked about the blonde actress with the strong back. "I've heard that a lot of beautiful movie stars are frigid," I said.

"Not her," Mantle said.

"Great lay?"

"I can't tell you," Mantle said. "I've been muff-diving for so long I've forgotten how to fuck."

He burst out laughing, not just at what he had said, but at what he perceived was success in his personal war-game against me and *Newsweek*. "I finally give you something good," he said, with a large smirk, "and there's no fucking way you can get it into the magazine."

"Thanks."

"Aaaah," Mantle said. "I gotta hit."

His wife, Merlyn, a fawnlike girl with reddish hair, was open, but nervous to the point of being frightened when I met with her and Bob Fishel in an office at the Stadium. "Mickey was close to his father," Merlyn said. "*Real* close. When his father died it really affected him. He's had big responsibilities since then, sending his sister and three brothers to school. He's what you, uh, call the nervous type. I mean he can't sit quiet. Still you can't hardly tell if he's worried. He keeps within himself. Uh, does that help you?"

"Sure. I wanted to ask you some things about baseball."

Merlyn's gaze fell. "I knew next to nothing about baseball when I married Mickey," she said. "Still don't. I'm sorry." I wondered, but was not harsh enough to ask, what in the world they talked about at home.

I dispatched a reporter from a Tulsa newspaper to visit Commerce. He filed information that became the basis for two telling paragraphs about the shaping of Mickey Mantle and one likely source of his terrible anger:

No stage-struck parent ever forced a child through routines more intensive than the baseball drills Elvin (Mutt) Mantle, a zinc miner and occasional semipro, organized for his eldest child. By the time Mickey was 10, it had gotten to be a joke in Commerce that when Mutt came home from the mine at 4 in the afternoon, Mickey had to stop playing and start practicing.

Mutt's first principle was switch hitting. Against his father, Mickey was allowed to use his natural righthanded swing, but against his grand-father, Charles, he was forced to bat lefthanded. "He didn't like it at all," says Mickey's mother, Lovell, "but I guess now he must be glad."

The cover story was well received and Ed Wergeles's clever photograph caused a splash. Everyone wanted to know how I had gotten so much cooperation out of Mantle. Wishing I'd been allowed to write about Jackie Robinson, annoyed at Mantle's crude, taunting humor, I managed to hold my tongue. Mantle had cursed me out in a variety of ways. My response was to put him on the cover of *Newsweek* and depict him as a nice sort. That wasn't entirely wrong. Once you got past all that bristling and obscenity, in many ways he was a nice sort: A snarling, sullen hero, true, but within that frame there lived a decent fellow, waiting to break out.

Mantle hit 52 homers in 1956. He knocked in 130 runs, scored 132 more, and batted .353. Stan Musial had, perhaps, a better season with the Cardinals in 1948, when he led the National League in hits, doubles, triples, runs scored, runs batted in, and hit .376. Musial in '48— for overall batting—and Mantle in '56—for Herculean power— remain, so to speak, twin benchmarks: best single-season performance by any hitter from World War II until today. Like Musial before him, Mantle won the Most Valuable Player award by an enormous margin.

After a bumpy, buckboard journey, the Mick had arrived. Carrying an inevitable touch of newsmagazine hyperbole, my *Newsweek* story summarized baseball thinking in 1956:

[With his speed as well as his power] Mantle has finally come to a point where he is widely regarded as the best baseball player in the world and is given a serious chance to become the best baseball player of all time. Only two elements weigh against him. The questionable soundness of his knees and the uncertain development of his personality.

So much was made in later years of Mantle's drinking, that it may seem odd my comments excluded whisky. Mantle was a hard drinker;

so were Billy Martin and Whitey Ford and Early Wynn and Bob Lemon, and a great number of other reigning stars. More games were played by day during Mantle's time, and that left many nighttime hours free. As a breed, ballplayers tended to spend off-hours with a drink. Dizzy Dean spoke for generations when he said, "Stay in your room like I used to do and you can drink as much as you want without getting into trouble." (But once after a night in his room, Dean showed up in the morning with a black eye. He attributed that to the telephone on his night table. "I was trying to use the phone," Dean said, "when it slipped in my hand and hit me.")

Like many of his contemporaries, the young Mantle drank heartily without immediate negative effect. His legs caused him to miss games—bad wheels jolted him, not hangovers. "Them young fellers," Casey Stengel said, "it don't matter [how much they drink] at night. Just give 'em a glass of milk and they're ready to play. When you get a great one like this boy, and he shows up regular, the best thing is leave him alone."

As far as I know, a hangover disrupted Mantle's performance only once. He felt so terrible one afternoon—I forget the year—that he couldn't get to the ballpark until the fifth inning. Stengel greeted him with fury. "Yer late. Get in and pinch hit fer me right now."

Trembling under a high, bright sky, Mantle took one swing and hit a 425-foot home run. He trotted around the base paths, trotted into the dugout and said to Stengel, "You'll never know how hard that was." Then he retreated to the clubhouse to lie down.

Some say that without drinking, Mantle would have been a better ballplayer.

Better than what?

Better than whom?

Stengel drank more than Mantle and look what whiskey did to him. Killed the Ol' Perfesser when he was eighty-five years old.

If Mantle never fulfilled his potential to become the best ballplayer of all time—and he did not—reasons include both his disinclination to practice hard and the nature of his physique: what Jerry Coleman called "the upper body of a god on decidedly mortal legs." I don't believe intemperance affected Mantle's play in any significant way.

# II

Mantle and I had our second extended encounter in the summer of 1961, by which time he had evolved and even matured. This time the driving engine was *Sports Illustrated*. I left *Newsweek* in 1960, after the death of my friend John Lardner.

"Why resign?" John Denson said. "If it's money, I'll get you a raise. I'll get you $20,000, if that's what you need."

"It isn't money, John. But thanks."

"Well, what is it then?"

What is it or what was it? Maybe I was going to set out and write a book, a big book, a big baseball book. Or take a look at Hollywood. Or write a sonnet sequence. I wasn't sure. I just wanted to move on. "Please don't ask me to explain myself," I said, and I parted from this strange, unusual, bigoted, and gifted editor with a feeling of great warmth.

Soon after that a new band of editors at *Sports Illustrated* decided to try me again, this time proposing that I become a contributing writer. I would essentially be a freelance on retainer not subject to a time clock or to corporate meetings or to three-martini lunches, unless I volunteered. Books? You'll have plenty of time to write all the books you want. I hopped onto the treadmill and returned.

Andre Laguerre, a former chief of *Time*'s Paris bureau, had deposed Sid James as managing editor. Laguerre sometimes squired Henry Luce around France, but how this sybaritic Frenchmen came to run an American sports magazine remains as mysterious to me as the winemaking secrets of Chateau Petrus. Laguerre liked horse racing, drinking, and the company of men, all helpful in his new job, but he had no background at all in American sports, and not much feel for the English phrase. Still, Robert Creamer insisted, Laguerre was a good man. He delegated authority well and was correcting earlier mistakes at *Sports Illustrated* in ways that were acceptable within the Time organization. Jack Tibby, for example, was no longer permitted to dictate to writers or to edit stories, but Tibby was not totally degraded. He was assigned full-time to review expense accounts.

Some said running *Sports Illustrated* was Laguerre's reward for connecting Luce with spirited Parisian belles. Others said he got the magazine because of his sure knowledge of the Time Inc. bureaucracy. Both hypotheses were probably correct.

Creamer quit baseball writing and emerged as articles editor under Laguerre. Creamer's skills and the demands of the job didn't mesh, but I worked for him as best I could. In August 1961, he asked me to travel with the Yankees and observe Mickey Mantle and Roger Maris in pursuit of Babe Ruth's classic record: sixty homers in a single 154-game season. Mantle fell short (54), but Maris, of course, eventually hit 61, albeit in a longer season.

I picked up the Yankees in Minneapolis and soon found the home-run numbers less interesting than a mostly off-the-field spectacle: Maris contending with the horde of reporters who swarmed and pelted him with questions every day. Mantle assumed an important, but relatively subtle role.

Maris had to field questions not only about baseball, but about his outside interests and his views of life. He was a pleasant fellow, but private and without much humor. The reporters' questions bothered him more than sliders, and the questions persisted day after day.

"Who's your favorite male singer?" one reporter asked.

"Frank Sinatra," Maris said.

"Female singer?"

"I don't have a favorite female singer."

"Well," the reporter said, "would it be all right if I wrote Doris Day?"

"How could you write Doris Day when I just told you I don't have a favorite?" Maris said. He was on his own. No one was helping him deal with the demands and the inanities of the press.

"Do you play around on the road?" asked a correspondent from *Time*.

"I'm a married man," Maris said.

"I'm married myself," the *Time* reporter said, "and *I* play around on the road."

"That's your business," Maris said.

"How about you, Mick," the *Time* character said. "You play around on the road?"

"I used to," Mantle said. "A *lot!*" He was having fun. He knew what *Time* could use and what it could not.

When the last newspaperman left, Maris walked over to Mantle and said, "I'm telling you, Mick, I can't take this anymore."

Mantle met Maris's gaze, which was both angry and sad. "And I'm telling you *this*: You gotta keep taking it. You gotta because it ain't going away."

"I wanna hit some of these guys."

"Turn your back," Mantle said. "Give 'em a stare. But listen to me. Listen! You hit fucking nobody." The words were a command. At twenty-nine, Mickey Mantle, his yokel days long gone, had become the leader of the New York Yankees.

In Chicago, a reporter asked Maris: "Do you really want to break Ruth's record?"

"Yes."

"What I mean is," the reporter said, "Babe Ruth was a great man."

"Maybe I'm not a great man," Maris said, "but I damn well want to break the record. And feller, I don't like your goddamn questions. Get outta here." That provoked a harsh Chicago piece suggesting that Maris was "cracking under pressure."

Hank Greenberg, now running the White Sox with Bill Veeck, took me to dinner the next night. He had signed Maris for a $15,000 bonus in 1952. "I know him," Greenberg said, "and he's just a boy. The reporters get him talking and he says things you just don't say to reporters. The year I hit 58 homers [1938] drunks called me Jew bastard and kike, and I'd come in and sound off about the fans. Then the next day I'd meet a kid all popeyed to be shaking my hand, and I'd know I'd been wrong. But the writers protected me then. Why aren't the writers protecting Maris now?"

Even if they chose to, reporters in 1961 could not have protected Maris. He was being covered more intensely and more competitively than any individual in sports history. Jack Dempsey, Babe Ruth, Jackie Robinson, Ty Cobb, Willie Mays—none was subjected to so much interviewing and so much shadowing for so sustained a period. That was one reason why reporters couldn't protect him: all that competition raised the risk of being scooped. Another reason was the failure of the Yankees to respond to the Maris Phenomenon. One ballplayer; thirty, forty, fifty devouring reporters. The Yankee staff felt overwhelmed and couldn't keep order among the journalists, or even make hotel reservations for everyone that wanted them. Scenes that should have been celebratory ended in hostility, and a hostile writer is unlikely to protect a subject.

Today interviewing rooms and prearranged question periods impose limits of place and time upon the media. No one thought to do that thirty years ago. Maris, as I say, rather a shy sort, was left naked to interrogators for hours before and after every game. In time, he lost clumps of his brown hair. By default, Mantle became Maris's buddy, press adviser, and counselor.

In Detroit, while he was suffering from a cold and leg pains, Mantle offered me thoughts, after I told him about Hank Greenberg's comments.

"Greenberg never played for a New York team," Mantle said. "He played in Detroit. New York is different. And I bet it was when Greenberg was playing, too. Hey, Detroit is easy. Detroit is Oklahoma."

"What do you tell Maris?"

"What you heard me tell him. That he's gotta put up with the horseshit. That he's gonna make some real money. And don't make such a big deal out of every fucking thing. I been through the writers' stuff myself."

"You feel much pressure?"

"What from?"

"Chasing Ruth's record."

"I ain't chasing Ruth. Maris is chasing Ruth. I already got my man. I nailed Lou Gehrig."

As we spoke, Mantle had hit 49 homers. In 1927, the year Ruth pounded out his 60, Gehrig hit 47. More and more, humor was becoming Mantle's good buddy.

Home runs were secondary to the story I wrote. Mostly it was about the press and Roger Maris.

"This is terrific," Bob Creamer said.

"Thanks."

"There are only two things I don't like."

"Namely?"

"Your first paragraph and your last paragraph. I don't like them at all."

"Well, they're part of my story, Bob, so you have to accept them."

"No, I don't. I'm the articles editor here. Your first paragraph and your last paragraph are out of the story. I've killed them."

Creamer had evolved from *Sports Illustrated* virgin, and something of an idealist, into a Time Inc. apparatchik, with ideas on authority dangerously close to those of John Knox Tibby. Perhaps Creamer was plotting someday to replace Laguerre; he may even have dreamed of leaving his old house in Tuckahoe and acquiring a Tibby-type mansion on the shores of Gatsby country.

Since the story—my story and in a sense Maris's story—was to appear in *Sports Illustrated*, Creamer believed it belonged to no one so much as the magazine. Editors in the bureaucracy, therefore, had a right to change the story in any way they chose. For many years that sort of thinking prevented *Sports Illustrated* from assembling a strong permanent collection of writers. You simply cannot write a sonnet by committee. (In later years, Creamer experienced a second coming and emerged as a serious baseball biographer. His better instincts triumphed. He still lives with his wife in the old house in Tuckahoe.)

I gave the magazine permission to reprint the Maris piece two years ago and reading it, I saw a story that lacked an appropriate beginning or an end. Both had died in someone else's wastebasket three decades before. Beyond that, I wished that in 1961 I had been able to do more with Mantle, in his new and impressive role as a supporting player.

The following spring at Al Lang Field, Mantle greeted me by name and said, "Maris is looking for you."

He walked me toward the dugout. Maris was working on a bat. "I read that story you wrote," he said.

"And?"

"Of all the horseshit that got written about me last year," Roger Maris said, "yours was the best."

Deep within every man there beats the heart of a critic. Maris, I had to concede, seemed like a good one.

# III

One essential element of Roger Maris had become clear and paradoxical: in the midst of sudden fame he wanted to remain the way he had been in obscurity. He intended to preserve himself as he had existed in the past. He had sought fame to be sure, as all ballplayers do, but Maris was comfortable only with the person of years gone by: a plain, blunt man who liked to speak his mind. Now when he spoke his mind, he fed a headline or drew boos. Change or perish, biologists tell us, is a rule of nature. Maris wanted to do neither.

Guile would have made his life more comfortable, but he regarded guile as suspect. Above all things Maris wanted to protect his own integrity, as he perceived it. He never had another great year, nor did he ever resolve his inner conflict.

For my part, after the remarkable 1961 season and the mutilation of my Maris story, I resolved henceforth to protect the integrity of my work, which in a sense was protecting myself. I did not regard myself as an artisan, crafting work to preconceived or arbitrary specifications. I was trying to become a creative artist and the best baseball writer I knew how to be. But creative fulfillment wasn't possible for a writer at *Sports Illustrated*, essentially an editors' magazine.

John Lardner knew that when he turned down a fat offer from Luce. Kurt Vonnegut, Jr. found that out and stalked away from a writing job at *MNORX*, even though he needed the money. Red Smith learned the *SI* lesson once. I had to learn it twice. Pursued by Jack Tibby, who said I owed him two expense accounts, I fled Harry Luce's rich sports magazine for a second time.

After that, for most of the 1960s, I worked as a contributing writer at the *Saturday Evening Post*, under marvelous editors, Bill Emerson and Otto Friedrich. I wrote more politics than sports, but I kept an eye on the game and especially on the three great center fielders, whose play and competition was so exhilarating. Time snared them all, slowed them all, and brought their baseball days to difficult conclusions.

Snider, five years older than the others, hit 40 homers in 1957, the last year the Dodgers played in Brooklyn. That was the fifth consecutive season in which he hit 40 or more. Snider was never the same triumphant ballplayer in Los Angeles. A bad knee weakened one steel-spring leg, and the absurd dimensions of the diamond at the Coliseum —440 feet to right center field—canceled some of his power. Snider wound down with stints at the Mets (.243 with 14 homers) and the Giants. At age thirty-eight, in windy San Francisco, Snider batted only .210 and hit his final four home runs. This was in 1964; some said only Barry Goldwater had a worse year. Still, counting the eleven Snider hit in World Series, his home run total reached a formidable figure: 418.

Willie Mays played into the 1970s, but after 1965, never hit .300 or drove out 40 home runs. At length, he too was exiled to the Mets where in 1973, past forty, he became a .211 hitter. Curiously, Mays never did hit a World Series homer, but despite the gales of Candlestick Point, his final total reached 660, third on the all-time list. Had Willie been permitted to play out his career in the Polo Grounds, like Mel Ott before him, he would have hit at least 800 homers and surpassed Babe Ruth and Henry Aaron. Or so I believe.

Late in the summer of 1973, when he was forty-two and playing for the Mets, Mays got his legs crossed chasing a routine fly ball and fell down in the outfield at Shea Stadium. Soon afterward in a small ceremony at home plate, he announced that he was retiring. He said: "When I see the way these kids are playing and fighting for the pennant, it tells me one thing: Willie, say goodbye to America." That brief speech tore at many hearts. Suddenly, everywhere, Americans felt the clutch of age.

Mantle's late baseball days became struggles against agony. The knee injury he suffered during the 1951 World Series was only partially repaired by surgery. After that he could not play without a knee brace, a cumbersome device of metal, canvas, and rubber. As the years continued to tear at his legs, he came to require literally yards of tape to hold himself together. Marvin Miller, who ran the players' union, saw Mantle getting into uniform near the end. "With all that tape," Miller said, "from the hips down the poor guy looked like a mummy."

The great Yankee dynasty came to an end with Mantle's last strong season, 1964. From 1951, when Mantle broke in, through 1964— a stretch of fourteen seasons—the Yankees won the American League pennant twelve times. (During DiMaggio's thirteen seasons, the Yankees won ten pennants.) Mantle leads all batters in World Series home runs, runs scored, runs batted in, walks and—inevitably—strikeouts. In 65 World Series games, he fanned 54 times.

It is exaggerating to say that all by himself Mantle carried the Yankees. He had great cohorts in Berra, Whitey Ford, Elston Howard, and Maris. But it is fact that when Mantle could no longer hit 30 homers and bat .300, when he could no longer disrupt quiet games with home runs that called up images of Hercules, the Yankees collapsed. They finished sixth in 1965, and then—to general amazement and a certain amount of rejoicing—they sank into the American League cellar.

By 1967, Mantle could no longer run well enough to play outfield and he shifted to first base. He had his final multi-homer game on August 10, 1968, hitting both drives righthanded against a tall lefty named Jim Merritt of the Minnesota Twins. This was Mantle's forty-sixth multi-homer game, formidable, but 26 games behind Ruth's record. Mantle hit his final home run batting lefthanded against Jim Lonborg of the Boston Red Sox on September 20, 1968. Including his World Series total of 18, Mantle finished with 554 homers, and a dozen or so of the longest ever hit. He stands eighth on the all-time homer roster, but did not crack the top ten in any other "offensive" department, except drawing bases on balls, and, to be sure, striking out.

For all that early speed, Mantle stands (through 1996) no better than twenty-third in scoring runs. (Cobb leads; Ruth and Aaron tie for second.) For all that power, he stands no better than thirty-fifth at driving runs home. Despite the speed *and* power, his ranking in extra-base hits is no better than twenty-eighth. He was a thrilling competitor. As to that early potential to become the greatest ballplayer of all time—he never came close.

When his big league career began to close down, the former Oklahoma poor boy worried about money. He grabbed tabs. He squired ladies. He felt he couldn't afford to quit playing ball. But by 1968, at thirty-seven, Mantle had become a .237 hitter. The power showed only in flashes, a thunderstorm rumbling into the distance. His speed was history. The Yankees retired Mantle and his $100,000 salary in the spring of 1969. Then they put him on a retainer to coach hitters and perform public relations work—make speeches to sell tickets to the Stadium. Mantle worked out his own, drawling opening for the talks.

"Sure Ah hit a lot of homers, folks, but let me tell you something else.

"Ah struck out 1,710 times.

"Ah walked 1,734 times.

"That means Ah come to bat in the major leagues 3,444 times when Ah didn't hit a single ball fair.

"How 'bout that?"

Mantle's retainer was $7,500 a year.

Just after Christmas, 1968, the *Saturday Evening Post* folded. Otto Friedrich told the disturbing story of the magazine's last years as well as the story could be told in his 1970 book, *Decline and Fall.* Mantle and the *Post*, a couple of considerable institutions, seemed to be going out of business at the same time.

For a number of writers, the *Post* shines in memory, like April sunlight. My own retainer there reached $30,000 and I was set free to write about presidential campaigns, urban politics, music, and, of course, sports. I listened to Barry Goldwater mouth the same speeches four times a day to all-white audiences. I unearthed the reeking politics that caused a strike of New York City garbage collectors. I heard the lonely eloquence of Eugene McCarthy, who lost his senate seat after challenging Lyndon Johnson and the war in Viet Nam. Unlike *Sports Illustrated*, with its robotic editing, the late *Post* encouraged a variety of writing styles, which is how the magazine came to publish work by Arthur Miller, Barbara Tuchman, Elie Wiesel, Lewis Lapham, Ed Linn, Joan Didion, and a score of other major talents.

As an editor-at-large at the *Saturday Evening Post*, I periodically took Jackie Robinson to lunch. The long-ago abuse had wounded him and now, adding to the old hurt, organized baseball refused to offer him a job. "Prejudice?" Robinson said, his high voice carrying through a crowded midtown restaurant called Jansen's. "Ask yourself this. Knowing baseball the way I know it, and having played as well as I played, don't you think if I was white, I could be managing today?"

"Do you want to manage?"

"I'm not sure. I just know I deserve to be asked." Then, in a quieter, defensive tone, "Anyway, I don't much care. Playing was fine, but, face it, baseball is boring to watch."

"Snider? Mays? Mantle? They were boring to watch?"

"Anyway, I wanted to talk to you about politics. We have to revive the Republican party's liberal wing."

Robinson was making his complex adjustment to life beyond second base. The torch he carried had passed to Martin Luther King. Now Robinson concentrated on finding a new career and making a living. As he himself said, his life after breaking baseball's color-line "was sort of an anticlimax. How could it be anything else?"

Considering Robinson, a brave hero, now adrift, I began to wonder about some of the others from that great team I covered in 1952, others whom I no longer saw. Where was Preacher Roe? Carl Erskine? Andy Pafko? They had fallen out of the public eye, but they were neither old nor decrepit. Though the cheering stopped, their lives proceeded. What happens to old ballplayers? I wondered. What becomes of them?

Al Silverman, Ed Fitzgerald's successor at *SPORT*, asked if I would contribute a memoir to commemorate the magazine's twenty-fifth anniversary. "Something like 'Twenty-five Years of Great Baseball,'" he said, in his earnest way.

The *Post* let me moonlight in noncompeting magazines. "Sure, Al, if you'll pay my way to visit Billy Cox."

"Cox? Why him? We'll pay your way to see DiMaggio."

"I don't know why him. I guess I just miss Billy."

That wasn't a wholly rational reason to go off reporting, but Silverman was a good enough editor to let me follow my inclination. Because Cox lived in Newport, Pennsylvania, the trip from New York was not a budget buster.

I believe my first baseball ambition had been to play first base, like Sam Leslie, who hit .332 for the Brooklyn Dodgers in 1934. But that summer when I was six, my father mentioned that first basemen should be lefthanded so they can throw back across the infield to second base, without having to pivot. "That makes for faster double plays," he said.

Oh!

I had to visualize that and then try it out on a miniature Brooklyn diamond. As it turned out, my father was correct. I had a bad day, but later rallied. If I couldn't play first base like Sam Leslie, I could play third like Jersey Joe Stripp.

Cox, a small, horsefaced fellow with what Clem Labine called "little blacksmith's arms," played third base for the greatest Brooklyn teams. He wore a small, cheap-looking black glove, with which he snared all manner of doubles before they had a chance to breathe. Cox was so good and so quick and so sure that during one World Series, Casey Stengel complained, "He ain't a third baseman. He's a fucking acrobat."

I felt no resentment, none at all, about Cox living out my childhood dream. He was pure ballplayer. He didn't seem to belong anywhere except on the field. He'd been pinned down by mortar fire for a long time during World War II. He suffered from bad dreams and homesickness, and drank so heavily in spurts that he missed games. Cox and I struck up a casual, odd-couple friendship.

I found him tending bar at an American Legion club, on an Allegheny hilltop, and now the lithe infielder carried before him Falstaff's belly. "Hey," he cried, when I came in. "Here's a fella seen me play. He'll tell you some of the plays I made. He'll tell you."

Three stone-faced old railroad men glared from the bar, where they were drinking beer.

"Billy, you were the best damn glove I ever saw."

"See," Cox said to the trainmen. "An' this man's a writer from New York."

The *Saturday Evening Post* folded just about when my baseball retrospective appeared in *SPORT*. Looking about for another retainer, I struck a deal with Harold T. P. Hayes, the editor of *Esquire*, to write a sports "column" every month. "Eight pages to twenty pages, you make the call," Hayes said, cheerfully. Then, in a rougher tone. "But the stuff better be good." Abrasive though he could be, Hayes was an editor of enormous inventiveness, and he also tolerated a variety of styles. His regular contributors included Budd Schulberg, Tom Wolfe, and Norman Mailer.

In the five years I worked for him, Hayes tried to impose column ideas on me only twice. A devout weekend tennis player, he asked me to play a set with Rod Laver, then the best tennis player in the world, "and pass on to our readers what you learn." Laver was busy, but I did play a set with Roy Emerson, number 3 in world rankings. I thought the gap between our games, Emmo's and mine, would be too great for me to learn anything at all. To my surprise I did learn a number of things: how hard a great pro serves; later how to use the topspin lob; and still later, over a beer, that some Japanese pronounce Rod Laver "Lod Raver." (Score? Emerson beat me by the predictable margin of 6–0. I did win a point, on an inside-out forehand. Emerson lost a point when he hit a forehand into the net. But to quote one of Ring Lardner's characters, speaking about a tough pitcher, "I didn't molest him none.")

In 1971, Hayes asked me to run down Mantle, spend some time with him and "write about the way life is for him now, the way you did about that Dodger third baseman whose name I forget."

"Billy Cox. He's an open sort of fellow if he trusts you. Mantle is closed-in. A box."

"I saw Mantle play a few times. His power was like nothing else. And he could bunt. Do you know how quickly he made it to first base?"

"Sure. Batting left he got to first in 3.1 seconds. That's a tenth faster than anybody else in the annals. But he doesn't write all that well. He's a bad subject."

Hayes continued to talk about Mantle's gifts and I recognized that I was listening to one good old southern white boy—Hayes was born in North Carolina—holding forth on someone he perceived as kin. "I wouldn't think of ordering you to write a specific column," Hayes said. "It's your sports column and you run it. But I'd *appreciate* it if you'd visit Mantle. Is your veal bird all right?"

"Fine, Harold. I'd like another wine."

"A lot of people have been noticing your column," Hayes said. "That pleases me. It's the first true sports column that has succeeded in a national magazine. It's so successful, in fact, that Murray Kempton wondered if he could take it over when your contract expires."

I told Hayes I would set out at once and visit Mickey Mantle.

Bob Fishel said Mantle would cooperate with *Esquire* and me "if he wants to keep working for us. He hasn't hit many homers lately for the Yankees, if you've noticed." Having outgrown Commerce, Oklahoma, but still tied to southwestern roots, Mantle had moved to Dallas. Fishel gave me a number and said to call in an hour or so after he'd had time to give Mantle marching orders.

"Yeah?" That was how Mantle answered the phone.

After I identified myself and told him what I intended to do, Mantle responded with another "yeah."

"I'm going to fly down on Tuesday night. Then we can spend Wednesday together and Thursday if we need it. Can you get me a hotel room near your house?"

"Why can't *you* do that?"

"I don't know Dallas that well. Just get me that damn room, will you, Mickey."

He mentioned a motel near the old Dallas airport, Love Field. "The manager will take care of you."

"And how will we get together on Wednesday?"

"I'll pick you up. Fishel says I gotta pick you up."

"Good. What are you driving?"

"A blue Caddy. You can't miss it."

"I'm looking forward to seeing you again," I said.

"Yeah," said Mickey Mantle.

He had just been burned—badly he believed—in *Ball Four*, the funny, gamey book created by Jim Bouton and Leonard Shecter. Mantle and such Mantle cohorts as Whitey Ford, Roger Maris, Joe Pepitone, and Clete Boyer disdained Bouton during the pitcher's eight seasons as a Yankee. Although he won 21 in 1963, Bouton worked out to be pretty much a .500 pitcher. Across his Yankee career, he won 55 and lost 51. He was also haughty, well read by base- ball standards, argumentative, and he bragged about sexual conquests and enjoyed hanging out with sportswriters. To Mantle and the others, Bouton embodied uncool. But at least Bulldog Jim was a big-league ball player.

Shecter worked as a sportswriter for the *New York Post*. He some-times knocked the Yankees and he consistently made fun of Yankee foibles. Typically he hung a droll nickname on a weak-fielding out-fielder from Panama. In Shecter's pieces the man was named Hector (What a Pair of Hands!) Lopez. Shecter's defenders see him as a fore-runner of later, more critical sportswriting. I thought he was a richly talented fellow, who didn't like baseball very much and didn't care for ballplayers. He died young of leukemia. He might have been happier as a book reviewer or a White House correspondent.

*Ball Four* was published in 1970 in the form of a diary. Bouton says he took notes every day for a season. When the book begins, the Yan-kees have sold Bouton to the Seattle Pilots. But if it is a diary, it is also a memoir, with extensive flashbacks to Bouton's Yankee years. Some of it is funny and some of it is about getting even. Mike Shannon summed up in his critical work, *Diamond Classics*: "*Ball Four* reproduced the unexpurgated speech (vulgar and obscene) of the locker room and candidly discussed ballplayers' . . . illicit involvement with and pre-occupation with sex and documented the numbing conformity of the thinking that ruled the game."

Here are some paragraphs that caught Mantle's eye:

Spot a good beaver and you could draw an instant crowd. One time in Fort Lauderdale we spotted this babe getting out of her bathing suit. The louvered windows . . . weren't properly shut and we could see right into her room. Pretty soon there were twenty-five of us jostling for position.

Now, some people might look down on this sort of activ-ity. But in baseball if you shoot [spot] a particularly good beaver you are a highly respected person. . . . The roof of the [Hotel] Shoreham [in Washington, D.C.] is important beaver-shooting country . . . a series of L-shaped wings make the win-dows particularly vulnerable from certain spots on the roof. The Yankees would go up there in squads of fifteen or so, often led by Mickey Mantle himself. . . .

I ached with Mantle when he had one of his numerous
and extremely painful injuries. . . . I often wondered, though, if
he might have healed quicker if he'd been sleeping more and
loosening up with the boys at the bar less.

This sort of writing provoked intense reactions. A reporter called
Mantle and said, "What do you think of the Jim Bouton book?"

Under pressure Mantle was quick. He said, "Jim *who?*"

I went to bed in a clean, undistinguished room at the Dallas motel
Mantle chose but my sleep was interrupted through the night by the
thunder of jet airliners taking off over my pillow. The motel was not
actually on a runway at Love Field. But it was close.

Mantle arrived on time in the blue Cadillac and asked me at once
how I slept.

"Not great. Damn jets were taking off over my head every twenty
minutes."

Mantle offered his best, innocent country-boy smile. "Oh," he
said. "You noticed."

We were playing a game, as you may have deduced. I forced Mantle to make a room reservation for me. Very well. He'd find a room
where sleep was impossible. He continued to smile and I had to grin
myself. It was nine in the morning; we were even.

"I didn't know it was you," Mantle said, starting the car. "You
know I meet so many people and I'm not real good on names." He
wore blue slacks and a blue polo shirt. His middle was thicker than
when he played, but he was reasonably trim and his manner—in his
fortieth year—still was boyish. "Growing up in a small town . . . New
York with all those people. It sounds stupid to say, but I'm kind of
inward. Not backward, I don't think. Just inward. You know. A country boy."

He said he was going to play golf. Would I like to join the group?

"Lousy golfer. I'd just embarrass you in front of your Texas
friends."

"But you look in shape," Mantle said.

"Tennis, Mick. I play three or four times a week."

"I'd like to play tennis myself," Mantle said, "but I can't run no more. Anyways, I'm gonna play a round of golf. Then I gotta make a talk tonight over in Fort Worth . . . anyways, come by the house and Merlyn will make you a cup of coffee."

We rode quietly. "I imagine you want to strangle Bouton," I said.

"I didn't read the book," Mantle said. "Just some chunk in a magazine. Anybody who's been on the road can write a book with sex in it. You could; I could. But I wouldn't do it. Why do you suppose the sons of bitches picked on me?"

"It was a commercial effort, Mick, and you're box office."

"Roger Maris hated Bouton. He always wanted to belt the bastard. Is the book rough on Maris?"

"He's hardly in it."

"The other guy, Shecter, was an agitator. I didn't speak to him for the last four years at the Stadium. I'd just give him the stare. Do you think maybe the son of a bitch was trying to get even?"

"Yes."

"Do you think maybe the book ought to read: by Shecter, edited by Bouton?"

"For lots of it, sure."

"One thing that really bothered me in the excerpt. It said I wouldn't sign autographs. New York was my town. For all those years, I couldn't walk a block without getting stopped. Hell, I've signed maybe a million."

"Well, I've seen you turn people down."

"In crowds, maybe. That's true."

"When *Newsweek* wanted me to write a cover story about you, Mick, you gave me fits."

He smiled again and winked. "I knew you was getting good money, from that magazine, and I figured it was up to me to make sure you earned it.

"Well, come on in and have your cup of coffee."

Until the final years, when his marriage burnt out, Mantle lived in a rambling buff ranch house, set on a cul-de-sac on the north side of Dallas. Merlyn greeted us with a nice little smile and said, "It's a big house. Let me start you with the den." She was approaching forty, but the vulnerable fawnlike quality still lingered.

She had decorated the den into a shrine. One wall showed twelve framed magazine covers of Mantle batting, running, smiling, glaring. "There's your *Newsweek* story from a long time ago," Merlyn said. "Mick really liked that article you wrote."

"Funny," I said. "He never thanked me."

"He was just doin' what he got paid to do, Merlyn. But you want it. Shit. Okay with me. Thanks."

Another wall was crowded with pictures of the Mantles and famous men: Babe Ruth, Bobby Kennedy, Dwight Eisenhower. Locked behind glass were the jewels of a great career: the silver bat he won as batting champion in 1956; his last glove, bronzed like baby shoes; three plaques celebrating the seasons—1956, 1957, 1962—in which he was voted the Most Valuable Player in the American League; a baseball signed by Mantle, Hank Aaron, Ed Mathews, Willie Mays, and Ted Williams, an aristocracy in which everyone hit more than 500 big-league home runs.

"I'm very proud of him," Merlyn said. "But do you think this room is a little, um, too much?"

"Not at all. It isn't as if you people were faking a lot of medals."

"Come on," Mantle said, grabbing my elbow. Then, to Merlyn, "He don't want to see no more of your shit." I must have blinked. Locker room language in front of this gentle lady, in her own home, in the den she created for her man, jarred like a klaxon.

"I got something to show you out back," Mantle said. There I saw a metal pole standing in the center of a large yard. A baseball was attached with a tether. Mantle worked some electrical machinery and the pole began to spin whirling the ball in a wide arc about belt high. First the baseball moved clockwise; then, after Mantle readjusted the controls, it stopped and started up again, this time counter-clockwise. "What we got here," Mantle said, "is the perfect machine to teach kids switch hitting. One way, it's like your facing a righthanded pitcher. The other way, you're up against a lefthander. Wanna try your luck?" He handed me a Mickey Mantle bat.

"How fast can you make the ball go?"

"Up to a hundred miles an hour, like an Allie Reynolds fastball. But it's a nice machine. It ain't like Allie. It won't knock you on your ass. You been playing ball, haven't you?"

"Central Park softball, Mick. Set the machine for sixty miles an hour, okay?"

"You got it," Mantle said.

I was wearing loafers. It was difficult to get a foothold in Mantle's lawn. Whoosh. The baseball rushed by me. The bat felt heavy. I suddenly remembered Ring Lardner's short story, *Alibi Ike*. It begins, "His name was Francis X. Farrell and I guess the X stood for Xcuse me."

After a while I began to swing, but late. "Pick the ball up earlier," Mantle said. "This isn't Central Park."

I kept swinging but I couldn't make solid contact with the tethered ball. At length I dropped the bat and ran over to the control panel, shouting, "Don't touch those levers, Mantle. Hands off."

I checked the speed dial. Ninety. He had set the machine to serve up ninety-mile-an-hour fastballs. "Dammit, Mick. How is somebody going to come off Central Park softball and hit ninety-mile-an-hour stuff? We agreed it would be sixty."

"One of the risks of playing games with me," Mantle said, "is that I'm not afraid to cheat." His tone changed. "I'd say you could do good at seventy-five," he said. And so I did.

"You still swing?"

"Oh, sure. Mostly lefthanded these days."

"I'd like to watch."

"Set it at ninety, will ya. I'll hit a few."

He didn't miss. The tethered ball came in at a constant speed and could not curve or drop, but his batting eye, against ninety-mile-an-hour stuff, was phenomenal. That and his power. He swung so hard that each swing made him grunt. He hit for ten minutes and never missed. I had never seen anybody swing so hard. As best I could tell, some power came up from the battered legs, but most seemed to flow out of the upper body and the mighty arms and wrists. Swing. Crack. Grunt. Swing. Crack. Grunt. His timing meshed arm strength and wrist strength and hand strength into an instant of phenomenally violent contact with the baseball. Again and again and again. It was only

68 degrees, but he was sweating when he limped away. I wanted to cheer.

"Leg bothering you?"

He shrugged. "No more than usual. C'mon. Let's get over to my club."

As he drove, Mantle said he and his lawyer, Roy True, were looking to market the pole-and-tether batting machine. "Best thing yet to teach a boy switch-hitting," he said. "No backyard in America should be without one."

"How much?"

"We're not sure yet. Fifteen hundred. Maybe a little more."

"Mick, how many parents are going to lay out that much for a pitching machine?"

"I'm gonna put my name on it. That'll work. It gotta work. I need the money. I made good, but I spent good. Damn. You know I got three kids. It costs me $2,500 a month to break even."

"It costs everybody with three kids $2,500 a month."

"Yeah," he said, "but that $2,500 for me don't count the broads."

Preston Trail Golf Club, limited to 250 members, no pool, no tennis, spread over rolling acreage twenty miles north of Dallas. Under the clear wide sky, city towers shaped a fringe of the horizon. "Good weather here," Mantle said, "but sometimes it turns. It's warm and then the wind shifts—a norther they call it—and the sky gets blue as a marble and you have to hurry to the clubhouse, it gets so cold. Hey, let's warm up."

He started with a double Jack Daniel's on the rocks. I countered with a Scotch and soda. It was going to be a day of drinking—that was a given—and I intended to drink enough to be social, without matching Mantle's pace. "They say," he said, "Whitey [Ford], Billy [Martin], and me was a bunch a rummies. But look at this. Whitey wins more World Series games than anybody in history. Billy's got a lifetime Series average of .333 and you know about me."

"The injuries," I began.

"I can give that to you quick. In fifty-one, my rookie year, I was in right. DiMaggio called me off a fly ball late. I tore up my right knee.

After that I started straining muscles; the bad knee was affecting the whole leg. In sixty-two I was running to first and a hamstring tore in my right leg and I went down with all my weight on my left knee. After that I had two bad knees. A matching pair. Next year I broke a foot and couldn't play at all for a spell. After that some bit of bone come off my right shoulder and worked into the muscle. So I have a sore arm all the time. Look at this."

He pulled up his blue slacks, showing me his scarred right knee. Then with his right hand, he moved the knee from side to side. You have that with normal knees, of course, front to back, but this was different, a bit grotesque. "The docs call a knee like mine a 'flail' knee. That's what was under the metal brace you saw.

"Booze got in my way? Hell, it relaxed me. All the pressure I was under all them summers, I needed something. Gimme good legs and I'd be playing yet. But like it really is today, I can't even walk eighteen holes. I gotta ride the cart, like an old man." He raised his glass. The waiter brought another double Jack Daniel's.

"You?"

"I'll pass from time to time, Mick. I have to take some notes, if I'm going to get this right."

"Fine."

"I have to be able to read my notes back. I need to have legible notes to get the story right."

"Fine. Get it right. Listen. That stuff . . . you know . . . I didn't care what people wrote. That was horseshit. I always wanted to get good write-ups, just so's I could send some to my mother. Today I must have fifty scrapbooks. Most of 'em people sent me, in exchange for autographs. Sometimes after breakfast I go into that den you saw and I sit all by myself and I take a scrapbook and I just turn the pages.

"The hair comes up on the back of my neck. And I get goose bumps. And I remember how it was and how I used to think that it would always be that way. Always. I never thought that it was gonna end."

"A big league ballplayer forever."

"You got it. That's about right. When I was a young guy with the Yankees, that's what I thought. I'd be a big league ballplayer forever.

"I loved it. Nobody could have loved playing ball as much as me, when I wasn't hurt." He sipped his whiskey. "But damn I did get hurt. Now sometimes late at night my knee hurts so bad it wakes me up. But first I dream.

"I'm playing in the Stadium. And I can't make it. My leg is gone. I'm in to hit, but I can't take my good swing. I strike out and that's when it wakes me. The pain. Then I know you can't be a big league ballplayer forever. Ruth. DiMaggio. Nobody can. When the pain wakes me up, I know it's really over."

Touched, I put a hand on his left forearm. "Nobody can have scrapbooks like yours."

Mantle shook his head. "Come on," he said, placing his empty whisky glass on the table. "There's a little nine-hole putting green outside. Let's go warm up."

The club professional, Gene Shields, introduced himself and described Mantle's golf game. "Swing is a little flat, like all ballplayers', but he's the longest hitter around here, maybe anywhere. Our tenth hole runs 495 yards, and last October with a little wind, he drove to within 70 yards of the green. Ed Hoffman saw it. I'll call Ed for you, if you want. No matter how you figure it, counting the roll and all, Mickey's drive went 425 yards." (The strongest pros can't hit a golf ball that far.) "Don't believe me or Ed Hoffman," Gene Shields said. "You're going around with Mantle. You'll see for yourself."

Mantle was impatient to begin what turned out to be a putting contest. He concentrated, the strong hands gripped the putter, but his touch was ordinary. He won the first two holes. I took the third, sinking an eighteen footer. "Great putt," Mantle said, really pleased. "Good goin.'"

He finally won four holes. I won three and we halved the other two. "You did good," Mantle said, "for a tennis player."

Mantle played his serious golf in a fivesome of serious, laconic Texas golfers, who bet as they rode along in golf carts. The cart that Mantle shared with me made the best time. He whipped up knolls and spun around turns, always the first to reach his ball. "You know the old rule," he said. "He who have fastest cart never have to play bad lie."

The wind gusted, eased and gusted, disturbing the precision of everyone's game. Mantle smacked enormous, low drives and his chatter was easy and professional. Landing behind a tree, he said, "Well, I can make a fine golf shot from here." On the eighth hole, hitting into a quartering wind, he drove an astounding 300 yards. He waited for the others to make their second shots, then found his ball dead center in the fairway. "You sometimes give up distance for accuracy," he said.

An attendant waited in a cupola at the ninth. This time Mantle's Jack Daniel's was mixed with 7-Up. A few holes later, as he roared along in his cart, someone drove up bellowing: "Mantle, Mantle. Goddammit. Gimme your spare putter."

"Another club in the water?"

"Never mind. Just gimme your spare putter."

Mantle obliged with a small grin. "I got some clubs in the water myself."

The wind hoisted scores and Mantle's 82 was good enough to win his bets. He bought a round of drinks and sat back on a chair in the clubhouse. He was smiling. Playing sports always made him happy, he said. Playing golf, fooling with a pitching machine, matching putts, and hitting mammoth home runs at Yankee Stadium—these were things that made Mantle a happy feller.

That night he made a talk in Fort Worth, using a variation of his basic opening. "They say I was a hitter, but I struck out around seventeen hundred times. Then I walked another eighteen hundred. Figure that out. It comes to five years I come up to the plate and never hit the ball fair."

The crowd, about six hundred, gave him a strong laugh. Say, you could feel people deciding, this Mantle isn't snooty at all—and he certainly was not. He's a regular guy like us—but he was not that, either. After he spent forty minutes signing programs and baseballs for no fee, he said he knew a nice club outside Dallas where we could have a nightcap.

"We still got some silly blue laws around here. The only nice places to drink late around here are private clubs, but it'll cost you to join."

"How much?"

"Two bucks."

"I have two dollars with me, Mick."

"Don't worry. You're my guest. We get up to New York and eat at '21,' then I'll be your guest."

A small rock band was playing at the Cobra Club, off route 100 near Mountain Creek Lake. The walls were decorated with paintings of naked women, but hardly Renaissance nudes. These women appeared in clinical detail; not a single curl was left to the imagination.

A blonde waitress fluttered about Mantle, putting a hand on his shoulder. He said, "Hi, Corleen," and ordered another double Jack Daniel's with 7-Up.

Rock music blared, making conversation difficult. Mantle leaned toward me. "The question," he said, "is not, is the piccolo player a son of a bitch? The question is, is the son of a bitch a piccolo player?"

"You want to manage?" I asked when it was quiet.

"If they got a major league team in Dallas. I had good managers. Casey gave me my chance. Ralph Houk kept saying as Mantle goes, so go the Yankees. He's the leader. That made me feel like I was a leader, not just a country boy. But I never really got used to New York. I mean whenever I went out, it was like I had a billboard on my back. 'Hey. I'm Mickey Mantle.' I was always feeling like I was being crushed. Maybe that's why I didn't get on with the writers so good. They crushed me, too." He drank. "What was your question?"

"Managing."

"Only if there was a team in Dallas. I wouldn't want to manage outside of Dallas. I've had enough time on the road. I guess that you have too."

"What's tomorrow?"

"More golf. Talk with my lawyer, Roy True. I got to keep the money coming in. Some other things. I stay in touch."

"You bored?"

"Hell, no. I enjoy what I'm doing. I miss baseball, but I like to play golf. My health is good, 'cept for the knee. I'm not worried any more than anybody else." His eye wandered to one of the pubic nudes, then fell on the waitress called Corleen. He put both hands on Corleen's waist. The whiskey was hitting him hard now. He said, slurring the words, "I want you."

He was not holding her tightly and she took a step backward and out of his grasp. "Mickey," she said. "You had me last night. Don't you remember?"

I had been drinking at a quarter of Mantle's pace, so I recall quite clearly what I thought. Wherever the hell you are, Mickey Mantle, you're always on the road.

When his attention turned back to me he said, in the gentlest way, "You got enough to write? I been trying to give you my best stuff."

Back in the blue Cadillac, Mantle pulled toward the highway. Then, slurring again, he said my name and asked, "Which way is Dallas and which way is Fort Worth?"

I told him not to wreck the car because if we both died, the headlines would go to him. He blinked a few times, then laughed and slowly chauffeured me back to the motel—"Easy, Mick," I kept saying. "There's no great rush." We said that we should see each other more often and, still limping, he walked me to the lobby. He still looked like a kid from Oklahoma, but the limp. . . . Not yet forty, he was The Walking Wounded. That was the legacy that baseball left him, along with the scrapbooks and the memories that gave him chills.

We did see each other again from time to time, but it was never again like that day in Texas when he let his soul lie bare. A drink. A couple of jokes. He was switching to vodka.

When he was working on his 1985 autobiography, *The Mick*, he told Sam Vaughan, his editor at Doubleday, he was having some trouble with his collaborator and wanted out.

"Who do you want in?"

"That feller that wrote *The Boys of Summer*."

"He'd had some drinks and had to grapple for your name," Vaughan reported, "but he certainly remembered you and respected you. I told him you were writing something else, but I thought you'd like to know that you have Mickey Mantle's good opinion."

"As a matter of fact that means quite a lot. You know he's a good feller when the walls come down."

Sam was publishing my book, *Good Enough to Dream*, which Christopher Lehmann-Haupt announced in the *New York Times*, was "knowledgeable, funny and heart-warming and better than the book about the Dodgers." I try not to take such wonderful notices seriously, because then I may take sour reviews seriously, too. But roused by the *Times'* commentary, Doubleday sent me on a long promotional trip, accompanied by a tall, attractive publicity woman, who had just finished making a similar tour with Mantle. "I want to explain up front," she said, "that even though we'll be traveling together, this is a business arrangement. I'm engaged. I'm getting married in three weeks."

"Fine."

"I had a strange experience with Mr. Mantle. He said he was too tired to do an important show in Chicago, but if I came to his suite and rubbed his neck, he might feel better. When he opened the door he wasn't wearing any clothes. I was raised in a strict Catholic family. I got upset. I hardly knew Mr. Mantle and he was naked."

"Had he been drinking?"

"Oh, yes. Quite a bit."

"Nothing personal, then."

The strict Catholic publicity lady blinked. I could not tell whether she was pleased or offended.

Mantle's marriage to Merlyn was coming apart. They never divorced, but Mantle moved from Dallas to Atlanta where he lived with a bright, media-wise woman named Greer Johnson. She was his personal manager and lover for at least his last five years.

Mantle and I bumped into each other at the restaurant on 57th Street, to which he lent his name, and he took me to a table and began telling me about Greer. "Like somebody says he needs twenty minutes for an interview, and I gotta be a good guy and I say fine. Really the guy wants to bug me for three hours. Hey, at the twenty-minute mark, Greer comes in and tells him his time is up. She's a great lady, and she knows about how to be tough, better than me."

"They tell me you're making millions."

"Quite a bit," Mantle said, "but I try to be fair. They want me in Atlantic City to sign for a day or so. Thirty thousand, I tell 'em, really Greer tells 'em, or Roy True. 'No, the fee is twenty-six thousand. Bring in Hank Bauer and Bill Skowron and pay them two thousand dollars each. Then you get Mickey.' Hell, Skowron and Bauer were my teammates and they really need the money."

He drank a vodka and tonic. "Christ," he said, "don't write that like it sounds I'm saying I'm a great guy. Okay? I'm not a great guy. I'm just trying to help a couple teammates who been sick."

"How's the family taking your split?"

"It hurts the boys." Mantle fathered four sons. "I don't feel good about that part of it, but I feel good about Greer."

Not very long after that the owner of a sports bar, in the town that is my home, telephoned at about ten p.m. "Could you come down here? Mickey Mantle's son Billy would like to meet you."

Billy must have been thirty. He had his father's broad build, but he looked smaller, shorter, and terribly vulnerable. He wore a black lumber jacket and he spoke with great intensity. "You knew my dad when he was playing ball. I know you did. He's talked about you. Well, I got an important question for you. Very important."

"Sure, Billy. Take it easy."

"Was my dad a nice guy?"

"Yes he was. Yes he is."

"I hear he could be a real shit."

Billy was drinking a beer. It wasn't his first. "You take the drinks, son, and your dad took some drinks, your moods swing around. There was a lot of pressure on your dad, particularly after Duke Snider and Willie Mays left New York. Your dad was suddenly Mr. New York baseball. I think that was hard for him, harder than hitting homers, so he could be sullen once in a while, sure. But he was a helluva good guy."

"Thanks," Billy Mantle said, "and I'm sorry to have bothered you so late at night. It's nothing to you but it's real important to me."

Billy died in 1994 of Hodgkin's disease.

His father, growing puffy and suffering from stomach pain, found out in 1995 that he was afflicted with cancer of the liver. On June 8 he received a liver transplant. He seemed to be improving, but on August 13, 1995, the cancer, which had spread beyond the liver, killed Mickey Mantle. He was sixty-three.

After the transplant story appeared, organ donations "greatly increased nationally." But numbers of doctors criticized the transplant team in Texas for giving "a healthy liver to a dying man who happened to be a celebrity." These doctors said the transplant team just had to know that Mantle was doomed "assuming they could read a cat-scan."

Mantle lived a life of courage and excess. He bridged eras, captured the nation, and if you got to know him and came to care for him, you had to wish that he enjoyed his sublime sporting gifts more than he did, drew more satisfaction from his greatness.

But this life he led, was he living his own dream or the dream dumped on him by a beloved, harsh, demanding father? I don't believe he ever knew.

If there was anything good about his death, it was just this. The agony was done. The knee and the shadow of cancer couldn't hurt him anymore.

With an awful sense of sorrow, I thought:

*The limp is gone now, Mick.*

Walk in green pastures.

# Say Goodbye to America

## Willie's Song

*T*HE WORLD SERIES MADE THE CATCH. You know that. It was the World Series so there were writers from all around the country watching, a whole lot of fellers who didn't see me play every day. They saw the catch and all those writers thought the catch was unusual and they made it such a big thing."

"It was such a big thing, Willie."

"But not an *unusual* thing. Leo got on a sportswriter after the game? That sounds like Leo. But there was truth in what he told that man. I *did* make catches like that all the time. In those days, if the ball was hit in the air, I'd get it."

I had made a pilgrimage to the California town called Atherton, a quiet peninsula village of large homes, tall redwoods, and stout eucalyptus trees with peeling bark. The *San Jose Mercury News* reported that twelve single-family homes sold in Atherton the month before. The newspaper recorded the average price at $1,669,833. On streets called Fairway Drive and Valley Road, the homes of Atherton sit far back from the road, remote from inquisitive eyes. Atherton is a wealthy and extremely private place. No one who lives there relishes privacy more than Atherton's most distinguished resident, Willie Mays.

"Come in," he said at the door. He was wearing a yellow polo shirt, just as he wore a yellow polo shirt forty-two years ago when he flew out of the Arizona sky and rejoined the Giants. He had just turned sixty-five, but there was still a boyish look to his smooth and mobile face. No gray hair. Eyes that seemed about to laugh. "Its been a while."

When we shook hands I noticed his forearms; these were not the arms of a senior citizen, eligible at last to enroll in Medicare. Mays's arms looked so thick and powerful I thought, "Willie could choke a horse."

For an athlete Willie is a smallish sort. He stands 5-feet 10-inches, or just a shade more, and he played at 175 to 180 pounds. Still, he hit 523 doubles—17 more than Babe Ruth—and 1323 extra base hits—133 more than Lou Gehrig—and 660 home runs. Mays hit more homers than Mantle, more homers than such huge characters as Willie Stargell and Frank Howard, and more homers, 299 more homers, than 6-foot 2-inch Joe DiMaggio. The coaches say hitting is timing, getting the bat on the ball at the instant when the swing reaches maximum speed. That is so, but before timing comes a more basic essential: physical strength. Every good major league home-run hitter, from Hank Aaron to Carlton Fisk, from Frank Robinson to Greg Luzinski, from Gil Hodges to Hammerin' Henry Greenberg, has been a very powerful man.

Why then be surprised at the might of Willie's arms? Because Willie was speed and grace and poetry, a bar of music. The arms remind me that Willie was also the strongest 5-foot 10-inch 175-pound athlete on earth.

Mays led me into a handsome living room and then into a hallway full of pictures.

"Presidents?" I said.

"Oh, sure," Willie said.

He gestured toward a photo of his wife, Mae, and Ronald Reagan, and one of himself with George Bush, the old Yale first baseman. Above his signature, President Bush wrote "To Willie Mays, from his longtime and steadfast fan." Quite humble for an American President, but Bush knows the game. Watching Willie play ball did that to those who knew the game. It made them humble.

We proceeded into a den. Some trophies graced the wall. "More in the pool house. I'll show you later. You've come a long way. Can I get you anything?"

I thought a Scotch on the rocks would not be out of line and Mays moved behind the bar, held up a bottle of Haig and Haig Pinch and said, with that old Willie twinkle, "This all right?" Haig Pinch is a premium Scotch and I suspect Willie understands that it is. He doesn't drink himself—he never smoked—but he is now quite a worldly man. The Mays I know is a deep and clever fellow, not at all the obsequious Negro some writers invented in the 1950s. As I mentioned, I never heard Mays call his manager anything as ridiculous as "Mistuh Leo." But Durocher said he did, and sportswriters picked it up. Mays called his manager "Leo" or "Skip," like everybody else. I never heard him exclaim "Say, Hey," either. "But the writers said I did and that's okay." Willie is a sophisticated fellow and—in a baseball sense—he was, almost from his major league beginning.

He mixed the drink, waited for me to sip. I said the Scotch was fine and then he began to tell me about the catch. The date was September 29, 1954. The Indians, who had won 111 games, were solid favorites to defeat the New York Giants. The teams were tied, 2–2, in the eighth inning, Sal Maglie working against Bob Lemon, a couple of gamers.

Opening the Cleveland eighth, Larry Doby walked. Al Rosen smoked a grounder to deep short. Al Dark knocked down the smash but had no play. Nobody out. Indians at first and second.

Lefthanded Vic Wertz, the next batter, had been hitting Maglie hard, two singles and a triple. Durocher replaced Maglie with a left-handed relief pitcher, Don Liddle, who threw a shoulder-high fastball as hard as he could.

Willie remembers: "I'm playing a shallow center field. It's the eighth inning, the score is tied and I don't want Larry Doby scoring from second base. One run could be the ballgame. The ballgame could be the Series. You never know.

"Wertz hits it. A solid sound. I learned a lot from the sound of the ball on the bat. Always did. I could tell from the sound whether to come in or go back. This time I'm going back, a long way back, but there is never any doubt in my mind. I am going to catch this ball. I turn and run for the bleachers. But I got it. Maybe you didn't know that, but I knew it. Soon as it got hit, I knew I'd catch this ball.

"But that wasn't the problem. The problem was Larry Doby on second base. On a deep fly to center field at the Polo Grounds, a runner could score all the way from second. I've done that myself and more than once. So if I make the catch, which I will, and Larry scores from second, they still get the run that puts them ahead.

"All the time I'm running back, I'm thinking, 'Willie, You've got to get this ball back to the infield.'

"I run fifty or seventy-five yards—right to the warning track—and I take the ball a little toward my left shoulder. Suppose I stop and turn and throw. I will get nothing on the ball. No momentum going into my throw. What I have to do is this: after I make the catch, turn. Put all my momentum into that turn." Mays looked at me intently. "Are you following this? To keep my momentum, to get it working for me, I have to turn very hard and short and throw the ball from exactly the point that I caught it. The momentum goes into my turn and up through my legs and into my throw.

"That's what I did. I got my momentum and my legs into that throw. Larry Doby ran to third, but he couldn't score. Al Rosen didn't even advance from first.

"All the while I was running back, I was planning how to get off that throw.

"Then some of them wrote, I made that throw by instinct."

I had thought from the first time I saw him in Phoenix that Willie Mays was the greatest natural athlete of our time. He well may be. But it was not until the visit to Atherton, twenty-three years after his last season in the majors, that I really recognized what a *conscious* athlete Mays has been. This great slugger and batsman and baserunner, the man who caught more fly balls than anyone else in history, was very much a thinking ballplayer. If you want to get along with Willie

Mays—and it is said that not everybody does—you best begin by dropping the old hackneyed cartoon of Willie Mays as a sort of gifted, comic simpleton, a Stepin Fetchit with a glove.

A salient factor in Mays's extraordinary and eventful life is the color of his skin. Mays is a black man. He is proud and self-aware. His way is not to march, like Martin Luther King, or to address Congress, like Jackie Robinson, or to renounce white Christianity like Muhammad Ali. Willie's way is to point out—and only to those he trusts to understand the message—that there is more to the black athlete than speed and strength and leaping. The great black athletes, Mays suggests, have deep intelligence even as he himself played with such profound intelligence in making the most famous of all baseball catches.

Still thinking of the catch, I remarked in Mays's den, that if he had gone into football, he would have been the greatest wide receiver of all time.

He laughed easily and said. "You may be partly right. Football was my best sport, but I wasn't a receiver. I played quarterback in high school. We used something like the shotgun formation. One of my favorite plays was the jump pass. Come up to the line of scrimmage, like it's a run, then jump and throw. We had a good team. We were unbeaten in my senior year in high school."

"How far could you throw a football?"

"In the air? While I was jumping?"

"In the air."

"Sixty yards."

"How many colleges came after you?"

"None."

"You could throw sixty yards in the air? Your team went undefeated? And not a single college offered you a scholarship?"

"I was a quarterback," Mays said, "and I was black. In 1950 a black kid wasn't allowed to play quarterback in a white college. Nobody came after me. Nobody offered me a football scholarship, even though football was absolutely my best sport."

How much American history, I wondered, has been etched by bigotry? I tried to contemplate baseball without Willie Mays. I attempted to imagine Mays as the greatest quarterback in football history, but the baseball uniform, the Giant uniform, kept getting in the way. My mind spun like Mays making his throw. Willie's manner has mostly been genial and, on the surface, accepting of the way things are. That may be why I never stopped and considered how profoundly racism determined his career. In his generation, Mays could not have played professional football or professional basketball or professional anything else, except baseball. In effect, this greatest of all ballplayers played baseball by default. Fortunately for Willie and for baseball, he loved the game.

Racism. Our own home-grown American *apartheid*. Then my thoughts turned to an episode that Willie and I shared forty-two years before, when both of us were very young.

Late in March 1954, the Giants and the Indians flew to Las Vegas to play an exhibition game. On a raw afternoon, Sal Maglie outpitched Bob Feller and the Giants won the exhibition, 3–2. After that the entire Giant club boarded a bus for free dinner and a show at a popular hotel on the Vegas strip. Executives had been advertising: If you want to meet the great New York Giants, come on by.

The Giant management felt some concern about letting loose its troop of energetic athletes among the bosoms and the gamblers of Las Vegas for a full night. A schedule was set up that left the players free to seek as much trouble as they could find, up until eleven. At that time another bus would take them to the airport for a flight to Los Angeles, where two more exhibitions were scheduled in a small Pacific Coast League ballpark called Wrigley Field.

We ate well—great slabs of prime roast beef. No one worried about cholesterol that long ago. I caught up with Mays in the hotel theater, where Robert Merrill was to sing. As I joined Willie's table, Merrill burst into "*Vesti la giubba*," the famous aria from *Pagliacci* in which Canio, the clown, sings of having to make people laugh, although his own heart is breaking. Merrill gave it full voice and all his passions. When he was done, Willie turned to me amid the cheering. "You know," he said, quite moved. "That's a very nice song."

An hour later he was in a gambling room, standing quietly amid a group of people close to a dice table. Monte Irvin and Whitey Lockman were fighting a ten-cent slot machine. Sal Maglie, glowering like a movie mafioso, was losing steadily, fifty cents a game, at blackjack. I walked over to Willie. "How you doing?"

"Oh," Willie said, while the dice clattered, "I'm just learnin' the game." We both grinned.

I moved on, thinking to try a little roulette. Bet red. If you lose double. If you lose again, double again. Continue until you are prosperous or dead broke. Suddenly a short, thick-shouldered man with a flat face seized my arm. "Hey," he said. "Wait a minute." He pointed at Mays. "That guy a friend of yours?"

"I know him."

"Well, get him away from the dice tables."

"What?"

"You heard me. Get him the hell away from the dice tables. We don't want him mixing with the white guests."

"Do you know who he is?"

"Yeah, I know who he is. He's a nigger. Get that nigger away from the white guests."

Too angry to speak, I tried to take the measure of this man. I noticed a small, significant bulge on his left hip. This fellow, some sort of security chief for the hotel, was carrying a gun.

"Do you know this is America? Do you know that fellow just got out of the Army?

"That don't mean nothing. I was in the Army myself."

"You bastards invited him down to your hotel."

"Who you calling a bastard?"

We were shouting. At length, moving slowly out of a prudent respect for the man's weapon, I took my wallet out of a hip pocket and withdrew my press card. It was red and shaped like a police shield. "I really have to thank you," I said. "You've given me one helluva story for the Sunday *New York Herald Tribune*."

The hood retreated. I walked over to Irvin, the senior black on the Giant ballclub—he was thirty-five—and told him what was happening. Lockman listened briefly and then, taking the conversation to be personal, stepped back. "Maybe Willie and I will get on the airport bus right now," Irvin said, quite calmly. It was his way to avoid confrontations and to strive for civil-rights progress by diplomacy, so to speak. But Irvin also was worried lest Willie be shocked or hurt.

Now a trim, sandy-haired fellow in a buckskin jacket appeared, leading a young woman, attractive in a hard-faced sort of way. He introduced himself as "Maury," a vice-president of the hotel. "Shana," the young woman, was his "special assistant." The two of them would appreciate it if I'd join them for a drink at The Ol' Wrangler Saloon, just down the walkway.

We proceeded to a bar, decorated in a western style with wagon wheels and a few skulls of longhorn cattle planted in the walls. The man said that neither he, nor anybody else at the hotel, had anything against "a Negro like Irvin or Mays," playing one-armed bandits. But the dice table was a different proposition.

"There's a lot of body touching around the crap tables," Shana said. "People brushing up against each other real close." She fixed her gaze directly on my eyes, to stress her point.

Maury, the vice-president, said that as far as he was concerned Negroes were as good as anybody, some Negroes, anyway, but that he had to consider the wishes of hotel customers. That was his business. And the customers who were shooting dice simply didn't want Negroes brushing up against their women.

"We're really in the South here," Shana said.

"I thought the South was Alabama, Georgia, Texas."

"That's it," Shana said. "We get a lot of customers from Texas."

Maury nodded at the bartender, who refilled my glass. Close-up, Shana was prettier than I first thought.

"We're really a very liberal place," Maury said.

"Even though we're in the South," Shana said.

"We not only book Lena Horne to sing here," Maury said. "When she performs, we let her live on the grounds. We're the only hotel that liberal in all of Las Vegas."

"I've met Lena Horne," Shana said. "She's a wonderful person."

"Why not stay over?" Maury said. "That way you can really get to know us."

"I'm on the Giants' charter to Los Angeles. It leaves at midnight."

"There are other flights," Maury said. "We can make the arrangements. I have some work piled up, even this late, but Shana is free."

"Yes I am," Shana said.

There it was. A lodging for the night. Food. Drink. A lady who was free. And in return?

Well, they'd surely expect me to forget the hotel hood who called Willie Mays a nigger.

Thinking about that got me angry again and I looked at the two of them, the liberals from Las Vegas, Maury and Shana. Then I said, "Why did you invite him to the hotel if you were going to shit on him?"

I kicked away from the bar and joined Monte and Willie on the bus. When Irvin got me alone in Los Angeles, he pleaded with me not to write the story. "This is something that Jackie Robinson handles all the time," Irvin said, "but Willie is only twenty-three. If you write what happened at the hotel, you could put Willie in the middle of a huge racial storm. I think that would be too much for the kid. If you don't absolutely need to write what happened . . . I'd appreciate it, and I know Willie will appreciate it in time, if you could sorta let this one pass by for now."

"Sure, Monte."

By the time I finally mentioned the episode in a magazine article, fifteen years had passed and Willie was established as the best ballplayer in the world. But the magazine editor, a decent but blue-nosed sort, cut back the language and the sexual innuendo. So I have never been able to write this story truly until now.

Willie grinned at me in his den at Atherton. "I didn't need to wait for you to write about what happened. I knew about what happened pretty soon."

"How could you have known?"

"Leo told me. Monte talked to Leo. Maybe *you* talked to Leo. And Leo talked to me."

"Look at it from my point of view, Will. I didn't get to write the story for my paper. *Plus* I didn't get to take a shower with that girl."

"What can I tell you?" Willie said. "You're on your own." Then the smile passed and Mays said seriously, "There *is* something I can tell you. One word. Thanks.

"I wasn't much for controversy. Not then. Not now, either. I guess not ever. If there's some controversy from what you're going to write, can you make sure the controversy comes from you, not me?"

"I just might be able to do that, Will. Yes."

He began to share his life and times with me in a warm, insightful, and completely open way, offering thoughts on yesterday and today, on the essence of playing baseball, on his father, on Muhammad Ali, on Michael Jordan, and on—quite literally—pride and prejudice. His talk was rich, illuminated as it was by years of contemplation, but some of what he said echoed and reaffirmed the very things he said in 1954.

"You met my dad?"

I had indeed met Willie Howard Mays, Sr., called Kitty-Kat when he played on Negro teams. "He's still alive, in a retirement home. My father was a very hard worker. You had to be where I grew up; you had to work hard just to make a living. My father worked in a steel mill. He was a sweeper. He swept out the mill. And he played for the mill baseball team. Different kind of player from me. Not a power hitter. Lead-off man. Left fielder. He worked in the mill and played for their team three days a week. Then four days, he was a porter on the Pullmans, going from Birmingham up to Detroit and back."

Racism was the way of life in Birmingham and the mill town called Fairfield, thirteen miles away, where Mays grew into his teens. It is hardly a coincidence that the most obnoxious of baseball's bigots, William Benjamin Chapman, called Ben, resided in Birmingham. As manager of the Phillies, Chapman ordered his team to join him in assaulting Jackie Robinson with epithets like "snowflake," "jungle bunny," and worse. (He later made the preposterous claim that he wanted his players "to get on everybody in the same way. That's baseball.") Nor is it coincidence that Dixie Walker and Bobby Bragan, the two Brooklyn Dodgers who demanded to be traded when Robinson joined the team, were Birmingham boys. The most famous police commissioner of Birmingham, Bull Connor, who responded to early efforts at integration by setting police dogs on blacks, had a mentality that would have worked well for a concentration camp guard.

Willie Mays grew up in black neighborhoods. All his playmates were black. The schools he attended were peopled only by blacks.

Lynching was not a dirty word in Birmingham's polite society fifty years ago. The dirty word was integration.

A poll tax barred most blacks from voting. How could blacks work for changes, when they had no pathway into government? In effect, the bounties of America were simply not available to Birmingham blacks. When Mays was a young man, an athletic scholarship, a first-class education, a good job, and of course major league baseball, were accessible only to whites.

Kitty-Kat Mays, in a conversation a few years ago, said proudly, "Things are a lot different down in Birmingham these days. They're better."

I asked him when he first realized that his son would be become a superlative baseballplayer. Kitty-Kat screwed up his face as he went backward in time. "Well, you know we lived right across from a ballfield, and when Willie was eight he played with older kids."

"I mean before that, before eight."

"Soon as he started walking," Kitty-Kat said. "When he was about a year old, I bought him a big round ball and then he'd bounce it and he'd chase it and if he ever couldn't get that ball, he'd cry.

"I knew he'd be a good one, with these oversized hands." Mr. Mays extended his own palms. His faced twisted in regret. "I was pretty good, but my hands are regular size. Willie gets those big hands of his from his mother."

Willie's parents separated and his mother, Ann, died at thirty-four. She remains shadowy. "My father did a lot for me," Mays said. "Working as hard as he did, he made sure I always got the best equipment. My spikes were called Featherweights. That was a brand name. The best metal spikes. Good gloves. My father made sure I played with the best equipment.

"When we'd chose up sides, I'd like to be picked last. You see I could play any position, any one of the nine, and I'd tell them, pick me last. That ways, I could look over the team and figure out which position I could play to do the team the most good."

"With your throwing arm, you must have done some pitching."

"I was a *good* pitcher," Mays said. "I had strong legs. A ballplayer throws from the legs up, you know, and I had a good curveball. But when I was fourteen or fifteen, my father made me stop pitching. I was playing pretty much every day with our local team, the Fairfield Gray Sox, most every day when the weather was good, playing short-stop, playing center field, and pitching. One day I was running across home plate, scoring a run, and I collapsed. I just passed out. It was exhaustion.

"After that, my father said I was burning myself out. He said no more pitching and that was that."

"If you'd gone on pitching . . ."

"I know what you're gonna say." Willie's eyes were laughing. "You're gonna say I could have been Babe Ruth."

"Willie," I said, "you *are* Babe Ruth."

He shook his head. "Now don't go trying to make me spoiled."

Kitty-Kat Mays, sweeper, Pullman car porter, semipro lead-off hitter, was a sound enough baseball man to recognize that his son could very well become something special, if only in the Negro Leagues. "He didn't want me to work at a job," Mays said. "He didn't want me taking all that time away from baseball. I think I had job as a dishwasher in a diner, but not for very long. He wanted me playing ball, learning the game.

"We didn't have big-league baseball around Birmingham, but there was a Southern Association team. My father used to take me into town sometimes to see them."

Birmingham also was home to a Negro League team, the Black Barons. While still in high school, Mays played for the Black Barons, whenever he could. By his middle teens, he had stopped rotating from one position to another and become a full-time center fielder. "I could throw," he said, "and I had good breakaway. I could always breakaway for fly balls pretty quick."

After Robinson integrated major-league baseball with the Brooklyn Dodgers on Opening Day, 1947, the Cleveland Indians signed Larry Doby and the St. Louis Browns added two black players. In 1949 the New York Giants brought in Monte Irvin. The next year speedy Sam Jethroe joined the Boston Braves. The men who ran baseball inte-

grated their business slowly and in many cases resentfully. Four years
after Robinson broke in, only five of the sixteen major league teams
had signed a black. Put differently, as the 1950s began eleven major
league teams still refused to hire any blacks at all.

Word of Willie's speed and power sped north to Boston and the
Red Sox actually sent a scout to Birmingham. But this was a pro-forma
scouting trip, no more. The scout reported that Mays moved well, but
couldn't hit a curve. Just about every young player has difficulty with
the breaking ball; hitting a curve is an acquired skill. You look for kids
with a quick bat, who can get around on hard fastballs. Hitting the
curve comes later. The Red Sox passed on Mays. There never was an
outfield in Fenway with Ted Williams playing left field and Mays
playing center (and as much of left as Williams' limitations
demanded). But for bigotry, there could have been. And then how
many pennants that the Red Sox failed to win would have flown
smartly in the fresh breezes of New England?

Negro League veterans—smart, decent men like Artie Wilson of
Springfield, Alabama—recognized Mays's potential and counseled him
not to sell himself cheaply. His time would come. But when a Yankee
scout named Bill McCorry looked at Mays, he too decided to pass.
(Or had been instructed to pass, whatever he saw.) So much for a Yankee outfield pairing Mantle and Mays and that is probably just as well.
A Stadium outfield with Mays and Mantle side by side would have
been downright unfair.

"You just gotta be patient," Artie Wilson said. Willie listened. He
wasn't making much money, but playing center field the way he could
play it. Man, that was fun.

The Giants found Mays quite by accident. They sent Ed Mon-
tague, a top scout, to look at one Alonzo Perry, first baseman for the
Black Barons. Perry made no impression, but Montague telephoned
New York—this was in 1950—and, as Chub Feeney put it, "just about
burned up the phone lines telling me about this kid named Willie
Mays. Great hands. Terrific speed. Quick bat. Amazing arm. Simply
amazing. Amazing Willie Mays." Montague told Feeney that if the
Giants never signed another player they *had* to sign Amazing Willie
Mays.

Feeney liked to tell a story that had Willie's Aunt Sarah, stereotyped as an old Southern mammy, handling the negotiations with the skill of a Hollywood agent and prying a bonus of $5,000 from the Giants.

"That isn't what happened," Willie said. "I handled the negotiations. I had good advice from Artie Wilson and some other older players. I didn't get $5,000 to sign. I got $15,000. I'd always wanted a nice car. I took a little of my bonus money and bought myself a Mercury. Better than a Ford."

On May 31, 1950, Willie Howard Mays, Jr. received his diploma from Fairfield Industrial High School. Then he moved north and at nineteen played a season for Trenton, the Giants' farm team in the Class-B Interstate League, four levels below the major leagues. He hit .353 in 81 games. The next season, at Triple-A Minneapolis, Mays exploded into stardom. That was when Scout Hank De Berry filed his gorgeous and prophetic report, which is worth considering again:

> . . . everything he does is sensational. He has made the most spectacular catches . . . Runs and throws with the best . . . Hits all pitches, hits to all fields and is now on one of the best hitting streaks imaginable . . . The Louisville pitchers knocked him down plenty, but it seemed to have no effect on him at all. Slides hard, plays hard. He is just about as popular with local fans as can be—a real favorite. This player is the best prospect in America; it was a banner day for the Giants when this boy was signed.

When the Giants called up Mays on May 25, he had played 35 games for Minneapolis. His batting average stood at .477.

The kid could hit a curveball, after all.


"New York was a fine town for me," Mays said. "It was a fine town for Duke Snider and Mickey Mantle, too. You remember all stuff the writers put out, about a terrific rivalry among us. Who was the best and all. That was just writers' stuff. You know what we said among ourselves, Mickey, Duke, and me?

"We said, as long as they keep writing about this terrific rivalry, it means one thing: All three of us will have jobs next season.

"Then Duke and I would say to Mickey. 'All right, Mick. Now

you go take care of things in the Little League.' That's what Duke and I called the American League back then. 'The Little League.'"

Mays started slowly at the Polo Grounds. He made out in his first twelve turns at bat. He hit a huge home run off Warren Spahn. Then slumped again. When his average dropped to .039, he began to wonder whether he was good enough for the major leagues. He had just passed his twentieth birthday.

"Now look, Willie," Leo Durocher said in the Giant clubhouse. "You better get one thing straight. You are my center fielder. Today. Tomorrow. For as long as I'm managing this club. I'm not sending you back down. You are my center fielder. Now stop your fucking crying."

Willie went on a tear. He got nine hits in his next twenty-four at bats, a .375 pace. That tear did not run down for something close to twenty-two years.

"Leo was a great manager for me. I was always thinking when I played. 'Am I doing anything wrong?' I'd check the other outfielders. 'Are they doing anything wrong?' Sure I made mistakes, but it was very seldom that I made the same mistake twice. Leo helped me there. If, say, I was playing a little out of position, Leo would talk to me about it afterward. Real quiet. Never in front of anybody else. Never bawling me out. Never hollering. He was a terrific manager for me and a real good friend."

"I missed you, Willie," I said, "at Cooperstown in 1994 when Leo was inducted [posthumously] into the Hall of Fame."

"I wanted to go," Mays said. "But here is what I thought. Leo really was like a father to me. He said I was like a son to him. Being that close, I thought I should be allowed to say a few words. Talk about my friend. But they wouldn't let me do that, so I thought what's the sense of going."

I remembered the Durocher induction from a hot July afternoon. The other inductees were Steve Carlton, who had not spoken to the media for most of his pitching career, and Phil Rizzuto, a soul of geniality. Carlton made a tense speech. Rizzuto rambled in high good humor. ("When the Yankees first signed me, they sent me to a minor league team in a southern town called Bassett. When I got off the train, I couldn't find the town. Then the train moved. The town was behind it.")

The Durocher proceedings seemed odd—to put it delicately. Leo's adopted son, Chris, stood on the dais; he could not speak for weeping. The other "family member" on the platform was Laraine Day, the movie actress Durocher married in 1947. Later they divorced; Day was the second, albeit most famous, of Durocher's three wives. Some wondered why an ex-wife was accepting an honor for a dead and divorced ex-mate. This led to a predictable rumbling among the sportswriters. "I guess," someone said, "Leo finally got caught up on his alimony payments."

I remarked that the politics of the Hall of Fame was sometimes hard to understand.

"I respect it," Mays said, "I'm proud to be a member. But the Hall of Fame isn't all of baseball. And it's not just a hall, it's a business. I just wish they'd let me talk about Leo."

"Baseball itself seems more and more a business," I said.

"I don't want to get into that." Mays said. "Not at all. How could I possibly say anything critical about baseball, after all I've gotten from baseball? I can just tell you how it was for me. Study. Learn. Improve your game. Have fun. Very, very important. Have fun. Then you'll play well and the money will come. I never played ball saying I got to make money. I played ball saying I want to have fun. I never thought about money on the field. I thought about hustling, hustling every minute. I thought about the game, the hitter, the pitcher. I thought about how to improve."

"Did you keep a book on pitchers?"

"No. Not a book really. I studied the pitchers and I learned every pitcher's best pitch. I memorized that. I knew what every single pitcher's best pitch was. You wonder why? Because in a tight spot, with the game on the line, what's the pitcher going to throw? His best pitch. Curve, slider, fastball, whatever. His best pitch. Because I'd studied and memorized, I'd be ready."

"How did you hit Sandy Koufax?"

"Not great. Only maybe four homers off him in my career. He pitched me whoosh, whoosh, whoosh. Fastballs. When a guy throws around a hundred miles an hour with the kind of control Koufax had, it doesn't help that much to be anticipating.

"[Don] Drysdale, with that big sidearm move, got me backing away. I didn't try to pull Drysdale. I took him to right. Bob Gibson was another pitcher who gave me trouble. His brush-backs didn't bother me, but Gibson threw very hard, like Koufax, with great control. You seldom got a pitch you wanted to hit."

Mays led the National League in batting at .345 in 1954. Four years later, in the Giants' first season in San Francisco, he hit .347, his high for a single season. Of course Mays hit for power as well as average. He led the league in home runs four times. His top output: 52 in 1965, truly remarkable when you consider that the unfortunate location of Candlestick Park, right on the bay, had Mays swinging into the wind for half a season.

He hit for power, he hit for average and he had great speed. Mays led the league in triples three times. For three straight seasons late in the 1950s he stole more bases than anyone else in the majors.

Defensive statistics don't always correlate with ability. An outstanding fielder reaches balls a lesser athlete does not, attempts more difficult plays and may make more errors than the leadfoot. An old baseball saying points out: "You can't miss what you don't reach." Willie reached more balls than anybody else and still made very few errors. In one characteristically fine year, 1962, while he was powering the San Francisco Giants into the World Series with 49 home runs, he made 429 putouts in center field. (In Joe DiMaggio's greatest year, 1941, he made 385 putouts.) Mays threw out six baserunners, giving him a total of 435 fielding chances. He made only four errors.

Six baserunners thrown out across the season? Where, pray tell, was Willie's wondrous arm? In the right place. Everybody knew about Mays's arm and nobody dared to run on him. You can't throw out runners who don't try for an extra base. Instead you freeze them in their tracks. No statistic exists to show how many hundreds of runners did *not* try to advance, did *not* try to score because of their respect for the Mays arm.

At times, Mays has been amused by reporters and fans pressing him to declare a single outfield catch as his greatest. He caught 7,095 balls in the outfield—high flies, sinking liners, short pops, and wallops rocketing toward the fence. He caught flies of every description and at just about every length. No other outfielder ever made as many catches. After a while, Willie offered a stock answer. Reporters quoted him as saying, "I don't rate 'em. I just makes 'em."

As Mays described playing center field, a critical element is preparation. He knew the hitter, the pitcher, and the game situation and positioned himself accordingly. Then he would check with a glance into the dugout, where a small gesture might indicate what pitch was coming. Durocher said, "Willie was an absolute wonder out there. If I moved a knuckle, just a knuckle, to reposition him, he always saw it and he always moved." Mays himself, always stressing preparation, said, "You don't want to end up surprised."

But on what Branch Rickey called the best catch in baseball history, Mays was indeed surprised. The Giants were playing the Pirates late in the summer of 1951 at old Forbes Field in Pittsburgh, where center field ran 457 feet deep. Rocky Nelson, a lefthanded hitter, smashed a tremendous line drive and Mays, calculating at a glance, turned and sprinted for the wall. Nelson had hit the ball so hard that there was a hook to it. While Willie ran the ball drifted slightly to the right.

At precisely the correct instant, Willie looked. He had gotten back deep enough, itself a mini-miracle, but now the ball was to his right and sinking fast. He might have been able to reach across his body and glove the ball. Or he might not. We will never know. He simply stuck out his bare right hand and seized the liner at the level of his knees. Then he slowed and turned, his face a great, wide grin.

"Silent treatment," Durocher ordered in the dugout. Nobody say nothing to him."

Willie touched his cap to acknowledge the crowd and ran down the three steps into the Forbes Field dugout. Everyone avoided Willie's eyes. Durocher was checking the line-up card. Bobby Thomson was pulling anthracite from his spikes. Monte Irvin bent at the cooler for a very long drink of water. The silence was suffocating.

"Hey, Leo," Willie piped finally. "You don't have to tell me that was a great catch. I know that was a great catch."

A minute later an usher passed a note from Rickey into the Giant dugout. "That," Rickey wrote, "is the finest catch I have seen in fifty years of watching baseball. And it is the finest catch I ever hope to see."

• • •

In his den Willie beamed as he remembered. "That was a good one. Then there was one in Ebbets Field off Bobby Morgan. To tell you the truth, I don't know. I was busy running down the baseball."

"I read somewhere that you called Stan Musial the best hitter you ever saw."

"Not quite accurate," Mays said. "Ted Williams was the best pure hitter I ever saw. But Ted was stubborn. When they shifted on him, everybody to the right side, he still kept trying to pull the ball for hits. If anybody shifted like that on Musial, he would have wrecked them, by slapping base hits into left.

"So what I really said is this:

"Ted Williams is the best pure hitter I ever saw.

"Stan Musial is the best all-around hitter.

"Is that clear? When you write this, I hope you can explain the difference."

"Sure."

"So much is mental. I believe if you can't think, you can't play [on a good level]. Baseball or any other sport. People don't appreciate that enough.

"Some people who watched Jim Brown play football said, 'Man, he's big and fast and strong. He's gotta be good.' But they don't realize that when Brown was running with the ball, he was always thinking. Cut back. Fake. Whatever. He was always thinking ahead, two or three moves ahead of the tacklers.

"Muhammad Ali. Sure he was big and quick. But he was such a good boxing thinker, he could figure the round he'd win in before the fight. Then he made his moves and it would come out like he predicted. He was another athlete great because he would think.

"Julius Erving in basketball. Dr. J had all the moves. He had a great body to play basketball, but he had the moves because he knew how to think."

"Like Michael Jordan today," I said.

"Right, and I see something else with Michael. You remember long ago I told you, a player has to love the game. I look at Michael and I see a player who loves basketball. He loves playing it the way I loved playing baseball. Intelligence, sure, but love is a big reason Michael can play basketball the way he does."

I mentioned that Willie is a deep and clever fellow. He is making several points all at once and the most important one is this: The four great athletes he singled out for high intelligence are African-Americans. In white America you still hear a variety of clichés:

*Sure blacks can run and jump and slide and dunk, but can they think? Hey, that's the white man's game. Let Willie chase 'em in the outfield. Let Jim Brown run for daylight. Let Michael slamma-jamma. Fine for natural athletes like those guys. But for thinking, we gotta have whites. White pitchers and white quarterbacks and white coaches. Know what I mean?*

Willie Mays knows what you mean. He's heard it on so many occasions. *Willie, you're just the greatest natural athlete. It must be wonderful to have baseball come to you so naturally.*

Mays doesn't respond directly. That isn't his way. But ask him to choose the smartest baseball player he ever saw and he answers very quickly.

"Jackie Robinson."

Willie has a marvelously gentle way of making a powerful point.

I recall that during the student movements of the late 1960s, some criticized Mays for not speaking up on behalf of protesting black college students. "How could I do that?" he said. "How could I deal with all those issues. It's not as if I went to college myself.

"But I'm aware of what is going on. Remember when I was growing up in Alabama, we couldn't play ball against white players. We couldn't play in what they used to call 'organized ball' and we weren't even allowed to play against white semipros.

"I remember when that changed. After Robinson made it in the major leagues, he came through barnstorming with Roy Campanella, came right through Birmingham. They played some white team, I think it was, and you know who was playing with Jackie and a lot of other blacks? Gil Hodges and Ralph Branca from the Dodgers. That was the first time baseball was integrated in Alabama. People should remember. Gil Hodges and Ralph Branca." ("I do remember," says Ralph Branca. "I remember a third white player, too, the late Bob Young, a second baseman with Baltimore. Was it hairy? Not particularly. We just played ball.")

Because of his gifts, Mays moved into places where no black man had been before. "So many times," he said. "So many kinds of things. Dean Martin and Jerry Lewis. A lot of Hollywood people. They always wanted me to play golf at a white club. Even in Mississippi once, someone took me to play golf at a white club. I'd always go. I figured some would see that a black fellow behaved okay, and maybe they'd ask more blacks afterwards. A reporter came to me once and said why didn't I go into one of these segregated places that wanted me and after I got inside there go make a fuss.

"I don't know if he understood, but I told him just this: Why make a bad fellow of myself?'"

Mays walked me from the den onto the grounds, past a line of red-woods. "Isn't it nice around here?" he said. The tasteful brick motif of his driveway extends to the pool area and the pool house, which he has turned into an office. Here I could see the treasures of a storied life.

Twelve Gold Glove awards. ("The game begins with defense. I'd have had more, but they didn't start giving out Gold Gloves until my sixth year in the majors.") Red boxing gloves signed to him by Ali. Awards for helping baseball and young people in San Francisco and New York. After a while the trophies began to blur until I saw the centerpiece of the display in Mays's inner sanctum. It was a framed diploma from Fairfield Industrial High School, awarded to Willie Howard Mays, Jr., on May 31, 1950.

"Now what are you going to call this chapter?" Willie said. He was getting ready to drive me back to Palo Alto.

"Willie's Song," I said.

"Why is that?"

"Because when you talk baseball, it's a bar of music."

"I don't like it," Willie said.

"Why not?"

"People will think its about the music I listen to."

"It's my book, Will."

"Sure, but let me give you a title. You don't have to use it. Why don't you call the chapter, 'Say Goodbye to America'?"

I remembered hearing Willie's farewell on a distant island, staring hard into a faint, flickering television picture. The Giants shipped him off to the Mets in 1972 and now on September 25, 1973, Willie the Met was stepping back from baseball.

I was off scuba-diving and the divemaster, sitting beside me at a Nassau bar, was a basic, faintly bigoted American. He had heard of Lou Gehrig's famous exit line, the dying man telling the crowd at Yankee Stadium, "I consider myself the luckiest man on the face of the earth." Now he was tolerating Mays's farewell, but only because I insisted.

Willie stood near home plate at Shea Stadium with his wife Mae and Joe DiMaggio, who had flown to New York from San Francisco, an act of tribute by a proud old Roman Senator.

Mays said he was hitting .211 and that the game couldn't be fun for him anymore, now that he could only hit .211. He said he didn't consider himself a superstar and never had. He did consider himself to have been a complete ballplayer. "I thought," Mays said, "I'd be crying by now. Maybe I'll cry tomorrow."

Then he said it . . . "When I look at the kids over there" . . . still he was dry-eyed. He pointed to young and gifted Met ballplayers. . . . Through a tiny television set in Nassau, on a faint flickering transmission from Miami, I heard, and the rugged divemaster heard the next words: "I told myself, 'Willie, say goodbye to America.'"

In the Nassau bar, the tough, white divemaster, dabbed at his eyes with a paper napkin. After a while, he said: "You know, New York is quite a town for farewells."

"Where did that farewell come from?" I asked.

Willie was driving me to Palo Alto, driving down the *Camino Real*.

"Out of my head. It just came to me. It meant that no one in this country, white or black, would ever see me play baseball again. No one in the country. No one in the world."

We rode quietly for a few blocks, past a Sizzler, an Olive Garden, ordinary places. How baseball can unify, I thought, and at its best surmount generations of bigotry, even hatred. "Did your father ever tell you how proud you've made him feel?"

"No," Mays said. "He never did. Did your father ever tell you he was proud of you?"

"Not really, Will."

"Well maybe your dad was like my dad is. Maybe he knew. If he made a big fuss and praised you, all you'd feel was uncomfortable, embarrassed."

More blocks in silence along the *Camino Real*. Willie Howard Mays, Sr., of Fairfield, Alabama and Gordon Jacques Kahn of Brooklyn, New York.

If they'd met, they could have talked a little baseball.

A red light. Willie stopped the car. Three children stared in. They called to their parents. Noise rose. People began to clap and wave and cheer.

Willie has said goodbye to America. America never wants to say goodbye to Willie Mays.

# CHAPTER TWELVE

# Walking at Midnight

Businessmen, politicians, judges—"people of substance" in my mother's genteel term—organized a celebration not so very long ago. The invitation promised guests a "rousing gala in Brooklyn's Fabulous Botanic Garden with real big-league baseball stars, Brooklyn's very own *Boys of Summer*." Big-league baseball had, in fact, deserted Brooklyn thirty years earlier and the boys of summer had evolved into senior citizens, as likely to talk about cholesterol readings as they were to recall the dust raised by a long-ago hook slide. But the chance to spend a summer evening with baseball friends proved stronger than my distaste for commercialized nostalgia. Besides, I wanted to deal with unfinished family business. I would attend.

After my father's death in 1953, my mother forged a remarkable widowhood. She continued teaching world literature at Thomas Jefferson High School in Brooklyn until urban violence exploded into the hallways and classrooms and destroyed the climate for her aesthetics. She grieved briefly, then resumed teaching in a program at the

New School for Social Research called The Institute for Retired Professionals. Here dentists, accountants, physicians, who felt they had been "too busy to read," turned to Olga Kahn for guidance through the worlds of Dostoevsky and Balzac and the poetry of Walt Whitman and Robert Bly. Teaching, she said, gave her life structure. Searching for new writers kept her feeling "like something other than an utter antique."

She declined to curtsy before the years. She traveled every summer and at seventy-eight returned from Egypt and announced in triumph, "I climbed the pyramid of Cheops."

"How was the view?"

"It's inside, dummy," she said, with a kind of noncommittal tenderness.

Suitors appeared and vanished. She dismissed a retired historian as too autocratic. She spurned a prosperous lawyer as too frugal. None had a chance, for none approached my father, as she came to remember him.

I telephoned to ask her to join me for the affair at the Botanic Gardens. "Is it going to be entirely baseball?" she said. "You and your father talked about nothing else for twenty-five years."

"There's going to be a band playing dance music. Fox-trots. That sort of thing."

"Then I'll go, if you promise to dance with me." She was eighty-six. "Do you realize," she said, "that in your entire life, you've never asked me to dance?"

At dusk, I parked in an asphalt lot behind the Brooklyn Museum. Our cherished neighborhood ballfield, where you *couldn't* lose a baseball, where homers always came rolling down the hill, had been paved over, buried without an epitaph.

My mother and I walked through a six-foot iron turnstile onto a narrow path edged with Japanese lanterns. On either side these grounds were tended with the care you find about the gardens of Devonshire.

"Oh," my mother said, suddenly sad.

"What's the matter?"

"I wish your father were here. He was the student of botany. He'd have known the names of all these shrubs and flowers. The Latin names as well."

At length we came to a huge striped tent and I guided my mother toward our table. We joined Clem Labine, George "Shotgun" Shuba, Carl Erskine, Pee Wee Reese, all of whom knew who she was.

Erskine mentioned his love of narrative poetry. He and Labine took turns quoting stanzas from Robert W. Service's "The Cremation of Sam McGee." Reese remarked that his son, Mark, was writing poetry himself and had found a hero in Jack Kerouac. Shotgun Shuba said that his favorite place in his hometown of Youngstown, Ohio, had become the public library. The venerable teacher of literature ordered her favorite drink—"a dry rob roy"—and glowed.

When we danced, she said, "Forgive me if I don't think of your friends here as ballplayers. They're gracious gentlemen."

I said that it was possible to be both. The dance band played Jerome Kern's sentimental classic, "All the Things You Are." Back at the table my mother audited tolerantly as we talked baseball.

But later on, toward midnight, when we left the tent, we plunged into an ominous night. You couldn't see what lay beyond the Japanese lanterns along the narrow path, but you could hear. Growlings of German shepherds. The squawk of walkie-talkies. To prevent this baseball reunion from becoming a crime scene, the police of New York City turned out in force.

We walked slowly, mostly in silence. The old ballplayers formed a close-ranked group around my mother. As she made her way forward, she was protected by a bodyguard of major leaguers.

A policeman's voice carried toward us. "Hey, Frankie. They didn't only rip the radio out of this one. They tore out the whole damn dashboard." Despite the police, the night felt full of menace.

After farewells, my mother said, "This isn't the way it was in the Botanic Garden when you and your father walked beside the babbling brook."

"We didn't do that," I said. "At least not that day. We went to a ballgame."

"I know."

"What? That was our secret. How could you have known?"

"When you came home, you said the phrase 'babbling brook' at least six times. I knew you had been rehearsed. But that's all right. Your father and you certainly got along."

She died on the Christmas Eve before her eighty-seventh birthday, at peace with her own rich life, her son, and even—so I like to think—the game of baseball.

# The Golden Dozen

*Some of my best friends are critics.*

—ANONYMOUS

*I* AM NOT ONE MYSELF. THE FEW BOOK reviews I've written—agreed to always in moments of carelessness—have been more trouble than they were worth. I am not comfortable holding forth in the required magisterial manner, on which books are good and which are bad, and why. That process feels too much like composing a term paper, which was, for me at least, a wretched form of writing.

But, of course, I have favorite books. The literature of baseball is richer than that in any other sport and I mean here to share some of my enthusiasms.

1. *Nice Guys Finish Last* by Leo Durocher with Ed Linn (Simon and Schuster, 1975). This book proceeded stormily from a magazine collaboration. Durocher was not comfortable with Linn, an author he could not intimidate. Linn, who had enjoyed working with Bill Veeck, found Durocher difficult and devious. Perhaps that spiky relationship is what gives this book its marvelously pugnacious tone. I've never read a baseball life story, biography or autobiography, that I enjoyed as much.

1. (Co-winner) *Bang the Drum Slowly* by Mark Harris (Alfred A. Knopf, 1956). A moving and magical novel, the story of Bruce Pearson, a third-string catcher, dying across a baseball season. The narrator is pitcher Henry Wiggen. The dying man is not a character of the dimensions usually assigned to Lou Gehrig. Nor is Wiggen as limited as Ring Lardner's Jack Keefe. Pearson's greatest pleasure is chewing Days O Work tobacco and spitting out of hotel windows. As death intrudes into the lives of Pearson and Wiggen, both grow in poignant ways. The end is spare, haunting, quite beautiful.

3. *The Glory of Their Times* by Lawrence Ritter (Macmillan, 1966). This oral history, compiled by a university professor, consists of twenty-two taped interviews with ballplayers prominent in the first two decades of the century. Their memories and Ritter's craft describe the game and the country, the way things were, the way they remain in the glorious country of memory.

4. *Baseball America* by Donald Honig (Macmillan, 1985). Creating a one-volume history of baseball is a job made difficult by the abundance of material. For some reason, the wheat surplus comes to mind. Honig's solution is to focus on the great stars. As the twentieth century began, he suggests, America had run out of heroes. Earlier generation admired adventurers (Davey Crockett, Daniel Boone) and men of action (Wild Bill Hickok, Buffalo Bill Cody). With the frontier gone, the country turned to baseball and the new heroes—Cobb, Ruth and the rest—were found not in "unpathed wilderness" but "playing America's own game on the bright green grass of home."

5. *A False Spring* by Pat Jordan (Dodd, Mead, 1975). A memoir of Jordan's life and torment in the low minors where his pitching career comes to an end. Depressed and despairing in one extraordinary scene, Jordan and his wife take to bed for solace. But their accommodations are minor league. The bed collapses. The title comes from Hemingway's *A Moveable Feast*. (Hemingway was referring to his attempt to revive a marriage that was done.) Jordan is focused on the death of his dream. He never will pitch in the major leagues.

6. *Lords of the Realm* by John Helyar (Ballantine Books, 1995). The author, a reporter for the *Wall Street Journal*, provides a smooth, well-researched account of Organized Baseball's struggles over some twenty

years. In the wrong hands, this could be dry and academic. But Helyar is a lively narrator of a story in which the people who run baseball collectively shoot themselves in the crotch.

7. *Cobb, a Biography* by Al Stump (Algonquin Books of Chapel Hill, 1996). Raw and real. Stump signed on to write Cobb's life story and found himself joined at the hip with a man equally brilliant and terrifying. Cobb was rich, mean, and menacing. He had been a portrait in rage since his mother murdered his father, who suspected her of cuckolding him. Unforgettable and not for children.

8. *A Whole Different Ball Game* (Simon and Schuster, 1991). Mild-mannered Marvin Miller is the architect of that powerful union The Major League Players Association. In this book, he dropped the "mild" and came out swinging from the ankles. Commissioner Bowie Kuhn was not terribly bright. Commissioner Peter Ueberroth was not much interested in baseball. Commissioner Bart Giamatti disgraced himself with his neo-fascist persecution of Pete Rose. Fay Vincent might have become a good commissioner but after the 1989 San Francisco earthquake interrupted the World Series, it was Vincent who ordered the Series resumed. Subsequently, Miller feels, Vincent began to confuse himself with Jehovah. Extreme? None of this seems extreme if you take the time to hear out Marvin Miller.

9, 10. Any collection of pieces by John Lardner or Red Smith. You can find Lardner's stuff in *It Beats Working* and *Strong Cigars and Lovely Women*. Two Smith favorites are *Out of the Red* and *Strawberries in the Wintertime*. Mostly you'll find columns in these books; two better columnists never lived.

11. *Fathers Playing Catch with Sons* by Donald Hall (Farrar, Straus, 1984). Renowned for his poetry, Hall brings a passion for baseball to wonderful short pieces on the game. Funny, insightful, charming and, oh yes, no surprise, poetic as hell.

12. *Man on Spikes* by Eliot Asinof (McGraw Hill, 1955). Better known for his nonfiction study of the Black Sox, *Eight Men Out*, Asinof poured youthful passion into this novel about a ballplayer who was not quite good enough to stick in the major leagues, but close enough to cling to his dream. Asinof bases his protagonist on Mickey Rutner, who played twelve games at third for the 1947 Philadelphia Athletics,

hit a homer, knocked in four runs and never got to play another big-league inning. Rutner was Jewish; apparently Connie Mack held that against him. Asinof's hero is not Jewish. He wears eyeglasses. The techniques of novelists can be every bit as fascinating as the techniques of lefthanded pitchers and center fielders.

*Roger Kahn*
January 2, 1995–December 17, 1996

# Index